CATALONIA : A COMPL

Barcelona. Incomplete Church of the Holy Family
(Templo Expiatorio de la Sagrada Familia).

CATALONIA

A COMPLETE GUIDE
JANE AND PETER HOLLIDAY

IBERIA PRESS

First published in 1992

by   Iberia Press, Bay Tree House,
        Stratton Audley, Oxfordshire, OX6 9BJ

Copyright © 1992 Jane Holliday

Maps and plans by Su Hopkins

Cover photograph by Peter Holliday

Black and white photographs courtesy of
    Spanish National Tourist Office, London

Typing by Debbie Mander

ISBN 0-9518767-0-8

British Library Cataloguing-in-Publication Data
A catalogue record for this book is available from the British Library

Printed and bound by Parchment (Oxford) Ltd, Printworks, Crescent Road,
Cowley, Oxford OX4 2PB

CONTENTS
Page

INTERIOR ROUTES

MAPS

TOWN PLANS

PREFACE

It was our fifth day in Catalonia. Already the floor of the car was littered with leaflets, maps and dog-eared plans. Information certainly was not lacking. Indeed it was heaped on us at every tourist office or town hall we stopped at, in a variety of different languages but most frequently in Catalan. Our irritation grew as we scanned both horizon and leaflets for a monument which we had, in fact, passed some miles back. Gradually it dawned on us that what was needed was a single comprehensive guide book to Catalonia – in English. So we decided to write it.

Many months of intensive study and searching visits, enriched by countless conversations with friendly people ranging from village bakers to museum directors, have enabled us to create this Guide. We hope it will serve, above all, as a framework for your wanderings in this altogether delightful, and very individual region of Spain. One can comprehend a foreign land at two levels: as a series of disconnected aesthetic/intellectual/pleasurable experiences to be remembered in no particular order other than that of time; or as a kaleidoscopic pattern within a frame, in which everything you see and hear and do falls into its logical place, either at the time or later on. The choice is yours.

It is hard to decide just how much information the average visitor with average curiosity and time will want to absorb whilst touring. Our main concern is to be accurate, clear and readable, and interesting enough to tempt you to visit the out-of-the-way places as well as the obvious sites. We hope this Guide will be compact enough to take with you each day, but absorbing enough to read, or perhaps re-read, in the evenings.

We make no apologies for our near obsession with Romanesque churches, for Catalonia is one of the richest repositories of religious art and architecture from this period anywhere in Europe. Monasteries too are everywhere, sometimes leaving only a cloister as evidence of past glories, sometimes fully restored. And we have included some of the most remote churches and monasteries, for which getting there along narrow mountain track is more than half the fun. The countryside belies description, from plains and vine-covered slopes in the south to stark Pyrenean giants in the north.

The Routes in this Guide are intended to take you right around the region in a clock-wise direction. We start with Barcelona because it is the capital, but you could equally well join the circle at, say, Girona (if coming from France) or Lleida (if coming from Zaragoza and/or Madrid). The circle is bisected by Internal Routes which cover the interior. Excursions are added so as to include monuments and outstanding towns and villages which do not happen to lie along the main Routes. Where possible we try to make Excursions circular; they can vary in length from 2km to 200km and the sites they include are in no sense less distinguished than those along the Routes.

Do not be deterred, either by volume of traffic or unattractive industrial suburbs, from entering the great cities – cosmopolitan and dynamic Barcelona, Roman Tarragona and the most ancient of all, which is Girona. All are rich in historic and artistic treasures and their museums, particularly Barcelona's, are outstanding. We recommend a stay of several days in Barcelona, and at least one in each of the other two. Equally fascinating and of more modest proportions are the cities of Lleida, Vic, Ripoll and Vilafranca del Penedes, to mention but a few. Always make for the city centre. We have tried in the Routes which follow to guide you in. In a case where a city has no particular attraction from a tourist point of view, we do not hesitate to suggest that you should by-pass it.

Because we aim to encourage you to visit not only the big cities but also the lesser known towns and, beyond them, the hidden delights of rural Catalonia, we are assuming the reader is motorised (and in possession of a good road map). If not, then there are excellent train and bus services which will cover many, though by no means all, of the places described. A combination of public transport and occasional taxis might just achieve this.

J.H., P.H. 1992

BACKGROUND INFORMATION

INTRODUCTION

Catalonia is an autonomous community within Spain, occupying a triangle of land hard up against the Pyrenees and measuring some 32,000 km^2. It is a land of infinite variety whose beaches are one of the most famous tourist attractions in Europe but whose ruggedly beautiful interior is still largely unknown. Physically Catalonia divides broadly into three zones: the Pyrenees to the N, the coast to the E, and the hinterland bordered to the W and S by the Spanish provinces of Aragon and Valencia.

The Pyrenees, a region of high peaks, alpine meadows, crystalline lakes and pine forests, are crossed by countless valleys, which once gave easy access to invading armies and now offer the same to visitors from the N. They are scattered with villages and churches, some as old as a thousand years, and their slopes offer splendid ski-ing in winter, and ideal opportunities for walking, bird-watching, fishing or just simply enjoying the peace of it all during the rest of the year. A serious environmental policy on the part of the autonomous government ensures that the region is respected and not despoiled by ungainly hydro-electric plants or over large tourist facilities.

Environmental purists will make for the *Park of Aigues Tortes*, one of only five national parks on the Spanish mainland, which extends over an area of 105 km^2, contains some of the highest peaks of all and still provides sanctuary to wild goat, ibex and capercaillie. Others, seeking a range of activities, will explore the towns and villages of the magnificent Aran valley. For those whose needs do not extend beyond small villages, simple accommodation and a rare wealth of Romanesque churches, the Boi valley is the answer. Fingers of the Pyrenees extend S-wards and include the dramatic *Cadi* and *Montsec* Sierras, whilst to the E is the extraordinary region of extinct volcanoes known as the *Garrotxa*.

The Coast, some 400 kms along and renowned for long, sunny days and temperate climate as well as everything else, divides naturally into three *Costas*. From the French border as far S as Blanes runs the aptly named *Costa Brava* which is wild and dramatic and full of rocky coves and picturesque fishing villages. From Blanes to Barcelona is the *Costa Maresme*, with long sandy beaches protected by coastal mountain ranges. S of Barcelona stretches the vast expanse of golden sand known as *Costa Dorada*.

The Hinterland is a region of plateaux and plains broken by outcrops of Pyrenean foothills. Parallel with the coast, S of the Ter river, run two significant ranges known as the *Cordillera Pre-Littoral* and *Cordillera Littoral*.

1

The former in particular is distinguished by some quite unique landmarks. One of these is the remarkable folded range of *Montserrat* (serrated mountain); another, declared a Conservation area by UNESCO, is the fertile and forested region of *Montseny*. Between the Cordilleras and the Pyrenean barrier to the N is the region known as the *Central Depression*. This is crossed from N to S by the rivers Segre, Noguera, Ribera and Llobregat and is, despite its name, largely mountainous. The lowest-lying areas, apart from the coastal strip itself, are the extensive marshlands of *Emporda* to the N and the *Ebro Delta* to the S, both now natural parks and conservation areas with an outstanding range of water and migratory birds.

In short, there is something to suit all tastes and the traveller will encounter a stunning variety of scenery in a surprisingly short time, and often only a short distance inland from the coast. Scattered across the changing landscape are the wheat fields, vineyards, olive groves and fruit orchards which man has cultivated in Catalonia since Roman times and which merge so naturally with the environment.

Not surprisingly, the **climate** is as varied as the geography and within a few hours you can move from the hard winter snows and perfect ski slopes of the Pyrenees to the warm and somewhat humid beaches of the Mediterrean. The latter become extremely warm in high summer. Once away from the coast, humidity drops and the air becomes fresh as the climate changes once again to that of the Spanish interior, with cold winters and hot dry summers. Only the Ebro Delta is different, with its very own sub-tropical micro-climate, its rice paddies and its mosquitos.

Since 1833 Catalonia has been divided by the Spanish state into four provinces, centred on the ancient cities of Barcelona, Tarragona, Girona and Lleida. Today over three-quarters of the population of some 6 million people live in and around Barcelona and other large towns near the coast. (Drive inland and you are soon in a very different world of wooded hills and rich agricultural land). Over and above the Spanish administrative division is the much older Catalan structure of *comarcas*, and there are 38 of these: 11 in Barcelona province, 10 in Tarragona, 10 in Lleida and 7 in Girona. Each *comarca* has its own capital and is justly proud of its history, its culture, its monuments and its gastronomy. The Department of Tourism produces a different leaflet about each *comarca* which lists main attractions and accommodation and these are usually available at local tourist offices and town halls.

THE COMARCAS OF CATALONIA

FRANCE

VALL D'ARAN

PALLARS SOBIRÀ

Llivia

Puigcerda ●
CERDANYÀ

La Seu d'Urgell ●

ALT URGELL

N

PALLARS JUSSÀ

RIPOLLÈS

● Ripoll

GARROTXA

ALT EMPORDÀ

● Figueres

BERGUEDA

SOLSONÈS

GIRONÈS

Girona ●

BAIX
EMPORDÀ

LA NOGUERA

OSONA

● Vic

LA SELVA

SEGARRA

BAGES

VALLÈS ORIENTAL

● Lleida

URGELL

ANOIA

VALLÈS
OCCIDENTAL

MARESME

SEGRIÀ

CONCA
DE BARBERÀ

LES GARRIGUES

ALT PENEDÈS

BARCELONÈS

● Barcelona

PRIORAT

ALT CAMP

BAIX
PENEDÈS

BAIX
LLOBREGAT

GARRAF

BAIX
CAMP

TARRAGONÈS

● Tarragona

TERRA ALTA

RIBERA
D'EBRE

MEDITERRANEAN

BAIX EBRE

Tortosa ●

MONTSIÀ

0 10 20 30 40 50 km

SCALE

3

HISTORY

There is evidence that man has lived in Catalonia since the Middle Paleolithic Age. A Neanderthal jawbone, probably from around 80,000BC was found at Banyoles; caves, particularly at Reus and Moia, have revealed hand axes and other stone tools. Cave paintings notably at El Cogul (in Garrigues) and at Ulldecona (Montsia) date from the Upper Paleolithic period (35,000-10,000BC). Settled farming probably started about 5,000BC (Neolithic), at a time when the post Ice Age vegetation had all but receded and been replaced by deciduous forests as a result of rising temperatures and abundant rainfall. These people left burial chambers in the form of dolmens and long galleries, particularly in the N of Catalonia, and an abundance of tools and pottery.

Agriculture, cattle-raising and copper mining were well established by the time the first invaders – the Greeks – arrived in the 6C BC. They came to Roses and Empurias and set up trading stations along the coast. The indigenous Iberians clearly benefitted from this civilised and non-aggressive invasion; they learned the alphabet and they were introduced to vines and olives.

In the 3C BC the Carthaginians arrived under their leader Hamilcar Barca. Their intention was to exploit the considerable mineral resources and to recruit for their armies fighting the Romans in the Punic Wars. But they also took pains not to upset the indigenous Iberians and to show them how to achieve a higher standard of living through the intrinsic bounty of their land. They intermarried with the tribes, founded Barcelona and built a fortress at Tarakon (which would later become Tarragona).

The Romans meanwhile had become aware of the growing military strength and general enrichment of their arch enemies in the west; the first legions set foot in Empurias in 218BC and then spread southwards with the specific purpose of chasing them from military bases such as Tarakon. They succeeded and those Carthaginians who were not killed fled back to reinforce Hannibal's army marching on Rome. The Romans adopted Tarakon/Tarraco as their main base and built it into the great city and capital of their province of Hispania Citerior (later Tarraconensis) which extended over the northern half of the peninsula. The Iberian tribes, particularly the legendary Illergetes, were fiercely resistant to these aggressive invaders and were only finally pacified by Cato who arrived with reinforcements in 195BC.

The Roman period was one of gradual but significant progress, and the Iberians were shown better agricultural methods so that great tracts of hitherto unused land could be brought under cultivation. The land was divided into roughly equal portions, each of which was worked by an individual family (a method which was to distinguish Catalan agriculture from the *latifundia* system of Castile in the future). Intermarriage between Iberians and Romans was actively encouraged. A wealthy bourgeoisie developed out of the thriving agricultural economy and people built sumptuous villas surrounded by orchards and farmland (the forerunners of the Catalan *mas*). Cities grew up and were linked by a network of roads; the most famous of these was the *Via Augusta* which crossed the Pyrenees, followed the coast through Girona, Barcelona, Tarragona and Tortosa and on to Alicante. It is interesting to note that during the early Roman period (before the arrival of the Goths), the cities were unwalled and were therefore totally integrated with the villas and agricultural economy beyond.

All of this material progress came abruptly to an end when the Franks and Alemanes swept in over the Pyrenees in the 3C, destroying cities and laying waste huge rural areas before passing on. Cities were rebuilt (and fortified with walls), but many of the villas remained in ruins. Romanisation declined from that moment on. Nothing however could erase the all important legacies left by the Romans. Firstly there was language: the Romans introduced Vulgar Latin which grew into Catalan over the centuries and remained undiluted by Arabic (and therefore a purer tongue in the eyes of the Catalans than Castilian). Of overwhelming significance too were the legislation and social structure (which would form the basis of the *Uzatges* when the Franks reintroduced it in the 8C).

There was also Christianity, unofficially creeping in already in the 3C and officially established by the time the Visigoths arrived in the early 5C but not adopted as their official religion until 589. By this time the Romans were seriously losing interest in *Hispania* and the legions were leaving for other parts of the troubled empire like Gaul and Britain which needed more urgent attention. The Visigoths briefly made Barcelona their capital but moved on to Toledo in 554. They brought with them a rigid class system, merging their own élite with the already installed Roman aristocracy to form a strong and highly privileged upper class; far below was the Iberian peasantry – without rights, without education or hope. Strangely, however, the Visigoths had no system of royal succession. Heredity played no part and new rulers had to be elected by the upper class. As each monarch came towards the end of his reign therefore, civil war would inevitably ensue between rival factions for the succession.

Into this unjust and unstable society came the Moors. The invasions began in 711 when an army of Berbers under Tariq set foot in what is now Gibraltar (deriving from *Jbel Tariq* = Tariq's mountain). They quickly despatched the Visigothic king Rodrigo at *Jerez de la Frontera* and proceeded slowly northwards, meeting with very little opposition until they reached *Tarraconensis* where a new Visigothic king had recently been enthroned. Here there was fierce resistance but it was not strong enough to counter the inexorable advance of the fanatical Moors who captured Barcelona in 717 and then crossed the Pyrenees and went as far as Poitiers before being checked by the Franks. In desperation the inhabitants of what was to become Catalonia turned to the powerful Frankish leader for help. This was willingly given in exchange for their agreement to becoming part of the Carolingian Empire. Thus was born the province of the *Spanish March* which owed allegiance to the Frankish king but under which individuals retained their rights to land (as instituted by the Romans), and limitations on the payment of taxes, and on military service (due only to the local overlord). Herein lay the seeds of the *Uzatges* and the subsequent Catalan constitution.

This powerful Christian alliance liberated Girona in 785 and Barcelona in 801 (though the latter was to pass to and fro several times thereafter). The reconquered lands, which extended roughly as far as today's road between Barcelona and Lleida, were divided into counties corresponding with the old Visigothic administrative boundaries. These were controlled by counts, who had political and judicial functions but were ultimately responsible to the Frankish king and were appointed or dismissed by him, at least in the beginning. Everyone had his place in this well-ordered feudal society owing allegiance to, and receiving protection from, his lord.

As the counts grew more powerful and began forming alliances and leaving their lands to their own sons, so the interest of the Frankish court in the far-flung province of *Spanish March* began to wane. Charlemagne was succeeded in 814 by Louis the Pious who, having twice tried and failed to reconquer Tortosa in the south, had become disillusioned and preoccupied with matters nearer home.

The most powerful count of all was Wilfred the Hairy (*Guifre el Pelloso*) (870-97) who managed to achieve subordination of all the other counties to that of his own – Barcelona. He it was who started the long process of separation from the Frankish empire, which would not however be formally recognised by the Franks until 1258. There is even a legend to illustrate the transfer of power from king to count: it is said that Wilfred was wounded one day when fighting the Moors alongside King Charles 'the Bald' (Charlemagne's grandson). On that day the King dipped his fingers in the blood and drew them symbolically across Wilfred's golden shield, creating thus what was to become the flag of independent Catalonia.

Alas, Wilfred died soon after, mortally wounded this time by the Moorish Governor of Lleida and his body was laid to rest at the Abbey of Ripoll which he himself had founded. His lands were divided amongst his sons who lacked the clear vision of their father and seemed undecided which way to turn, at first making fresh overtures to the Franks and then openly flirting with the Moorish Court at Cordoba.

All this came to an abrupt end when Barcelona was ruthlessly (and some would say, surprisingly) sacked by the notorious Moorish leader, *Yacoub el Mansour*, in 985. The then Count, *Borell II*, no doubt wishing he had remained more staunchly loyal to the Carolingian Court, urgently called for help from that quarter. The response was luke warm and much delayed. By the time it arrived el Mansour had done his worst and passed on to other territories. The event was significant in that it jolted Borrell into the realisation that hence-forward Catalonia could only survive as a sovereign state, owing nothing to either Franks or Moors. He therefore formally withdrew his allegiance to the Frankish king.

There followed a period of immense and fruitful activity in Catalonia. Defensive castles were quickly constructed in case the Moors should return (though with the death of el Mansour in 1002 this began to seem less likely), dioceses were created (or recreated from the old Visigothic ones), religious orders poured over the Pyrenees to build monasteries and churches and vast tracts of land were repopulated. Christianity was energetically established and the movement known as 'Romanesque' got under way, with its amazing proliferation of small stone churches often with every interior surface painted or carved to the glory of God.

The monks were very much in control because at first they were the only people who could read and write. And the greatest of these was *Abbot Oliva* of Ripoll (971-1040) who taught not only religious matters but medicine and science, mathematics, agriculture and even small industries. The Catalan language was by this time fully formed and in current use. The earliest Catalan text ever found dates from the early 11C; it is a collection of sermons known as the '*Homilies d'Organya*'.

And it was a monk (*Ponc Bofill March*) who drafted the *Uzatges* – a code of conduct which defined and made legally binding the rights and duties of every individual in the realm, from sovereign down to meanest vassal. It in effect legalised the feudal system introduced originally by the Franks, and failure to observe the stated obligations became punishable according to the code. Catalans are justly proud of the Uzatges which was first ratified in 1068 (though considerably amended throughout the following century) and was therefore in place almost 150 years before Magna Carta.

It is generally accepted by historians that by the late 11C Catalonia differed fundamentally from the rest of Spain, in language, in feudalism and also in the astonishing progress of its education in the capable hands of the religious orders.

Progress continued as the descendants of Wilfred the Hairy came and went. An unusually wise and visionary count acceded in 1096. This was *Ramon Berenguer III* who was the first to create a fleet of ships and send them out into the Mediterranean to explore. He also managed to oust the Moors finally from Tarragona (in 1118). However, it was his son, *Ramon Berenguer IV*, who changed the direction of history by marrying in 1137 the infant daughter of the King of Aragon, *Petronella*, thereby combining (on the death of the king) the two realms into one powerful kingdom known henceforth as 'the Crown of Aragon'.

The invincible combination proved too much for the Moors who were soon driven from their remaining enclaves of Tortosa and Lleida. By the middle of the 12C all Catalonia was back in Christian hands and the newly liberated territories came to be known as 'New Catalonia'. Much credit for this must also go to the Templars – a renowned order of Christian knights who had been invited by Ramon Berenguer III to help clear the country of Moors. That done, they became something of a liability, exacting a high price in the form of castles and land, until they were eventually disbanded in 1308.

Totally free now from the Moors at home, the kings of Aragon-Catalonia (as the counts were now known) sought to drive them from the Mediterranean. Greatest of the kings was James I (1213-1276), nicknamed 'the Conqueror', who took Majorca and Ibiza, followed by Valencia and Murcia. His motto was said to be 'War with the Moors and peace with the Christian princes abroad'; to this end he signed the *Treaty of Corbeil* with France in 1258 renouncing any claims on land N of the Pyrenees (except for Rousillon, Cerdanya and Montpelier) and thereby ending the recent troubles with the religious sect of *Albigensis* which had culminated in the defeat and killing of his father, *Père I*, by *Simon de Montfort* at the Battle of Muret.

The years that followed saw further conquests in the Mediterranean, including Sardinia and Sicily, and a massive expansion in trade. The liberated territories were systematically repopulated with ordinary people who were encouraged by being taught the latest methods of cultivating rice and fruit and, of course, vines. (Here too is another noteworthy difference with Castile where reconquered lands were distributed as vast estates to the nobility only, leaving them to exploit the peasantry at will).

At the same time, cities in Catalonia were burgeoning with skilled craftsmen and opportunists of all kinds, especially merchants taking advantage of overseas trade to supply the citizens with all they had ever dreamed of. A rich bourgeoisie began to emerge.

This growth in prosperity and confidence was behind the flowering of Gothic architecture in the kingdom and many of the great cathedrals – miracles of soaring space and light – date from this period. So do the famous shipyards in Barcelona (*Dressanes*) and countless palaces. Much of this was paid for by rich merchants who would often encrust altar-pieces and paintings with gold for good measure.

James I was not only a conqueror but also a very wise man who saw the urgent need for dialogue between the sovereign and his subjects. And so was born the great institution of the *Corts* – a consultative body in which were represented three classes – the nobility, the clergy and the urban bourgeoisie (the peasants and working classes would however wait another 700 years). Under James' successor, *Père II*, the Corts were transformed into an institution with full legislative powers whose approval the king must obtain, for example, before collecting taxes to finance a war. Later, as wars became more frequent and more costly, a special administration was formed specifically to collect taxes which was called the *Diputacio del General* – and became known as the *Generalitat*).

Catalonia's Golden Age was brought to an end by a combination of factors, principal amongst them being the onset of the Black Death in 1350. The population was decimated to the point where there simply were not enough people to work in the fields. This led gradually to serious unrest as peasants found themselves forced to work even longer hours for lower wages. Some landowners brought in labour from outside and profited from the misery of the less fortunate. The peasants revolted and the King briefly took their side against the landowners, many of whom were in fact clerics. The last two kings of the House of Barcelona, *John I* and *Martin the Humane*, reigned unhappily over sick and unruly populations.

All of these problems might have been overcome in time if only King Martin had left an heir to the throne. Unfortunately (and crucially for Catalonia) his only son was killed on an expedition to Sardinia. King Martin died in 1410 and with him died the great dynasty which had brought Catalonia from dependent principality to prosperous and independent Mediterranean power.

Predictably there was no shortage of claimants to the throne. These were narrowed down to two – *James of Urgell* and *Ferdinand of Antequera*, second son of John I of Castile. After months of intrigue, (much of it caused by the powerful Anti-Pope, *Pedro de Luna*, who needed the support of Castile and so threw his weight behind Ferdinand) a body of representatives from Catalonia, Aragon and Valencia met in 1412 in a town called *Casp*. For better or worse they chose Ferdinand. By handing the throne of the Crown of Aragon to a Castilian dynasty, this decision (known as the *Compromise of Casp*) ended at a stroke the separation of Catalonia from the rest of Spain.

Ferdinand took over a population already seething with unrest which grew rapidly worse when he imprisoned James of Urgell, whom many had encouraged to rally and fight back. Moreover, as a Castilian, Ferdinand had very little knowledge of, or interest in, the domestic affairs and traditional laws of his new realm. His son, *Alfonso the Magnanimous*, spent most of his time as monarch as far away from his irksome subjects as possible and irritated them the more by demanding huge sums of money for further Mediterrean adventures. Once more it was the peasants who suffered, being called upon to work for less and less money with their feudal rights forgotten. They formed their first syndicates and tasted 'people power' for the first time, much to the consternation of clergy and nobility. King Alfonso, meanwhile, successfully conquered the Kingdom of Naples and liked it so much that he established his court there and never returned to Catalonia. By the time his son, *John II*, came to the throne, the rift between peasants (whose role was fundamental in sustaining the economy) and the privileged clergy, nobility and merchants, had seriously deepened. It took a dispute between the king, who imprisoned his own son, and the Corts, who claimed he had no right to do so, for the rift to explode into a full and costly civil war, which was to continue savagely for over ten years. The people ranged themselves behind King or Corts, whichever suited their own personal interest best. The King tried unsuccessfully to enlist the help of France and England. Finally he turned to neighbouring Castile where a possible solution was waiting, in the form of the *Infanta Isabella*, still unmarried and therefore a most suitable match for his young son, *Ferdinand*. The two were duly married in 1469. And with this historic union the whole of Spain (except Granada which was still in Moorish hands) came under one and the same royal house, though both Castile and Catalonia-Aragon retained their own separate *Corts*.

The war came to an end and a formal peace treaty was signed between king and Corts. It was generally agreed that nobody had won, but that all of Catalonia had lost since its economy and national confidence had suffered untold damage. It was up to Ferdinand to settle matters between peasants and the rest. This he did by convening in 1486 a Council at the *Monastery of Guadelupe* (one of Spain's most revered shrines) which granted to peasants a right to the use of the land they occupied and the suspension of any agreements which had bonded them against their wills to landowners. The landowners also received certain privileges. Both sides seemed well satisfied and the stricken agricultural economy began slowly to revive. It was not helped however by the scourge of the Inquisition, rigorously enforced overall by Queen Isabelle and which caused the death or imprisonment of thousands of *Conversos* (Jews converted to Catholicism) who had often occupied key positions. Nor was it helped by the royal couple's total preoccupation with the struggle to drive the Moors out of their last enclave of Granada. This caused long absences from Barcelona and grave inroads into both Castilian and Catalonian exchequers. To everyone's relief, they succeeded in 1492.

1492 was also the year of Columbus's triumphal return from the New World to Barcelona. Barcelona was, and still is, justly proud of this event even though Columbus was a Genoese, not a Catalan, and returned there because the couple happened to be in residence at the time. It is well known however that Castile reaped more than its fair share of the rich merchandise coming in from the Indies, and that Catalonia-Aragon benefitted little. This had perhaps more to do with the distant location of the latter and the exhaustion of her fleet and funds after so many costly Mediterranean expeditions, than it had with the greed of the Castilians. Seville, and later Cadiz, were ideally sited to receive the laden galleys and enjoyed a virtual monopoly of the trade.

In fact, Catalonia's marginalisation at this time inclined her to develop her own independent trading links, and Ferdinand can be given credit for encouraging home industry, in particular that of cloth which was then profitably exported to Sicily and Naples. This gradual revival of commercial activity was to stand Catalonia in good stead in the future when Castile began to suffer from an economic decline caused by profligate spending of immeasurable riches by the nobility with scant regard for the worsening plight of the peasantry.

The election of Charles I, (son of Ferdinand and Isabella's mad daughter, Joan) as Holy Roman Emperor meant that all of Spain was now ruled by a single monarch whose main interests lay outside the country in Northern Europe, and specifically in fighting against the rise of Protestantism there.

The troubles which arose in Castile when the absent Charles installed his Flemish friends in key roles of state fortunately passed Catalonia by. It had more pressing problems anyway, in the form of damaging attacks by Barbary pirates and an increasing threat from the Turks advancing inexorably into Europe by land and sea. Faced with these dangers, the Catalans sprang into action, built ships with almost the same fervour as they had under James I 300 years earlier and sailed to meet the Turks under Charles' half-brother, *Don John of Austria*. The result is well known: a resounding defeat for the Turks in the Battle of Lepanto in 1571. This triumphant naval adventure did much to restore Catalonia's self esteem, even though at home social conflict continued between landowners and peasants in rural areas, and between merchants and craftsmen in the cities.

The dominant figure on the Castilian scene in the first half of the 17C was *Olivares*, Philip IV's chief minister, who argued passionately that if Spain were to survive intact, all the disparate elements most come together under one law – that of Madrid. As a mere province of Castile, he believed Catalonia-Aragon should pay appropriate taxes and provide troops to defend the empire.

When France declared war on Spain in 1635 Catalonia was asked for money and men. Since (according to her constitution) Catalonia should pay only those taxes which were approved by her own Government, and only recruit soldiers when her own territory was threatened, the answer was a firm no.

Olivares, determined to bring the rebellious province to heel, then launched a campaign into the Pyrenees from Catalan territory which went badly and involved the deaths of up to 10,000 men who had been recruited against their will. Far from satisfied with this sacrifice, he then forcibly billetted hundreds of Castilian troops in Catalonia, even in Barcelona itself. Riots ensued and the situation came violently to a head in June 1640 when a mob of *segadors* (reapers who assembled each year to help with harvest) revolted, burned down official buildings and murdered King Philip's viceroy. In a desperate bid to prevent complete anarchy, and to fight off the Castilian army which now had ample reason for every kind of atrocity against the Catalans, the Corts turned to the French king, Louis XIII, for help. They pledged obedience and a free passage across the Pyrenees in return for French observance of the Catalan constitution.

The constitution was not however observed; French troops poured in and caused as much damage as the Castilians had. A combination of plague, famine and Olivares' retirement in 1643 brought this pointless war of the reapers to an end. Philip IV signed the *Treaty of the Pyrenees* with the French in 1659 under which he ceded Rousillon and neighbouring counties to France but firmly regained Catalonia, whose brief separation from Castilian Spain had lasted only 19 years.

Philip IV died in 1665 and was succeeded by his son Charles II, a half-wit who himself died in 1700 without leaving an heir. Before he died Charles had been asked to nominate an heir. The choice lay between Archduke Charles of Austria and Philip of Anjou (nephew of Louis XIV). He chose the latter. The Catalans however preferred Charles of Austria whom they named

Carlos III of Catalonia-Aragon. England and Holland also preferred him because they feared a strong Spanish-French alliance. So it was with the support of the British fleet that Charles of Austria entered Barcelona in 1705 and was immediately welcomed by the Corts, also by Aragon and Valencia. There then followed the inevitable clash between this faction and that of the Bourbon Philip V, already established in Madrid. Soon after this, the Austrian Archduke's brother died and Charles was recalled to Austria to take his place as Holy Roman Emperor. At this point the English and the Dutch decided the cause was no longer worth fighting for and, having signed with France the *Treaty of Utrecht*, left the Catalans to defend the Austrian cause alone against the might of Castile and the enthroned king. The Catalans fought on most heroically for a year till finally defeated in 1714 by Philip's army of over 200,000 men with reinforcements from the French. The surrender was unconditional. Philip then inflicted a devastating retribution. The *Generalitat* and the *Council of One Hundred* were formally disbanded, the centuries-old rights and privileges were abolished, and it became an offence to speak, write or teach in Catalan. A huge fort (*ciutadella*) was erected in the city of Barcelona as a threatening reminder and the university was removed to the small and remote town of *Cervera*. The cathedral (*Seu Vella*) in *Lleida* became a military barracks and military governors were appointed overall under the control of a Captain General. Pacification, it seemed, was assured. Olivares would have been proud.

Subdued and with no further battles to fight for the time being, the Catalans gradually got back to work and the disrupted economy began to improve, especially textiles and the production of wine. To encourage a new climate of cooperation the next king, Charles III, allowed Barcelona and neighbouring ports to trade direct with the New World which resulted in renewed prosperity for the whole of the coastal region, and Barcelona in particular.

Peace was shortlived and in 1792 Spain declared war on the French in protest at the revolutionary execution of King Louis XVI. Catalonia's troops (willing this time) formed a vital part of the Spanish army and so much were they valued that they even received their orders in Catalan. They were no match for the powerful French forces however who occupied much of Catalonia by 1794. A treaty was signed in 1795. Incensed by this humiliating defeat caused, it was generally agreed, by the incompetence of the weak Charles IV and his unpopular favourite, Godoy, the Catalans reconstituted their Assembly and sent an army of peasants to chase the French back over the Pyrenees. The demoralised Madrid government did nothing to stop them. At this particular moment the balance of power was once more with the Catalans and it is tempting to speculate why they did not reclaim their independence then and there.

The French returned after 6 years of relative peace, Napoleon having assured Godoy that he wanted only to pass through Spain in order to subdue Portugal and would then leave. In the event French troops occupied the whole peninsula and Napoleon enticed the royal family out of the country 'to discuss peace' and enthroned his brother, *Joseph Bonaparte*, in their place. All over the country people were outraged at this high-handed behaviour and fought back. The English were amongst those who responded to the Spanish cry for help and sent the Duke of Wellington and the cream of the army. The Germans and Dutch and Portuguese also became involved, only too keen to teach Napoleon a lesson. The war continued for four long years, causing huge devastation of cities, monasteries and churches especially in Catalonia. In 1811 the Spanish army decided to evacuate Catalonia and leave it to its fate, which was to be annexed to France and divided into 4 departments. Bitter fighting continued and famine weakened soldiers on both sides. By 1814 Napoleon had withdrawn all his troops from the Iberian peninsula because he needed them on the Russian front.

By this time liberal leaders across Spain had become sick and tired of the inadequacies and corruption of their sovereigns who had recently led them from one disaster to another. They declared a new constitution – the *Constitution of Cadiz* – which proposed an elected parliament, a constitutional monarch, one law and one tax system for all. It effectively transferred power from the Crown, the aristocracy and the church to the people themselves and it stood for a united Spain, which would of course include Catalonia. The whole country was divided between *Constitutionalists* (who favoured it) and *Absolutists* (who preferred the old system of royal absolutism).

On his return from exile, the King rejected the constitution out of hand and its leading supporters were persecuted and imprisoned. Later there was an uprising of liberals and he was compelled to accept it. Tragically, however, the nation was not used to law and order without repression and it relapsed into chaos: it wasn't enough just to tell people they were free; they simply did not have the structures through which to work towards democracy and elimination of poverty. The rest of Europe became worried by the turn events were taking in Spain, fearful lest similar thoughts should beset their own people. The French, now with monarchy restored, once more poured their troops over the Pyrenees and, as usual, Catalonia bore the brunt of the fighting. Peace was declared in 1827 but an exceptionally repressive French captain general was appointed and subjected the people of Barcelona to a reign of terror until he was removed in 1832.

The Spanish King Ferdinand died in 1833 leaving only an infant daughter, Isabelle. He did however have a brother – *Carlos* – in whom many Spaniards perceived the quality of Catholicism and moral strength which would make the country great once more. These people – the Carlists – were to cause three civil wars, the first of which was sparked off by the 13-year old Isabelle's coronation. The Absolutists in Catalonia strongly supported Carlos who promised investment in their industries, though he made no commitment on the re-establishment of their traditional rights. The Constitutionalists on the whole supported the Queen. They in turn were divided between the moderate bourgeoisie and the more radical working classes. The Queen abdicated after reigning for only 3 years, leaving a country bitterly divided within itself and with no acceptable ruler in sight.

A republic was proclaimed. Intermittent fighting continued, less now between Absolutists and Constitutionalists, more between workers and the rich bourgeoisie between whom the gulf in living standards was widening fast. Despite the growing prosperity of Barcelona, wages and working conditions were low and miserable. Strikes became commonplace and Marxist-inspired anarchism began to creep in.

The anomalies at the turn of the century were characterised by grave and violent social unrest on the one hand, and the great Exhibition of Barcelona (in 1888) on the other. Catalonia had become the most dynamic economic force in Spain, with its textile factories working overtime to supply the demands of the Crimean war and later the First World War. The profits were ploughed back into resplendent houses and the whole Extension *(Eixample)* of Barcelona dates from this period.

Confidence grew and with it a resurgence of interest in Catalan autonomy, particularly on the part of the middle classes. The Catalan language was once again used overtly and the Regionalist league – *Lliga Regionalisata* – was formed which asked not for separation but for regional autonomy within a Spanish federation. By 1906 it had gained the support of Republicans, Socialists and Carlists throughout Spain as a respectable bourgeois organisation which could strengthen the cause against Monarchists and of course the workers and their anarchist fringe. It was therefore decided in Madrid to grant some concessions to Catalonia and in 1914 the *Mancomunitat* was set up in Barcelona (in the former Generalitat palace) with the power of regional administration financed by local taxes but with no political power. The Mancommunitat was also to provide an essential infrastructure which would form the basis of Catalonia's eventual modernisation. They built roads and a basic telephone network. In rural areas they encouraged cooperativism and peasant farmers were given courses in modern agricultural methods. The medical services were improved, and schools were allowed to teach in both Catalan and Castilian.

Whilst all this was happening, the Monarchy had been restored in Madrid in the person of *Alfonso XII*, Isabelle's young son and a fervent Catholic. When he died 11 years later his widow, *Maria Christine*, became regent and the move back towards Absolutism and Catholicism became even more pronounced which inevitably led to polarisation between the haves and have-nots. When her son, also *Alfonso*, acceded to the throne, he faced a deeply troubled country united only in its growing hatred of the established church. He relied more and more on the army to protect him. He finally lost their support when he made a gross error of judgement, ordering the commander in chief to march 10,000 soldiers into what turned out to be a Berber ambush in Morocco, which resulted in the massacre of most of them.

Bloody retribution was avoided only by the immediate appearance of *Miguel Primero de Rivero*, the Captain General of Catalonia, who proclaimed himself Dictator in 1923, promising even greater autonomy to Catalonia in exchange for her support. Once in full power, he went back on his promise, disbanded the Mancommunitat and came down harshly on the powerful trade unions. He spent large sums of money on monuments thoughout Spain and paid scant attention to the economy. In 1930 he gave up, disillusioned and exhausted and the king returned very briefly. In 1931, however, national elections returned a republic and Alfonso XIII quietly and sadly took himself into exile.

Two days later a federal Republic of Catalonia was declared from the balcony of the Generalitat building. The elected leader, *Fransesc Macia*, who had the solid support of the working classes, went to Madrid to present his constitution to the new *Cortes*. After long negotiation it was approved. The new government was to be called *the Generalitat de Catalunya* and the process of autonomy would be initiated.

The Generalitat was once more in control of its own regional administration, justice and culture (though not defence, foreign affairs or the church). This seemed to satisfy Catalans for the time being who began working together in a new spirit of co-operation for the greater good of their fledgeling republic. Widely supported at first President Macia soon found he could not please both industrialists and trade unions at the same time. He died in 1933 and was succeeded by the greatly esteemed left-wing lawyer, *Lluis Companys*.

In Madrid chaos was descending once more. The Republicans were actually defeated in elections by the Right who promised to restore order throughout the country. In Catalonia they suspended the Generalitat and replaced the President with a Captain General of their choosing.

In 1934 there was a rebellion in Asturias which was brutally crushed with the help of Moroccan troops under *General Franco*. Election followed election and by 1936 a new left-wing coalition was formed nationally in a concerted effort to stamp out the Right. It comprised Socialists, Republicans, Anarchists and Communists and was called the Popular Front. It won an overwhelming victory in elections. In Catalonia the Generalitat was restored under President Companys and the people were jubilant.

The Right had also become firmly entrenched nationally. It consisted of the new Fascist Falange party led by Primo de Rivera's son, *José Antonio*, the army, the church and the Monarchists. Left and right, Communist and Fascist, stood face to face across the land. The stage was set for civil war. And the spark which ignited it was the assassination of the Monarchist leader, *Calvo Sotelo*, by Republicans on July 13, 1936. Within days every military garrison in the land had risen to put an end once and for all to the Popular Front and re-establish the traditional God-fearing values of old. They called themselves the National Movement and believed they could win their crusade in 3 days. In fact it took three years of appalling slaughter and misery from which few Spanish families escaped and which shocked the world.

In Barcelona clerics and wealthy industrialists donned labourers' clothing in a bid to escape the dominant Popular Front. The Generalitat appealed for calm and managed to smuggle some of them out to France. Many more were murdered, churches, monasteries, palaces were looted and burned. Workers' collectives took over factories. Barcelona was a cauldron of hatred between Left and Right. In 1938 it was systematically bombed by Mussolini's airforce in support of the Nationalists under Franco, resulting in the destruction of many historic buildings and the death of over 1,500 civilians. The Nationalists with their superior might and powerful allies were advancing over all. The Catalans made a last stand on the banks of the Ebro at Tortosa but were finally overpowered and the armies swept northwards towards Barcelona.

The Civil War officially ended on March 28, 1939. The surrender of the Popular Front to the Nationalists was unconditional and the task of rebuilding Spain fell to the new Head of State, General Franco. The Generalitat de Catalunya was of course abolished. Catalan culture was forced underground and even the use of the language became a punishable offence. Politicians, intellectuals and artists either fled the country or were imprisoned or shot. President Companys escaped to France only to be handed over in 1940 by the occupying Nazis to Franco who had him executed at the Castle of Montjuich in Barcelona.

By the 1950s a slight softening in the Madrid Government's attitude to things Catalan could just be detected. By the 60s certain cultural institutions and periodicals were beginning tentatively to reappear. In 1974 the movement known as the 'Assemblea de Catalunya' come out into the open, uniting all the previously clandestine intellectual, artistic and political entities into one irresistible force whose slogan was 'Liberty, Amnesty and Statute of Autonomy'. The impetus gathered strength.

After Franco died the following year there was no holding back. On Catalonia's National Day, 11 September 1976, a million and a half people came out into the streets of Barcelona from all over Catalonia to demand autonomy. A year later the Generalitat was provisionally re-established under *Josep Tarradellas*, a former president in exile. A Statute was drawn up by Catalan parliamentarians in Madrid which in October 1979 was passed by the majority of the Catalan people. It did not allow for the full recognition of Catalan rights but it marked the beginning of the road to self-government. On March 20, 1980 the Catalan Parliament formally opened, with 135 deputies elected by the people and the election of a new President of the Generalitat – *Jordi Pujol.* This completed the recovery of Catalan institutions.

ROMANESQUE CHURCHES

So much has been written about Catalonia's uniquely rich heritage of over 1800 churches built between 1000 and 1250 (the period known as *Romanesque*) that the average visitor could find himself understandably confused. The following paragraphs are an attempt to summarise how, why and when the movement began, and what you should look for.

The northern region, known as 'old Catalonia', was freed from the Moorish yoke by the late 10C; (this is remarkable for being more than two centuries before the decisive defeat of the Moors at *Las Navas de Toloso*, and 5 centuries before the fall of *Granada*, the last Moorish enclave, in 1492). Already the first primitive stone and mortar churches with vaulted roofs were beginning to appear, in the style known today as *pre-Romanesque*. By the end of the 10C the Counts of Barcelona had achieved separation from the Carolingian Empire and were proclaiming their sovereignty over other Catalan leaders. The first people's charter (*Uzatges*) followed in 1060 which defined the rights of the individual and codified existing feudal systems and land rights. In 1137 Count Ramon Berenguer IV of Barcelona was betrothed to the Princess Petronella of Aragon, thereby uniting the two powerful realms under one *Crown of Aragon*. 1149 saw the final ousting of the Moors from their two remaining strongholds in Catalonia – the small kingdoms or *taifas* of Lleida and Tortosa – the region which came to be known as 'new Catalonia'.

Small wonder that this period of approximately 250 years was one of immense confidence, vigour and growing prosperity. The first gold coins were minted, the population increased and communities felt safe by and by to come down from the mountains and live on the fertile plain. Above all, there was a felt need to express freely and in hard and tangible form the glory of victorious Christendom and a one-ness with the rest of Christian Europe.

So it was that in the 11C the early Romanesque style was born, an explosion of robust and unwavering spirituality manifesting itself in painting, sculpture, metalware, country houses, bridges, monasteries and, of course, churches. The earliest churches are to be found in the Pyrenees, for the obvious reason that Christianity was established there first. These churches tend to be the purest in style: this is because populations moved southwards as danger receded and abandoned their churches, leaving them free from later 'improvement'.

The style is essentially a blend of the basic architectural traditions of Rome with the influences of France and Italy (Lombardy in particular) and the native vigour of the Catalans superimposed. French (or rather Frankish) influence was never far away: the ways of communication across the Pyrenees had always been open for the armies of Charlemagne and his successors who had ensured the early defeat of the Moors. The Italian influence came across the Mediterranean with the merchants who brought their ships in to the ports of Barcelona and Tarragona.

The early churches were (and are) immensely simple, single nave structures with stone walls massive enough to support the heavy barrel vault; there is usually a single east-facing apse, a doorway on the south side and a small wall belfry. Already in the early 11C the influence from Lombardy was moving in and even the earliest churches show bands of arcatures and pilaster strips (known as 'Lombard bands'), usually on the apse and frequently forming the only decorative feature. Inside there were often wall paintings of rich and vibrant colours, again showing the influence of Lombardy, as painters followed architects across the Mediterranean. A very few of these frescoes remain *in situ* but most have been removed in recent times to museums. The technique for this is highly skilled and is described at the end of this chapter.

It is fascinating to consider for a moment the degree of organisation and will-power which must have been needed to erect these stone churches in the first place. The Romans, after all, had a ready supply of slave labour; the Catalans on the other hand were a fiercely free people with no obvious labour source but themselves. These monumental structures can therefore only have been erected with huge effort involving the faith and determination of whole communities for whom the church meant not only spiritual guidance but also education, health and sometimes refuge.

As Christianity spread southwards, so the churches grew bigger and ever more complex. Side aisles appeared, separated from the central nave by columns and semi-circular arches; there would be three or five apses, a crypt, and a tall slender bell tower with pairs or triplets of windows separated by Lombard bands. (Even some of the simplest and most isolated country churches have this last, most delightful feature which can add a sublime lightness of touch to an otherwise heavy structure).

During the course of the 11C, stonemasons (usually from Italy) transformed the basic style, introducing lavishly carved capitals, and distinctive monumental doorways with many archivolts often covered with a plethora of sculptures. These carvings, so refreshingly alive and frequently amusing to the modern eye, represented not just pleasing decorations but a behavioural code to the congregation of the time, many of whom were illiterate. Much of the mythology represented was undoubtedly familar and the moral behind scenes of monsters devouring the wicked, and farmers spanking their wives, was presumably plain for all to see. One is constantly amazed by the fertility of Romanesque-period imaginations and the shrewd insight into what must have been the hopes and fears of people at that time.

The monastic orders arrived in force and established themselves all over the region. The Cistercians were busiest of all and created the monasteries of *Santes Creus* and *Poblet* in the early 12C. The monks themselves were a powerful motivating force, as were the pilgrims who trod the well-worn routes across the Pyrenees, and for whom particularly large churches must be built in order to accommodate their numbers. Cathedrals were built in the main cities and a few retain still their Romanesque beginnings. (A good example is at Vic). Other large churches, like the one at Agramunt, retain a superbly carved doorway in an otherwise unremarkable and many times rebuilt surround. Different styles of Romanesque emerged, ranging from the early Cistercian austerity typified by Poblet monastery to the ornate decoration of the *School of Lleida*, following the example of the old cathedral at Lleida.

Many of the smaller Romanesque churches still form centres of lively village communities, often scattered along Pyrenean valleys (*Boi* and *Aran* are prime examples). For security reasons these churches are usually kept locked. Do not be put off by this. There will be a keyholder somewhere in the vicinity (it could be the priest, or the owner of the local bar, or simply a helpful neighbour) who will usually be pleased to show you round, so long as you do not call in the middle of his siesta on a hot summer afternoon. Other churches lie right off the beaten track and occasionally in complete isolation, their villages having long since crumbled away; these may or may not be locked, may not even have been restored. The sudden and unexpected discovery of a humble and beautiful church standing alone in a mountain wilderness is a joy which needs no description.

The keen and adventurous visitor will take as many side roads as possible, armed perhaps with the free information sheet, attractively produced by the Department of Tourism and available at most Tourist Offices. It lists a fair number of Romanesque churches along six specific N-S routes. but there is no reason why, with good eyesight and a road-worthy vehicle, he should not discover one or two which do not appear on the list. There are, after all, 1800 in Catalonia. Natural curiosity is the key, combined with a degree of patience and a love of simple things.

It is a constant source of wonderment to many people – the writers included – that mural paintings over 800 years old can be removed from their mother walls and perfectly re-constituted in some present-day city museum. The technique, known as *strappo* was imported originally from Italy. It has been followed in Catalonia since the beginning of the century, and is still used today, albeit with some refinements.

* when the painting is first discovered (and it may well be behind a coat of plaster which will need careful chipping off), four coats of fixative are applied to prevent further deterioration

* squares of cloth are soaked in hot, brown, soluble glue, which is (or was) made by boiling rabbit skins

* the cloth squares are applied hot to the painting, slightly overlapping it. A tent-like structure is erected overall to prevent the heat from escaping

* the glue-soaked cloths are left to dry out completely, which can take as long a day; machines are used to detect any trace of humidity before it is deemed safe to proceed

* the cloth, with painting adhering, is then pulled off the wall in sections and carefully rolled up before being transported to its permanent museum site. (There are early photographs in one museum of the rolls being brought down some remote mountain side by donkeys)

* in the museum, a piece of cloth, the same size as the painting, is covered with permanent, non-soluble, white glue

* the sections of painting are carefuly fixed to this, face up

* when this glue is dry, hot water is thrown over the original sections of cloth which can be sponged off the painting, once the 'rabbit glue' has dissolved

* any areas of backing cloth not covered by fresco are painted over in a natural colour and then stippled to look like stone showing through. No attempt is made to re-create the original painting in areas where it has been lost, though a little delicate re-touching may be done to any sections damaged during the process of transfer

* after a final cleaning off of any extraneous material, and the application of a coat of varnish, the painting is attached to a fibreglass backing and placed in its permanent site.

MONASTERIES

There is evidence that small monastic communities existed in Northern Spain as early as 4C and that under the Visigoths who arrived in 5C these grew and multiplied. Many monasteries still standing today have Visigothic foundations (*Sant Pere de Terrassa* is one notable example) and it is known that in the early 6C, Councils were held in Barcelona, Girona, Tarragona and Lleida which gave bishops power to regulate the lives and works of monks in their respective dioceses.

This energetic and increasingly diversified Christian activity was abruptly ended by the arrival of the Moors in 717; it re-emerged less than a century later (in old Catalonia) within the more unified framework of the Rule of St Benedict. The Benedictines came over the Pyrenees in large numbers during 9C and 10C, actively encouraged by the Frankish kings to whom the Catalans owed allegiance under the *Spanish March*. Hundreds of Benedictine churches and monasteries sprang up in regions liberated from the Moors and now undergoing intensive re-population. Many of the new settlers were immigrants from the still Moorish-controlled southern region (to be known later as 'New Catalonia'), whose influence gave a distinctly Mozarabic flavour to some of the earliest Romanesque churches.

The Benedictines were committed to disciplined lives of prayer, sacred reading and manual labour and their communities tended to be inward-looking and generally closed off from the growing population. Many monasteries were founded, or at least supported, by members of the nobility, or even by the Counts themselves, and became increasingly dependent on the largesse which followed. The benefits to the communities were obvious and the protection was deemed especially necessary in view of the ever-present threat of returning Moors; the nobles in turn gained prestige and looked forward to ending their days in a peaceful monastic setting.

Inevitably such a dependent system led to a relaxing of the Rule, and a misuse of the trust placed in them by some nobles who were not above using the richer establishments as political bargaining counters in their quest for ever more power. Much the same thing was happening on the other side of the Pyrenees until the Monastery of Cluny in Burgundy led the way to reform in 949 by declaring itself free from its overlords and answerable only to the Pope. Catalan monasteries were not slow to follow suit. Two notable examples were the monasteries at *Montserrat* and *Ripoll* which, in 1025 and 1032 respectively, broke free and became outstanding centres of learning and creativity thanks to the inspirational leadership of *Abbot Oliva*. Lesser establishments, lacking the vision and determination of the Abbot, were less fortunate and became embroiled in petty quarrelling and empire-building on the part of unscrupulous clerics.

It was not until Count Ramon Berenguer IV liberated 'New Catalonia' after 1137, and the Cistercians arrived to help fill the vacuum left by the Moors, that lasting monastic reforms took place. The Cistercians were dedicated to a return to the Rule of St. Benedict and all the austerity and purity of being for which it stood. They came from the Monastery of Citeaux in Burgundy and their desire to expand coincided with the sudden appearance of vast tracts of available land, ripe for repopulation, particularly around Lleida, Tarragona and Tortosa. The role of the Cistercians was as much economic and social as it was spiritual and intellectual. They built large monasteries in hitherto barren areas of land and taught the new settlers how to plough, how to rotate crops, how to make their own tools and how to be self-sufficient. Forested areas were reclaimed, grazing animals were introduced and a highly efficient agricultural system was born.

The greatest and most influencial establishments were *Santes Creus* (Alt Camp), *Poblet* (Conca de Barbera), and *Vallbona de les Monges* (Urgell). The first two were founded in 1150 and 1151 respectively in remote, undeveloped but potentially fertile areas. The female community of Vallbona was incorporated into the Cistercian Order and given its first Abbess in 1175.

These three were quickly followed by smaller, dependent monasteries and Cistercian influence was soon felt all over the southern part of the Province. Many were blessed with royal patronage and protection and much of Poblet was paid for by Ramon Berenguer IV. Poblet, Santes Creus and Vallbona de les Monges incorporated sumptuous state-rooms and apartments to accommodate visiting royalty and the first two became royal mausoleums. So much attention and ostentatious spending might well have led to lax morals and even corruption. In reality, the discipline and high motivation of the Cistercians were not in any way compromised and this was largely due to the fact that their abbots were elected from amongst themselves and no longer imposed on them by noble families seeking suitable occupation for their younger sons. Order and efficiency were therefore maintained to a very high degree.

The austere life style of the Cistercians was reflected in their architecture, particularly in the churches which were spacious and simple almost to the point of emptiness, relying on delicate line and perfect proportions rather than ornamentation for their effect. Cistercian churches brought *Romanesque* to an end in Catalonia and ushered in the Gothic period with what was known as the *Transitional* style.

In the south the Cistercians were protected from Moorish incursions by the military Order of *Templars* whose fighting skills had proved invaluable to Ramon Berenguer IV in 1137 and thereafter. They were rewarded with land and erected several fortress-monasteries in the Ebro region, the best known being at *Miravet*. When they were instructed to leave and physically driven out of their last refuge at Miravet, their place was taken by a gentler race of Christian knights known as the *Hospitallers*, who stayed on there until 1835. Meanwhile, other Orders had crossed the Pyrenees and established themselves throughout the region. These included Carthusians, whose Priory at *Scala Dei* (Priorat) was established as early as 1163, Franciscans and Dominicans.

By the 14C, demoralisation, jealousy and corruption were once more taking hold of monasteries, particularly in the northern region. *Sant Pere de Rodes* was just one example of a once great and dominant community reduced to a state of decadence and self-indulgence by too much attention and too little control. Many monks left and the monastic treasures were plundered by local lords and by the French.

1469 saw the union of the Catalan-Aragonese throne with that of Castile and it was during the reign of the 'Catholic Monarchs', Ferdinand of Aragon and Isabella of Castile, that the *Inquisition* was introduced. It arrived in Catalonia in the late 15C and effectively put an end to all forms of indiscipline. Rigid othodoxy became the order of the day. Outside, wars raged, corrupt monarchs came and went during the centuries which followed and, in 1811, Napoleon's army sacked monastery after monastery in the Peninsula War. The period of political chaos which followed Napoleon's withdrawal in 1814 was characterised by anti-clerical violence with religion seen by the population as an obstacle to progress, and to industrial growth in particular. Churches were desecrated, monks and priests were ostracized, assaulted or even murdered, and monastic buildings were turned into factories, or simply destroyed to make way for new roads and houses. This was particularly so in Barcelona. A second period of violence against the church was to follow in the Civil War and again Barcelona suffered desperately.

Today it is little short of miraculous that so many monasteries throughout the Region have been restored to something approaching their former splendour. Many exhibit pictures of 'then' and 'now' to explain the tortuous process of rebuilding they have undergone. A few, such as *Poblet, Vallbona* and *Montserrat,* are once more occupied by religious Orders. Others, such as *Santes Creus,* have lost their monks and are now fully integrated into village life. A few, like *Scala Dei,* are still waiting for the restorer's magic wand, their majestic silhouettes and broken columns providing poignant reminders of the power of religion and the viciousness with which that power was broken.

All – almost without exception – are open to visitors, with obvious restrictions imposed where monks or nuns are still in residence, or where restoration work is still in progress.

MODERNISM

All over Catalonia museums contain evidence of the late 19C artistic movement known as *Modernism,* in the form of sculpture, painting, ceramics, jewellery, metalware and so on. Far and away the most striking and accessible category from the visitor's point of view, however, is the architecture with which Catalonia – and Barcelona in particular – is richly endowed.

A reflection throughout Europe of relative economic prosperity and of growing artistic and cultural awareness amongst the bourgeoisie, Modernism first manifested itself in Catalonia in the late 1880s. Despite grave social unrest and inequality at this time, a mood of optimism prevailed in the region. Language and culture were once more free and humiliating defeats were things of the past. The mood was in tune with *La Belle Epoque* which much of Europe was enjoying at the turn of the century.

Modernist architecture is characterised above all by its energy and by its exuberant disregard for the classicial norms which have gone before. It derives mainly from the neo-Gothic style but, at the same time, seems to rebel against it, showing scant respect for the rules, and the occasional lapse into downright poor taste, spiced with a few touches of genius. The frequent use of undressed red brick in early Catalan Modernism, followed by such innovative materials as sheet iron and industrial glass, was in itself a form of revolt against the more customary use of stone. It ensures that these buildings stand out from their more seemly neighbours like overdressed ladies at a vicarage tea party.

Moreover, Catalan Modernism carries an extra layer of meaning – that of Nationalism. The not uncommon representations of St. George, the patron saint, and the inclusion here and there of a coat-of-arms or some other patriotic symbol, signify a resurgence of interest in autonomy (which was to lead to the setting up of the *Mancommunitat in 1914).*

Three great masters dominated Modernist architecture in Catalonia. They were *Antoni Gaudi* (1852-1926), *Lluis Domenech i Montaner* (1850-1923) and *Josep Puig i Cadafalch* (1867-1957) and they attracted a host of disciples. All three worked mainly in Barcelona which has a greater concentration of Modernist buildings than any other European city – over 1,000 in fact. From here the movement spread to the main industrial towns, such as Reus and Tarragona, to the wine-growing areas in the form of wine co-operatives, like the one at Gandesa, and to the main holiday resorts such as Sitges.

The prolific and varied output of Gaudi, a deeply religious man, was quite extraordinary. Perhaps he is best known for the still unfinished and highly controversial church of *La Sagrada Familia;* is it an inspired work of deep spirituality or simply a monstrous fantasy which has got out of hand? Liberally scattered throughout the town are residences commissioned by the rich and famous. In lighter mood is his surreal *Parc Guell* intended as a garden city and named after his patron, the prominent textile manufacturer, *Eusebio*

Guell. For him Gaudi designed a rather grim looking palace in the crowded *Carrer Nou de les Ramblas*, which is now a museum.

The other two architects were prominent figures in political life who found time nevertheless to design public buildings and extravagant houses for the newly prosperous merchants who wanted to show off their wealth along the wide avenues of Barcelona's new Extension (*Eixample*). *Ciutadella Park* – venue for the International Exhibition of 1888 – is generally accepted as the birthplace of Catalan Modernism and the building which started it all off was Domenech i Montaner's Restaurant, known as *Castell dels Tres Dragons*, a paradox of medieval inspiration executed in innovative materials such as uncovered brick. Today however it looks quite tame compared with, say, the Concert Hall (*Palau de la Musica*) which he designed 20 years later.

Puig i Cadafalch's style was similar, but was characterised by his tendency to combine both local and foreign traditions in one building: *Casa Amattler* on *Passeig de Gracia* presents a striking example of this, with Flemish-style stepped gable over typical Catalan arches and floral decoration. Prominent amongst other early Barcelona Modernists was Josep Vilaseca, responsible for the Great Exhibition's *Triumphal Arch* (in the same year as Domenech i Montaner's Restaurant), and for a well-known Ramblas landmark – the *Bruno Quadros* house – decorated with umbrellas and a Chinese dragon.

But there are rich pickings to be found almost everywhere in Catalonia and nowhere more than in the wine-growing areas of Penedes and the Ebro region where the design of magnificent wine co-operatives became an art form in its own right. Often completely out of step with surrounding town or village – an infringement of unspoken rules which is rendered more striking (and to some more unforgivable) by the harmony of the surrounding countryside – they should nevertheless be studied with respect and with an open mind. Inside, many of them are quite cathedral-like with huge vaults designed to control the light which filters through carefully placed windows, and sometimes supporting tiles which contract or dilate with temperature changes. Above all, they speak of the great wealth and confidence of the wine-growing syndicates whose produce was rapidly gaining renown all over Europe.

In the Routes which follow we attempt to draw the visitor's attention to the principal Modernist buildings in the vicinity. Many of these proclaim their presence so stridently anyway that it would be difficult not to notice them. The Department of Tourism's illustrated guide – 'Discovering Modernist Art in Catalonia' – is recommended to anyone with an overriding interest in the subject.

The careless exuberance of Modernism was brought to an end in the early 1920s by a new movement known as *Noucentism* whose exponents deplored the perceived descent into artistic decadence. They preached a return to classical origins in all the plastic arts; their works reflected a precision and an orderliness bordering on puritanism, and represented total disapproval of the subjective extravagance which had gone before.

A leading 'Noucentist' was Josep Goday, municipal architect of the city of Barcelona in 1923, an example of whose work can be seen on *Passeig de Lluis Companys*, known as *El Grup Escolar Pere Vila*. J. M. Jujol, a pupil of Gaudi and creator of the marvellous undulating bench in Parc Guell, became a convert to Noucentism and one of its leading practitioners. One of the best places to become aware of the movement's influence is Barcelona's *Montjuich*, where numerous neo-classical and Italian Renaissance-style buildings were created as pavillions for the 1929 World Fair. It is fascinating to note how far the spirit of architecture had moved from the adventurous creations of the 1888 International Exhibition in Cuitadella Park.

TWENTIETH CENTURY ART

The turn of the century produced various artists of formidable talent and originality in Catalonia who went on to become world figures. Foremost amongst these were Picasso, Dali and Miró.

Pablo Picasso was in fact born in Andalucia – in 1881 – but moved with his family to Barcelona when he ws 15 and held his first exhibition shortly after. He soon became friendly with established Catalan painters like *Santiago Rusinol* and *Ramon Casas*, and joined the dynamic group of artists which they had formed and which met regularly at the Barcelona café called '*Els Quatro Gats*'. Picasso then went briefly to Madrid but found the Barcelona atmosphere more to his taste and closer to influences from France.

He went to Paris in 1900 where his first exhibition was not a great success and his work was criticised as derivative of *Toulouse-Lautrec* amongst others, probably because many of his early sketches did indeed portray café society. There followed a period of exploration and experimentation, partly in Barcelona, partly in Paris, during which time he participated in just about every *avant garde* movement there was. He then went on to lead the creation of Cubism together with *Braque* in 1908 and this was followed by Analytical Cubism and Surrealism.

The Spanish Civil War distressed Picasso deeply and triggered a huge output of distinctive and often agonized paintings including the famous *Guernica*. He spent the last part of his life in the south of France and died there in 1973. Some interesting examples of Picasso's early work are on show at the Picasso Museum in Barcelona.

It is often said of **Salvador Dali** that his extraordinary life style and exuberant behaviour detracted from his work as a serious artist whilst he was alive; and that it is really only now that the dust has settled and the more outrageous memories are fading that his creativity can be appreciated objectively and without prejudice. Be that as it may.

Dali was born in Figueres in 1904, studied there and soon discovered the work of the *Impressionists* and the *Pointillistes*. In 1928 he attended the Madrid School of Fine Arts but was expelled two years later for misconduct. His first trip to Paris was in 1928 where he met and worked with the Surrealists, including Picasso and Miró, and held his first exhibition the following year. From that moment on, his prodigious talent manifested itself throughout Europe and the United States – frequently shocking, always controversial, never dull. He often let himself be inspired by great works of literature which he proceeded to illustrate; these included the *Bible*, the *Legend of William Tell*, *Macbeth*, *Faust*, and *Dante's Divine Comedy*. When inspiration faltered, he wrote something himself, often explaining his ideas about art – as in the *Mystical Manifesto* published in 1951 – sometimes expanding his extraordinary obsession with self, as in the *Secret Life of Salvador* (1961). The writer and friend of Dali, *Robert Descharnes*, describes his work as a mixture of reality, imagination, madness and passion, which neatly sums it up. Perhaps one could add that there existed also the occasional touch of genius.

In 1970 Dali inaugurated his own Museum in Figueres. The metamorphosis of old theatre into modern and entirely suitable setting for much of his work was personally conducted by himself. It is a sight not to be missed. The French Academy admitted Dali to its ranks as a 'foreign associate' in 1979 and the Tate Gallery in London held an important retrospective exhibition in 1980. He died in 1989.

Joan Miró was born in Barcelona in 1893. He was both painter and sculptor and lived for 90 years, a prolific and brilliant artist to the end. He studied in Barcelona, first at a business college and then at the Academy of Art in *La Lonja*, and made friends with the artists *Ricart* and *Artigas*. His interest in the French *avant garde* movement did not start until 1916 and he made his first trip to Paris in 1919 where he promptly made friends with Picasso. As in the case of Picasso, Miró's first solo exhibition in Paris was not a success. However he soon became part of the Surrealist movement and, after a longish period of experimentation and travel, he made his first breakthrough with an exhibition at the *Georges Bernheim Gallery* in Paris in 1928. From that moment on, his work was in demand all over Europe and in the major cities of the United States.

Over the years Miró produced a wide and exciting variety of paintings, sculptures and ceramics and his work was widely sought after. The ceramic walls of the UNESCO building in Paris were his inspiration, together with fellow artist, Artigas. He designed the ceramic walls for the IBM building in Barcelona and was also responsible for the huge ceramic installation at the airport. Even Osaka in Japan did him honour and commissioned a mural for the World Exhibition in 1970.

Miró spent the latter half of his life in Palma de Mallorca where his friend, the architect J. M. Sert, had built him a studio house. Sert was also responsible for the design of the highly imaginative *Miró Foundation* building, commissioned by the City of Barcelona in 1968 to house paintings by Miró himself and other contemporary artists. Towards the end of his life Miró experimented with tapestry, incorporating all manner of every-day materials such as skeins of wool, strips of sacking, lengths of rope, which are often left hanging loose, thus adding colour and excitement to what hitherto had been a rather restricted art form. There are some superbly vibrant examples of this medium at the Miró Foundation.

It must not be supposed that these three international giants emerged from a vacuum. Their first contacts and friends, long before they found their way to Paris, were Catalans such as Casas and Rusinol already mentioned. Rusinol was particularly known for his meticulous observation of the effects of light in his paintings; besides forming the *Els Quatro Gats* group in Barcelona, he also started a colony in a row of fishermen's cottages in the seaside town of *Sitges*, which acted like a magnet to contemporary painters and sculptors from both inside and outside Catalonia. Also painting at this time were *Juan Gris* (1887-1927) and *Jose Maria Sert* (1876-1945) whose masterpiece is the arresting and beautiful set of murals which cover the interior walls of the cathedral at Vic. The first set was lost when the cathedral was badly damaged by fire during the Civil War; the second set was sold by the painter in Paris because he was not satisfied with it; it is the third attempt which we are privileged to see today in Vic. Elderly locals maintain that even these paintings are not as sublime as those which were tragically destroyed.

To end this short resumé of modern Catalan art on a truly contemporary note, we come to two artists who are still working and who are no less original and exciting than their predecessors: **Antoni Tapies** was born in 1923 and is hailed by the popular press as the new Picasso, his paintings appearing all over Europe and in his own Foundation in Barcelona (255 *Carrer d'Arago*, just off *Passeig de Gracia*). He is preoccupied with texture and seems to let the materials he used dictate the process of creation. He performs much of his work on the ground, drawing with sticks and stones, sometimes tipping powdered marble into paint with devastating effect. Recognisable objects or figures may or may not appear. The result is vast primaeval patches of colour, crudely assembled and immensely powerful, with perhaps somewhere on the surface a small mark made by finger or brush dipped in paint and casually suggesting a human imprint. He also creates ceramics.

Josep Subirachs was born in Barcelona in 1927 and studied sculpture there at the *Escola de Belles Arts* before travelling in Europe and meeting, among others, *Henry Moore* and *A. Pevsner*. Since 1950 Subirachs' figures have become powerfully dramatic with special importance given to the contrast between positive and negative, concave and convex, male and female. Two examples of his work are readily accessible in Barcelona: one, the bronze door of the Archives of the *Crown of Aragon* (described in Route 1) illustrates to perfection his preoccupation with full and empty spaces, projections and hollows; the other, for which posterity will judge him, is the set of figures on the Passion façade of Gaudi's *Sagrada Familia* church in Barcelona. The architect Gaudi left no instructions as to how this work should be continued after his death, so the inspiration is wholly Subirachs' own. Already his distinctive style is being harshly criticised by some, hailed as revelatory by others. He is also responsible for countless public monuments, mainly in Barcelona, one in Cervera and one in Vilanova i La Geltru (in memory of President Macia), and has received many awards for his contribution to Catalan art.

These pages have given no more than the briefest summary of the rich and varied creativity which has taken place this century. A visit to some of the many galleries, foundations and museums which abound in all the big cities will testify that Catalan art is still alive and very well, and that a number of exciting artists and sculptors are emerging as worthy successors to the people described above.

FOLK-LORE

Catalonia possesses a wealth of colourful folk-lore and tradition which has joyfully reappeared during the last few years after who knows how many years of suppression. On religious feast days and festivals, there emerge from the town halls all manner of giants, demons, fire-eating dragons and big heads (masks known as *cap-grossos*), and the squares and streets come alive with music and dance. Many towns have their own particular festivals and customs, and some of these are very ancient indeed. There is the *Patum* at Berga on the day of *Corpus Christi*, and the extraordinary *Dance of Death* enacted every Maundy Thursday through the streets of Verges, and believed to go back to the medieval days of plague and pestilence.

You are very likely to come across the *Sardana* – an elegant ritual in which young and old alike join hands and trace and retrace delicate steps in a large circle. This is the Catalan national dance – not as simple to perform as at first appears – and claimed by some to go back to sun worship. It is accompanied by an assortment of wind instruments called a *cobla*, or perhaps just by a drum, and it is always taken extremely seriously. Sunday morning is the favourite time and the *Plaça Mayor* (main square) the preferred part of town. In Barcelona it happens in front of the Cathedral on Sundays and sometimes in *St. James' Square* on Saturday evenings.

The human pyramids, locally known as *castells*, are a rarer and frankly almost unbelievable sight. The *castellers* use their own bodies as building blocks, usually with four hefty specimens forming the base, and create a tower some five, six, seven, even eight storeys high. The crowd below stretch out their hands to support the human foundation as the tower grows methodically higher to the sound of flageolets and drums. The motto of castellers is "strength, balance, courage, common sense" and one can see why: all of these qualities are necessary to create a form of such breathtaking precision; one slip could cause disaster.

There are some twenty teams of *castellers* in existence, all in the south and mainly around Tarragona, the most famous of all being at Valls. El Vendrell, Vilafranca del Penedes and Sitges would probably dispute that, and there is friendly competition between the various towns. The first mention of the *castells* goes back to 1805 (at Valls) but no-one seems clear as to their origin except that it is linked to certain feast days: in Valls for example you could see it on 24 June (the feast of St. John) and 21 October (the feast of St. Ursula); in Vilafranca it would appear on 30 August (Sant Felix) and in Tarragona on 23 September (Santa Tecla). Local tourist offices can provide lists of dates.

FOOD AND WINE

Catalan gastronomy is dominated by three factors: the mountains, the sea and the proximity to France. The Pyrenean towns and villages and the mountain regions of *Montseny* and *Montsant* offer a variety of succulent local meats – wild boar, goat or lamb, chicken or partridge – either grilled over charcoal (*à la brasa*) with herbs rubbed in and served unpretentiously on a wooden board, or slow-cooked in a strong sauce with garlic and mushrooms and tasting far more French than Spanish. The higher and more remote the region the richer the sauce and more generous the helpings, and the Aran Valley is renowned for its casserole called *Olla Aranesa* which contains all manner of goods things. And don't miss jugged boar (*civet de senglar*) or partridge in red wine (*perdiu à la cacadora*), which tastes unbelievably good after a morning's outdoor exertion.

The sea cuisine must be one of the best in Europe thanks to the great variety of fish (*peix*) available along the coast. It ranges from the humble cod (*bacalla*) through all manner of Mediterranean fish and may be quite simply grilled, or served with creamed garlic, or in a traditional sauce known as *Romesco* which has an almond base and includes red peppers. High point of the fish menu is the *sarsuela* – a kind of fish stew with peppers and tomatoes and very reminiscent of the *bouillabaisse* of southern France. Shell fish (*mariscero*) is good and, on the whole, cheap with mussels (*mejillones*), prawns (*gambas*) and crab (*cranc*) well to the fore. Some stylish restaurants mix fish and meat in one creation and *llagosta amb pollastre* (lobster and chicken) is a favourite combination with almonds, anis and even chocolate making up the sauce. The use of fine grated chocolate to darken a rich sauce is quite common in traditional Catalan cookery and was probably introduced by returning *conquistadores* who would have discovered this originally Aztec custom in Mexico.

Dedicated fish eaters should certainly find their way down to the Ebro Delta. Here fishing is a way of life and hotels and restaurants vie with each other to put up the longest and most tempting menu outside their doors. Elvers are a particular speciality here (with 5 tonnes netted in the delta every year) but your best bet is probably a mixed grill of fish containing some seven or eight freshly-caught varieties which – with salad, bread and wine – should cost less than the equivalent of £10. A bowl of mixed shellfish (*sarsuela de mariscos*) is another mouth-watering option.

On the plains between mountain and sea, fish and meat dishes exist side by side along with a multitude of home-made sausages – *llonganissa* (cured) and *botifarra* (boiled), often served with haricot beans (*mongetes*) or with local mushrooms (*moixernons*). The flavour of each sausage changes subtly with the region depending on the meat used, but seasoning is kept to a minimum and La Seu d'Urgell claims to have the 'cleanest' sausage of all, seasoned only with salt and pepper. Rabbit (*conill*) too is eaten widely, sometimes cooked with mushrooms, or with pears, or garlic or, for grand occasions, stewed in a chocolate sauce, with tomatoes, peppers and brandy. A number of Mediterranean style sauces tend to appear over and over again. Besides the almond-based *Romesco* already mentioned, there is *Sofregit*, a gently fried blend of oil, onion, garlic and tomato, or *Samfaina*, with the same ingredients and chopped pepper, aubergine and courgette added; both can accompany fish, meat or poulty, or form the base of a dish from its inception. *Picada* is another favourite, consisting of almonds, filberts, garlic and sometimes saffron and/or chocolate, all ground together in a stone mortar with a wooden pestle; it too is often an integral part of a dish, serving as a thickening agent. Lastly there is the ubiquitous *Allioli*, a blend of olive oil and garlic which is eaten warm with fish or combined with egg to make mayonnaise and eaten with charcoal-grilled meat.

Do not miss *Escudella*, a hearty broth containing vegetables, pasta and slices of sausage – a kind of permanent stock pot varying greatly from one region to another; or that rarest and most typically Catalan dish – *Calçotada*, a speciality of the Valls region which consists of the tenderest baby onions grilled and usually accompanied by Romesco. The season for this is from December to March. Vegetables are often eaten as starters and favourites are spinach with nuggets of smoked bacon (*Espinacs à la Catalana*) or green beans (*Judias verdes*). Salads too tend to come as starters and are frequently so generous that they constitute a meal in themselves; there might be a winter salad of curled chicory with salt cod, anchovies and olives (*xato*), or a raw fish, bean and tomato concoction (*esqueixada*), or a plate of some five or six varieties of sliced sausage with lettuce, peppers etc (*l'amanida Catalana*).

Visitors are often puzzled by the appearance on the restaurant table as soon as they arrive of a thick slice of toasted bread accompanied by a clove of garlic and a half tomato. This is *pa amb tomaquet* and a very popular rural pre-starter it is. Rub the garlic and the tomato into the bread, pour on olive oil (a jug of which will surely be on the table), add salt and tuck in.

Unless you take advantage of the predictable range of Mediterranean fruits, the sweet course can be disappointing and an excellent meal can all too often end with an unexciting ice cream straight out of the freezer. But there is one notable exception which, when properly made, can rival the most delicate of international creations. That is a *Crema Catalana* – a *crème brulée* with its caramel topping burned on with an iron, specially made to culinary dimensions, and available in local markets for those who want to try it at home. Refuse any *crema* which has been standing around for a long time and whose topping has gone soft. It really should be ironed a few minutes before it is eaten, so that the dark brittle toffee layer contrasts crisply with the creamy egg custard below.

Perhaps one of the best things about Catalan cookery is its basic simplicity. Moreover, it is true to its origins, and generally resists the temptation to cosmopolitanize and become bland, except perhaps in the big urban restaurants. Touring the rural areas and trying the local specialities really can be fun.

Wine: Catalonia is now recognised as one of Spain's principal regions for quality wines and *Penedes* in particular is rapidly becoming as well known as, say, *Rioja* or *Valdepenas*. Penedes is just one of the seven wine-producing areas in Catalonia and lies SW of Barcelona in a depression protected by the mountains of the *Cordillera Littoral*. It is especially the whites which are achieving international recognition with nine different varieties ranging from dry and aromatic to full-bodied and sweet. It is said that the reds have yet to achieve their full potential. There are eight varieties, all of which tend to be softer and fruitier than the typical Spanish reds and can be the perfect complement to the fine local meats of the mountain areas.

But Penedes is probably best known for the highly successful *Cava* – a sparkling white which comes in *Brut* (dry), *Seco* (nearly dry), *Semi-seco* (medium dry) and *Dulce* (sweet) and is now exported all over Europe and the United States. To qualify for the name *Cava*, wine must be made in the traditional method of second fermentation in bottle. The first tentative experiments with the *methode champenoise* were made by *José Raventos* in the town of *San Sadurni d'Anoia* in Penedes in 1872. It took a long time to perfect the intricate process which really only got underway after an outbreak of phylloxera in 1887 when affected vines were replaced with healthy American stocks, on to which were grafted different varieties. In 1902 it is said that the

King, Alfonso XIII, made the wine fashionable throughout Spain by drinking it at court. Certainly it has never looked back and today the Penedes region produces more than 90% of all Spanish Cava.

The two largest Catalan producers of Cava are *Cordorniu* (head office at Gran Via 644, 08007 Barcelona) and *Freixenet*, (PO Box 1, San Sadurni de Anoia, Barcelona) and both receive visitors. There are also some 70 other Cava producers. Cava, like the champagne it so closely resembles, will add zest to any occasion. Devotees insist that it should be drunk in a conical glass with a pointed bottom to encourage the bubbles to rise.

Moving southwards from Penedes you come to Tarragona which is the largest demarcated wine region of Catalonia and is sub-divided into three zones – *Campo de Tarragona, Comarca de Falset* and *Ribera de Ebro*. The first, with its sea breezes and long hours of sunshine, produces a high quality white similar to Penedes; Falset, a mountain area with a low yield per hectare, gives a dark, full red which is high in alcohol content; the third zone which stretches along the Ebro valley, produces the full gamut – dry and sweet white, rosé (*rosado*) and dry red.

Furthest south in Catalonia is the mountainous zone of *Terra Alta*, where a limestone and clay soil and continental climate produce predominantly white wines. *Priorato*, west of Tarragona, is named after the Priory of the Carthusians at Scala Dei who introduced the vine to the area in 12C. Its rugged mountain terrain and slatey soil produce some wonderful dark full reds which are greatly appreciated throughout Spain, though not much exported. There are also some choice *rosados* and whites. A tasting session at the cellars at Scala Dei is highly recommended.

North of Barcelona are two more regions. Smaller of the two is *Alella* with very fresh drinkable whites, and several liqueurs made at the seaside resort of Arenys de Mar. The other regions is *Ampurdan-Costa Brava* which is close to the French border and produces both red and dry rosado.

The seventh and newest area to achieve full status as an official wine producer is *Raimat* which lies somewhat inaccessibly to the W of Lleida. The costing of planting and labour is said to be higher than anywhere else in Catalonia but the drainage and composition of the soil is excellent and successful experiments are being carried out with all kinds of wines, some of which are already being exported.

Serious wine-lovers are advised to contact *Wines from Spain*, 22 Manchester Square, London W1M 5AP for detailed information before leaving for Catalonia. And, once there, should be sure to visit the splendid Wine Museum at Villafranca del Penedes (54 km SW of Barcelona).

PRACTICAL INFORMATION

TRAVEL TO CATALONIA

By Air – There are regular British Airways and Air Iberia flights from Heathrow and Birmingham to Barcelona. Air Iberia also flies from Gatwick and Manchester and Air Viva (Iberia's sister line) flies from Gatwick. Charter flights go from Gatwick to Girona and Reus.

There is a half-hourly train service from Barcelona airport to Plaça Catalunya in the centre of town.

For those already in Spain there is an hourly shuttle service from Madrid to Barcelona.

Package holidays are too numerous to list here; many of them are excellent and information on these is widely available in tourist offices everywhere.

By Rail – British Rail offers a return fare of (currently) £153 return from London Victoria to Barcelona. The journey takes 30 hours and there are daily departures at 11.10 am. Details are available from BR Continental Enquiries, tel: (071) 834 2345. French Railways (179 Piccadilly) offer further possibilities).

By Bus – National Express–Eurolines buses depart from London for Barcelona on Mondays, Wednesdays, Fridays and Saturdays and the journey takes about 24 hours. For details ring (071) 730 0202. SSS International also runs regular services to Barcelona – details: (071) 388 1732.

By Sea – The only direct passenger route from UK to date is run by Brittany Ferries from Plymouth to Santander in Northern Spain (706 km W of Barcelona). The crossing takes 24 hours. There are two departures weekly between mid-March and mid-December and one weekly thereafter. P & O European Ferries plan to start a new, twice-weekly ferry service from Portsmouth to Bilbao in Summer 1992.

By Car – There are altogether 14 border crossings from France. For Catalonia the easiest is probably the coastal route from Perpignan to Figueres and Girona via Portbou. Pyrenean routes include Auch or Tarbes to Vielha in the Aran Valley, and Toulouse via Andorra to either La Seu d'Urgell or Puigcerda.

From Madrid to Lleida via Zaragoza is a journey of 475 km.

From Alicante and Valencia the motorway passes through Tortosa and Tarragona to Barcelona and continues up to Girona and on in to France.

TRAVEL IN CATALONIA

By Rail – There are 1,341 km of railway in Catalonia, run by the state company, *RENFE*, and *Ferrocarriles de la Generalitat de Catalunya*. The network links most major cities and many of the coastal resorts. Trains are clean and reliable and come in several categories: the most luxurious is the *Talgo*, an air-conditioned super express which links major cities throughout Spain, including Barcelona; the *Ter* is slightly slower because it makes more stops than the Talgo. Both offer first and second class accommodation, sleepers and or couchettes. *Expreso/rapido* are long-distance trains and *Omnibus tranvia automotor* are local trains with frequent stops.

From May to October RENFE offers a number of tempting excursions to and from Barcelona including a trip on the sumptuous *Al Andalus Express* between Barcelona and Santiago de Compostela.

Information and tickets are available from local tourist offices as well as railway stations. Anyone planning to use trains frequently would do well to contact the Spanish National Tourist Office, 57 St. James Street, London SW1 for timetables and detailed information. Or you can phone RENFE direct (Barcelona 322 41420).

The city of Barcelona has four railway stations. These are the *Central Sants* (central station) for national inter-city lines, international lines, trains to the southern coastal resorts, and to the airport; *Estació Terme-Franca* for international lines and trains to northern coastal resorts; *Estació Plaça Catalunya* for trains to Vic and Puigcerda and *Estació Plaça Espanya* for trains to Montserrat.

By Bus – Virtually every town and village with a made up road is served by some kind of bus and this can be a delightful, if slow, way to travel. Inter-city coach services are efficient and cheap and there are many of them. There is no national bus service in Spain. Timetables for the major routes should be available at the Spanish Tourist Office in London (57 St. James Street, SW1) and local tourist offices will provide details of services throughout Catalonia.

By Car – To drive in Catalonia (as in the rest of Spain) you need either an International Licence or an EEC pink licence. Cars drive on the right and give priority to traffic coming from the right and the International Highway Code is in force. Speed limits are as follows: 130 kph on motorways; 90-110 kph on other roads and 60 kph in built-up areas.

Motorways (*autopistes*) are few: there is the A7 which follows the coast from France, sweeps past Girona, Barcelona and Tarragona and on to Valencia; and there is the A2 which goes off the A7 N of El Vendrell and continues inland to Lleida and on Zaragoza. They are expensive but worth every *peseta* if you are in a hurry, since trunk roads (*carreteras*) are often very congested, especially those anywhere near Barcelona and/or the coast.

How much more pleasant it can be – and sometimes quicker – to take the "C" roads (marked yellow on Michelin map no.990), or even the unnumbered "white" road which may well take you over a mountain range or two. Many of the Routes and excursions in the Guide use such roads.

In general Catalan roads are extremely well maintained and drivers, especially truck drivers, tend to be courteous and helpful. Moods can quickly change in the big cities however where traffic grinds easily to a hot and impatient standstill in the rush hour. The answer for the visitor – apart from avoiding the rush hour – is to park the car as soon as possible, either on the outskirts or in one of the parking areas marked by a white "P" on a blue sign, and either walk or take a bus or taxi or, in Barcelona, the metro which is by far the quickest way of crossing the city at any hour.

Car hire is readily available and all the major companies are represented. A recommended option for those who are short of journey time but want to see the countryside as well as the main cities, is to buy a fly-drive ticket from the airline, which works out considerably cheaper than paying for an air ticket and then arranging a car on arrival.

HOTELS, PARADORS, YOUTH HOSTELS AND CAMPING

There is a wide range of accommodation available, closely controlled by the tourist authorities in all but price which varies considerably according to category. A complete list of hotels with prices is produced annually by the Catalan Government Tourist Department and is available free of charge from the following address:- *Direcció General de Turisme*, Passeig de Gracia 105, 08008 Barcelona; it is also available from local tourist offices.

Official Categories are as follows:-

H　　Hotel (one to five stars)

HR　　**Hotel Residencia** (the same but without meals)

Hs　　**Hostal** (one to three stars): cheaper than a hotel and sometimes offering better service, especially in rural areas. Generally recommended as a category.

HsR　　**Hostal Residencia** (the same but without meals)

P　　**Pension** (one to three stars): rather more homely and usually cheaper

CH   **Casa de Huespedes**: guest house

F   **Fonda**: a very simple guest house, with or without meals: usually very cheap.

However basic the accommodation it is fair to say that it is generally spotlessly clean. For anyone wanting to meet local people and understand something of the culture, the evening meal in a small country *Hostal* (often a family affair) can be a friendly and relaxing experience; there is usually nowhere else but the restaurant for spending the evening so it will be used for TV viewing, playing cards, or simply chatting over a bottle of wine. Quite apart from anything else, this is a pleasant and effective way of discovering what there is to see and do in the locality.

At the top end of the market are the State-run **Paradors** (seven in Catalonia). These are usually historic buildings such as monasteries or castles, suitably modernised inside but scrupulously and correctly restored and/or preserved outside. A few, such as the *Vall d'Aran* at Vielha, are modern and built in traditional style in local materials. Other paradors in Catalonia are to be found at Aiguabrava, Arties (Aran Valley), Cardona, La Seu d'Urgell, Tortosa and Vic. Staying in a parador anywhere in Spain is an experience which should be tried at least once; anything more may prove expensive since paradors can charge the equivalent of £60 a night or more for a double room. It is fun to live like a grandee for a night, to mount a magnificient marble staircase to one's room, or to dine in a vast and vaulted hall. All bedrooms (even those tucked away in castle turrets) are equipped with modern bathrooms, and the public rooms with antique furniture and fine paintings on panelled walls are often quite splendid. Sometimes the food can be disappointing however and the service slow.

Youth Hostels are to be found in Barcelona, Tarragona and Arenys de Mar. Detailed information about these can be had from the International Y H Federation, Howardsgate, Welwyn Garden City, Herts. They are usually clean and well run. They get very crowded in the high season and one should book well in advance.

Camping is well organised and categories go from *Luxury* to *3rd class*. There are some 300 camp sites in Catalonia and the Costa Dorada has more sites than any other Spanish resort area. Nearly all have electricity and running water and some even have restaurants and swimming pools. The Catalan Government Tourist Department will send a free list of all sites on request (address as above).

RESTAURANTS

These are plentiful and quality is controlled by the provincial authorities. In the big cities 'international' cuisine prevails and prices are relatively high, especially in Barcelona. But it is still possible, in the narrow streets of the old sections of town, to find modest establishments where a 3-course meal (usually Catalan or Spanish) with bread and wine included costs less than the equivalent of £10 a head. This will appear as *menu turistico* or *menu del dia* or *plats del dia* (Catalan).

Serious eaters, having read the chapter on **Food and Wine** in this Guide, and perhaps delved into the very excellent book on *Catalan Cuisine* by Colman Andrews (pub. Headline), will confidently seek out restaurants with Catalan specialities. Local tourist offices usually have annotated lists but often the best advice can be had from your hotel porter or taxi driver. Don't miss Aranese cooking in the north (Aran Valley) and wonderful fish anywhere on the coast, especially in the Ebro Delta.

Meal times are late, but not as late as they are in Southern Spain (perhaps because of the proximity of the French). Generally speaking, lunch is served from 13.30 hours but people often linger on till 16.00. Dinner will not start before 20.30 but 22.00 hours is more usual. Breakfast is rather a non-event and most people make do with a large *café con leche* (half coffee, half hot milk) with or without a sticky pastry or a croissant.

Snacks can be had throughout the day in the numerous bars, cafés (known as *cafeterias* – which does not mean self-service) or café-restaurants. Most bars and cafeterias produce *tapas*, which are mouth-watering morsels ranging from huge black olives to crunchy fried squid. In the old days these would be offered free with drinks; now they are charged for and there is usually a price list on the wall. They are often irresistible and it is easy to end up paying more than the price of a full meal.

Raciones are slightly larger morsels; *Bocadillos* are open sandwiches. *Platos combinados* are platefuls of mixed grill or salad and are chosen from wall charts often displaying 20 or 30 varieties. Many of the cheaper restaurants and café-restaurants go in for these which are fine for large appetites and small budgets. The best known fast food chains have arrived in Barcelona but are difficult to find elsewhere.

TOURIST INFORMATION

The Spanish National Tourist Board's address in UK is 57 St. James' Street, London SW1. Telephone: (071) 499 1169.

The address for the Department of Tourism of the Catalan Government is *Direcció General de Turisme*, Passeig de Gracia 105, 08008 Barcelona. It will provide, free of charge, a useful range of materials including lists of hotels and camp sites. A letter to that address, or even a phone call (Barcelona (93) 237 9045) will usually trigger a swift response.

Catalonia is extremely well served with tourist offices in both major cities and small towns. The *Oficina d'Informació i Turisme* is indicated with a large *I* and will probably be located in the town centre. Barcelona and Girona airports and most railway stations throughout Catalonia also have tourist offices. In small towns and villages where there appears to be no such office, do not hesitate to go to the town or village hall, called *Ajuntament* or *Casa de Vila*. A smile and the magic word *tourisme* will certainly produce a local leaflet or two, and could even lead to a personal guided tour of a church or museum.

The Department of Tourism produces a colourful leaflet for each of the 38 *comarcas* in Catalonia. This will feature a simple map, basic information on local sport and cultural activites, dates of fiestas etc and a brief accommodation list. The leaflets tend to come all too often in Catalan only, but this may well change in 1992. A full range of *comarcal* leaflets is available at the airports and at other major offices. They are not, so far, available outside Catalonia. Also recommended and similarly available at the airports and in most city offices, are attractively presented itineraries relating to Gothic art, Romanesque churches and Modernism.

PUBLIC HOLIDAYS, OPENING HOURS, BANKS AND CURRENCY

Catalonia observes the **national holidays** of the rest of Spain and, on these days, banks, offices, shops and even some restaurants will close.

These are: January 1, New Year's Day; January 6, Epiphany; March 19, St. Joseph's Day; May 1, Labour Day; July 25, St. James' Day; August 15, Assumption; October 12, National Day (Discovery of America Day); November 1, All Saints' Day; December 8, Immaculate Conception; December 25, Christmas;

In addition there are the movable dates for Easter and Corpus Christi.

There are also local holidays in honour of patron saints, and in many areas the feast day of St. Peter and St. Paul (June 29) is taken as a holiday. Local tourist offices usually have local details.

Shop Opening Hours are 9.00 to 14.00 hours and 16.00 to 20.00 hours from Monday to Saturday. Everything stops for the siesta except the large department stores which stay open all day. Food shops, especially rural ones, are often a law unto themselves and frequently open on Sunday mornings.

Banking Hours are from 9.00 to 14.00 on weekdays except Saturdays when they close at 13.00 hours.

With the proliferation of exchange offices (marked *Cambio*) which are usually permanently open, and the widening acceptance of internationally recognised credit cards, the embarrassment of being caught without currency on a public holiday is now (almost) a thing of the past. Eurocheques and travellers' cheques are also generally accepted.

The monetary unit of Catalonia, as in the rest of Spain, is the *peseta* (often abbreviated to pta) and this divides technically into 100 centimos. Bank notes exist in the following denominations: 200, 500, 1,000, 2,000 and 5,000 pesetas. Coins come in 1, 5, 10, 25, 50 and 100 pesetas.

MUSEUMS

Catalonia rightly claims to be more richly endowed with museums, on a *per capita* basis, than most European countries. Museums (a term which also covers contemporary art collections) are a source of great pride and are generally of a very high standard which is sustained by the Service of Museums of the Department of Culture. A full list is available from the Department of Tourism (*Dirrecció General de Turisme*, Passeig de Gracia 105, 08008 Barcelona) or from local offices.

Barcelona itself is particularly rich in treasures with its unique City Museum (*Museu de la Ciutat*) incorporating the town's Roman foundations *in situ*, its Museum of Catalan Art (*Museu d'Art de Catalunya*) containing one of the world's greatest collections of Romanesque art, and its Maritime Museum (*Museu Maritimo*) housed in the medieval shipyards known as *Dressanes*. And this is to mention but three out of some 46 in the capital.

In preparation for 1992 and beyond, most of the bigger museums are taking on the mammoth task of labelling their exhibits in something other than Catalan. Ideally this will be done in French, English and German, as well as

Catalan and Spanish. Opening hours are usually from 9.30 to 13.30 and again from 16.30 to 19.30 but this can vary enormously. Many are closed on Mondays. There is usually an admission charge of *200 pesetas*. All worthwhile museums are briefly described in the text of the Routes which follow.

SPORT

Ski-ing: There is an excellent booklet which is free from the Department of Tourism in Barcelona (see *Tourist Information*) which describes in detail each of the 18 Pyrenean ski stations in Catalonia. 12 of these are downhill and 6 cross-country. The season lasts from December to April and facilities, as well as access to resorts, have developed significantly over the last decade. Opportunities range from the large, sophisticated *La Molina* (Girona province) with numerous hotels, a sports centre, 2 stadiums and 6 internationally approved competitive ski runs (with 100 cannons of artificial snow ensuring permanent coverage over 18 hectares), to the wholly delightful small station at *Aranser* in the Cerdanya range (N of La Seu d'Urgell) with remote cross-country trails (no downhill).

Mountaineering and Hiking: Many of the ski stations serve as bases for these popular sports in summer. Some of the best scenery and most challenging walks can be had in and around the splendid *Aigues Tortes National Park* in the Pyrenees with its well organised mountain refuges. The *Aran* and *Boi* valleys are equally rewarding, if slightly less dramatic. Information about organised excursions, trail networks, refuges, advice on weather conditions etc is always available from local tourist offices.

Water Sports: With a magnificent coastline and a moderate climate everything is possible from sailing to water-ski-ing and wind surfing. Full details can be had from the Department of Tourism which lists 36 *Recreational Ports* with all their facilities. Under-water fishing is popular but requires a licence from the local Maritime Authorities (*Comandancia de Marina*).

Hunting and Fishing: The Pyrenean regions offer exciting opportunities. Game includes quail, pigeon and partridge, wild boar, chamois, rabbit and hare. The mountain streams are full of trout. Of exceptional interest for water fowl is the Ebro Delta (which also offers very good fishing) and there is a reserve behind Tortosa where hunting of the rare Spanish mountain goat is permitted under very strict control. Information regarding permits and seasons is available from the Department of Tourism, or from local offices.

Golf is one of Catalonia's favourite sports and there are some excellent courses in and around the coastal resorts. The principal course at Barcelona is the *Real Club de Golf El Prat* which is near the airport and has 27 holes.

Football is a passion throughout Spain and nowhere more so than in Catalonia. Barcelona is justly proud of its magnificent *Camp Nou* stadium (off Carrer d'Aristides in the W of town) which has recently been enlarged for the Olympics. Matches are normally played on Sundays.

LANGUAGE AND USEFUL WORDS

Catalan is a Romance language derived from Vulgar Latin spoken by the Romans during the period of occupation which started in 218 BC. It is closer to the *Langue d'Oc* of Southern France than it is to Castilian, the official language of Spain; and Catalans claim that it is a purer language because there is no admixture of Arabic.

Throughout the stormy years of Catalonia's history, the Catalan language has become a potent emblem of independence, devastatingly forbidden either to be spoken, or written or taught by the Bourbon King Philip in 1714, and again after the Civil War in the 1930s up until the death of Franco. Now, with the establishment of democracy in Spain and autonomy for Catalonia, the language – and indeed Catalan culture as a whole – is flourishing. Most Catalans prefer to speak it all the time, though they will easily slip into Castilian if need be. French is also widely understood, particularly in the north. English is not much understood, except in the big cities and on the coast; it seems to have been beaten into third place by German, at least as the language of tourism.

In this Guide we have used Catalan place names rather than Castilian ones, *eg.* Lleida rather than Lerida. This is partly out of respect to the people of Catalonia and partly out of consideration for you, the visitor, since road signs and general directions appear increasingly in Catalan only. There follows a list of basic words which are likely to crop up during your wanderings. It includes the usual words of greeting which are subtly different from their Castilian equivalents and give great pleasure if used appropriately.

Catalan	English	Castilian
Bon dia	Good morning	Buenos dias
Bones tardes	Good afternoon	Buenas tardas
Bona nit	Good evening/night	Buenas noches
Gracies	Thank you	Gracias
Si us plau	Please	Por favor
Adeu	Goodbye	Adios
Bienvinguts	Welcome	Bienvenido
Hola	Hello	Hola
Avinguda	Avenue	Avenida
Carrer	Street	Calle
Plaça	Square	Plaza
Palau	Palace	Palacio
Castell	Castle	Castillo
Comarca	Region	Comarca
Cuitat	City, town	Ciudad
Pobla	Village	Pueblo
Mercat	Market	Mercado
Esglesia	Church	Iglesia
Retablo	Altar-piece	Retablo
Museu	Museum	Museo
Monestir	Monastery	Monasterio
Mas/Masia	Farmhouse	Hacienda
Ciutat antic		
Casc antic	Old city	Ciudad antigua
Conjunt Historic		
Ajuntament, Casa de Vila	Town hall	Casa consistorial
Eixample	Extension	Ensanche
Pa	Bread	Pan
Forn de pa	Baker, bread oven	Panaderia
Carnisser	Butcher	Carniceria
Carn	Meat	Carne
Peix	Fish	Pescado
Aigua	Water	Agua
Llet	Milk	Leche
Vi	Wine	Vino

ROUTES BETWEEN MAIN CENTRES

ROUTE 1

BARCELONA

History Montjuich has revealed traces of Iberian occupation but it was the Carthaginians who founded the first city in 3C BC, naming it after their leader, *Hamilcar Barca*. The Romans came to Empurias in 218BC and quickly moved down the coast in hot pursuit of the Carthaginians. *Tarraco* (later Tarragona) was their main base, and later their capital, but they built a settlement on *Mons Taber* in Barcelona, which they later named *Colonia Julia Augusta Paterna Faventio Barcino* and endowed with a temple of Augustus, sections of which survive today in the heart of the old city. Much of what they built was destroyed by hordes of Franks and Alemanes who swept in from the N in 3C AD, but fortunately did not stay. The Romans encircled what remained of their town with defensive walls at this time and important chunks of these can still be seen.

The next invaders were the Visigoths in the 5C who briefly made Barcelona their capital before moving on to Toledo. Worse was to come and there was no stopping the Moors who devastated Barcelona in 717 and went on to cross the Pyrenees before being checked by the Franks. The powerful Christian alliance of Franks and Catalans freed Barcelona in 801, only to lose it again to *Yacoub el Mansour* in 985. With the death of this invincible Moorish leader in 1002, Christian spirits revived and the Moors were inexorably and finally driven southwards.

Barcelona emerged as the capital of Catalonia and, from 1137, the seat of the Catalan-Aragonese Confederation. Here began Catalonia's Golden Age and the great King James I expanded into the Mediterranean and brought the State unprecedented wealth and influence. The government institutions of Council of One Hundred (*Conseil de Cent*) and *Generalitat* were founded at this time, and many Gothic masterpieces were built including the Cathedral and the famous shipyards (*Dressanes*).

This era of success came abruptly to an end in the 14C when the Black Death decimated the population and set in motion an inevitable sequence of social problems. Countless wars of succession weakened the economy during the centuries which followed and Barcelona's lowest point was reached when, in 1714, the victorious King Philip V punished the city for siding with the defeated Austrian pretender to the throne, Archduke Charles; it lost all privileges, its government and university, and came under the direct control of military governors from Madrid who erected fortresses at Montjuich and La Ribera (now Ciutadella Park).

Out of this humiliation there grew in time a renewed determination to succeed and the city experienced a second 'Golden Age' in the late 19C and early 20C when industrialisation arrived on a large scale. Textile factories sprang up and the city expanded to meet the needs of the growing population. Much of the new building was in Modernist style, a flamboyant and exciting expression of restored confidence. Barcelona suffered greatly however during the Civil War and in the ensuing 36 years of dictatorship. Catalan culture was completely paralysed whilst urban and heavy industrial expansion continued apace, often to the city's detriment aesthetically. Now with autonomous government in place, with language and culture intact, Barcelona has regained its sense of identity and pride.

Sight-seeing The casual observer could be forgiven for initially writing off this thriving metropolis as a dirty, noisy, overcrowded city with a severe traffic problem. It is of course all of these things on the surface. Scratch the surface and you will find immaculately preserved relics of virtually every period of Barcelona's turbulent history, architecture of quite stunning beauty, outstanding museums, parks and restaurants and, above all, an infectious cultural dynamism and generosity of spirit. Could it be that Barcelona, suppressed for so long, is now quite simply making up for lost time?

It is a huge and daunting city of over 2 million inhabitants. Anyone intent on discovering its charms and avoiding exhaustion (if on foot) or frustration (if by car) should plan their visit carefully and stay, if possible, in or near the old city, also known as the Gothic Quarter (*Barri Gotic*). Here many of the principal sites are within easy walking distance of each other, and the streets and squares offer a fascinating mix of traditional gravity and Modernist flamboyance. Sorties to the modern section of town, known as the Extension (*el Eixample*) can easily be undertaken using the efficient Metro which criss-crosses the entire city more rapidly than any other form of transport. Entrances to stations, which are clearly marked by red diamond-shaped insignia, display detailed maps of all lines.

In an effort to produce both clear exposition and logical itinerary, we have divided the city into the following sections:

The Gothic Quarter
The Ramblas and the Waterfront
Behind the Waterfront: Santa Maria del Mar and Carrer de Montcada
The Extension and Modernism; Ciutadella Park; Pedralbes
Montjuich
Environs of Barcelona

The Gothic Quarter (Barri Gotic)

Arrive by car from any direction and you will eventually find yourself on one of the broad avenues which cross the modern city (from the airport and the south: *Gran Via*; from Madrid: *Avinguda Diagonal*; from France and Girona: *Avinguda de la Meridiana*). Follow signs for *Barri Gotic* or *Plaça de Catalunya*. The latter is a huge square where bus and metro lines converge and which connects up with the Gothic Quarter and the Cathedral by way of *Portal del*

BARCELONA

1. Cathedral
2. Pl. de Sant Jaume
3. Hospital de la Sta.Creu
4. Gran Teatre del Liceu
5. Palau de Guell
6. Dressanes
7. Sta.Maria del Mar
8. Picasso Museum
9. Museum of Modern Art
10. Triumphal Arch
11. Casa Amatler
12. Palau de la Musica
13. Museum of Catalan Art
14. Archaeological Museum
15. Military Museum (castle)
16. Olympic Stadium
17. Plaça Nova

CIUTADELLA PARK

Estació Terme Franca

Passeig de Colom

Plaça Portal de la Pau

Ramblas

PORT

MONTJUICH

Paral·lel

Gran Via de les Corts Catalans

Plaça d'Espanya

Passeig de Gracia

Plaça de Catalunya

Ferran

Plaça Reial

N

46

Angel, emerging from its SE corner into *Plaça Nova.* Since the Cathedral is the most obvious landmark, we start the itinerary there, but readers will join it at whatever point is nearest to their hotel, car park or personal inclination.

The Cathedral of Santa Eulalia Excavations have revealed traces of a very early Christian church on this site. The first Christian bishop of Barcelona was *Praetextatus* who, it is recorded, attended the *Council of Sardica* (in the Orient), together with 5 other Spanish bishops, in the year 343. It can be assumed that Praetextatus had a church or cathedral even then and there exists a document which records the dedication of the Cathedral of Barcelona to the Holy Cross (*Santa Cruz*) in 599. The relics of Santa Eulalia (patron saint of Barcelona) were not brought here until 877, having previously lain in the *Church of Santa Maria del Mar.* The cathedral was almost completely destroyed by the notorious Moorish leader, *Yacoub el Mansour,* when he sacked the city in the late 10C.

In 1046 a Romanesque cathedral was built over the ruins by the Count of Barcelona, *Ramon Berenguer II,* which was consecrated in the year 1058. Nothing remains of this today except the door to the Santa Lucia chapel and some relief carvings on the St. Ivo door.

The present cathedral was begun in 1298 at a time of increasing Catalan-Aragonese prosperity. It was constructed in four stages: the first consisted of the apse with its 10 radial chapels, the presbytery and crypt and the false transept with 2 octagonal towers; the second saw the addition of the nave and 2 aisles and side chapels as far W-wards as the back of the choir (*trascoro*). The third stage was the building of the W-end which was closed off by a plain and unadorned façade in the year 1417. Lastly – in 1448 – the cloisters were completed. The whole process had taken 150 years. Designs had been presented by a French architect known as *Carli* (Charles Galtes of Rouen) for the main façade but these were not taken up at the time and the drawings were locked away in the Cathedral archives. It was not until the end of the 19C that a philanthropic industrialist commissioned a local architect to construct the present neo-Gothic façade. The architect is said to have been inspired by the original plans, which explains the recognisably French character of today's W-end with its delicate pinnacles and gables. The cupola with spire above was added in 1913 (financed by the industrialist's sons).

The **exterior** of the cathedral, with the exception of the W-end, is uncompromisingly severe, in typical Catalan-Gothic style; but it is pierced by some remarkable doors and enlivened here and there – particularly around the apse – by some splendid gargoyles depicting unicorns, lions and other heraldic beasts.

On the N side, is *St. Ivo's door.* This leads in to one arm of the false transept and supports the mighty bulk of the octagonal bell tower. The door dates from the first construction phase of the cathedral (early 14C); it is carved from local sandstone and marble (probably from Montjuich) and is generally considered to be one of Barcelona's principal sights. It does indeed have a superbly simple Gothic elegance combined with undoubted strength to enable it to take the weight of the bell tower. Notice the two relief carvings on either side of the door – refreshingly earthy and obviously predating the surrounding stone work; the one on the left of the door depicts a man fighting a lion; that on the right a man struggling with a dragon. These carvings undoubtedly survive from the earlier Romanesque church.

On the other side of the apse, at the angle between it and the cloister, is the *Door of Compassion* (*Porte de la Piatat*), built about 150 years later than that of St. Ivo, with richly decorated side pillars, plain archivolts and the very fine sculpture figure of Mary holding the body of Jesus in the tympanum. On the S wall of the cloister is the *Door of St. Eulalia*, similar in design and roughly contemporary with that of Compassion. Its archivolts are decorated and the tympanum holds a carved image of St. Eulalia between two heraldic shields. The remaining Door, that of *St. Lucia*, is to be found on the SW corner of the cathedral leading into the Romanesque chapel of the same name. The door – and the chapel which is a separate building joined on to the cloister by a short passageway – is described on page 54.

Inside, the cathedral has buttresses which project inwards and form a continuous series of chapels going right round the walls (another classic Catalan-Gothic feature). It has a wide central nave lit by an octagonal lantern over the crossing and by the rather dim light which filters through the rich but narrow windows, many of which are partially obscured by the horizontal line of the high galley which runs above the chapels. The purest lines and highest elevations are to be found in the apse, which is the oldest part of the church, and it is necessary to walk right up to the crossing to appreciate this masterpiece of Catalan art in its full uncluttered glory; from the W end it is almost completely obscured by the Choir (coro).

There is a great deal to see and the most logical place to start your tour is from the great neo-Gothic *W door*. As you enter notice the *cupola*, unusually sited at the beginning of the nave, and added in the 19C along with the W façade. It too, had been planned – and even started – in the 15C but was then abandoned in an unfinished wooden state until interest in the cathedral rekindled at the turn of this century and it was duly completed and topped with its fine spire.

Immediately to the right of the door is the *Chapel of the Immaculate Conception of Mary*. In the portrait Mary holds the keys to the city which were a votive offering made by the people of Barcelona during the plague of 1651. The sepulchre is that of *Bishop Francesc Sapera* who died in 1430, having played a major role in the construction of the cathedral and particularly in the addition of the cloisters.

Next come *eight side chapels*. The first and largest – *Chapel of the Holy Sacrament* – is dedicated to *Saint Ollegarius*, Bishop of Barcelona and later, the first Archbishop of Tarragona after its reconquest from the Moors by *Count Ramon Berenguer III* in 1099. Ollegarius became a staunch reformer of the

Catalan church and died in 1137. The majestic recumbent statue was carved by *Pere Ça Anglada* in 1406. Beside the altar is a staircase leading to a small room (not open to the public) wherein lie the mortal remains of the Bishop. The altar itself reflects a mixture of styles and, at the time of writing, is missing its crucifix, known as *Christ of Lepanto*, which has been moved to the *Chapel of Saint Serverus* on the N side.

The second chapel – *St. Anthony of Padua* – contains the splendid alabaster sepulchre of *Sancha Ximena de Cabrera*, who was an early benefactress. A figure of St. Anthony is placed over the altar. The dominant figures on the painted *retablo* (mid 15C) are those of the saints and martyrs *Cosmas* and *Damian*.

The third chapel – *St. Joseph Oriol* – contains a white marble figure of the saint who was a notable priest at the church of *Santa Maria del Mar* and had the power to work miracles. He died in 1702 and was canonised in 1909 by Pope Pious X. On the left is the sepulchre of *Cardinal Salvador Casanas y Pages* who helped bring about his canonisation.

The fourth chapel – *St. Pancratius, martyr, and St. Rochus, confessor,* contains a rather overbearing gilded and polychromed 18C retablo with images of the two saints.

The fifth chapel – *St. Raymond of Penyafort* – contains two related objects of considerable beauty. These are a 15C polychromed marble sepulchre raised up on 8 white pillars and showing scenes of the saint's life and, lying beneath it the marble figure of the saint, carved on a memorial tablet. Both come from the now destroyed Dominican convent of *Santa Caterina* where he was originally buried. He was canon of this cathedral and confessor to King James I and died in 1275.

The sixth chapel is dedicated to *St. Paul*, the Apostle, and other saints. St. Paul's figure occupies the central section of the neo-classical retablo; either side are the figures of *St. Dominic* and *St. Peter*; above is a painted panel portraying *St. Cecilia* and *St. Martha*.

The seventh chapel – *Our Lady of the Pillar* – has an 18C retablo and the niches, going from left to right, contain figures of *St. Barbara*, our Lady of the Pillar, and *St. Thecla*. On the left-hand wall is the mausoleum of *Gregorio* who was Archbishop of Barcelona until he died in 1972.

The eighth chapel is dedicated to *St. Pacianus*, Bishop of Barcelona in the 4C and *St. Francis Xavier*, confessor at that time. The carved figure of the latter reposes on the altar steps. There is a good Baroque retablo but the finest items in the chapel are undoubtedly the relief carvings on the side walls showing scenes in the life of the Archbishop and also in the life of Christ. It is worth going up as close as possible to this work to look right in to the carvings, particularly the medallion of the Last Supper with all its remarkable detail.

Turn left now and walk back to the rear of the choir (*trascoro*). It has a very fine carved marble screen which was designed and started by the Renaissance sculptor from Burgos, *Bartolomé Ordoñez*, and finished after his death in 1520 by *Pedro Villar* from Aragon. The four panels of the screen depict scenes in the life and martyrdom of *St. Eulalia*.

(There appear to have been two Eulalias venerated in Spain during the early Christian period: this one and Eulalia of Merida (in Extremadura). The relics of the latter were taken to Oviedo (in Asturias) during the 8C and laid to rest in the cathedral there, possibly to protect them from Moorish desecration. Many scholars believe that the cult may have spread from Oviedo eastwards to Barcelona and that the Barcelona saint could be a mistaken transformation of the Merida one. This theory is obviously not popular with Catalans who firmly claim Eulalia as their own. What is certain is that the concept of a 12-year old Christian martyr has fired the fertile imaginations of generations of sculptors and painters throughout Spain, who have produced a gruesome and seemingly endless catalogue of her punishments).

The *Choir* itself is one of the most homogenous and quietly satisfying sections of the cathedral and it is well worth paying the extra 25 pesetas to go in. Here is a double row of wooden stalls, the upper row carved in 1399 by the master craftsman *Pere Ça Anglada* (who carved the prone figure of *St. Ollegarius* in the Chapel of the Holy Sacrament). The misericords of the upper row present wonderfully earthy scenes of everyday medieval life and, as in so many great cathedrals, offer a welcome contrast to the sometimes overpowering seriousness of the architecture all around. The lower row of stalls was added a century later and the carving is somewhat less fine.

Above the stalls, on both sides of the choir, is a splendidly rich sequence of coats-of-arms. These belonged to the Knights of the Order of the Golden Fleece who assembled here in 1519 by order of the Grand Master the Emperor, Charles V of Spain; included are the royal arms of England, France, Holland and Portugal. All this is surmounted by a canopy of finely worked pinnacles, somewhat lighter in colour than the stalls, which finish the whole sequence with an almost ethereal delicacy of touch.

The *pulpit* on the left at the E end of the choir is another piece of work by *Pere Ça Anglada*. It is an object of great beauty and has three carved figures on each of its five sides with a canopy over each. Movement is added to the whole structure by the arches at the base, each of which rests on a flying angel. Facing the pulpit is an important *Episcopal Throne*, probably 14C, sculptor unknown. The quality of the work, and particularly the carving of the small statues, incline some experts to believe that this too was the work of *Ça Anglada*. Before leaving the choir notice the fine oak screens (at both ends) made in the early 16C by *Bartolome Ordoñez* (creator of the *trascoro* marble screen) and showing Old and New Testament scenes.

Leave the choir now and move back towards the W end of the cathedral to the *Baptistry* alongside the main door. Behind the 15C marble font with its clean uncluttered lines is an appealingly simple scene of the baptism of Christ in alabaster, set off to perfection by its rather ornate canopy. There is a good late 15C window, designed by an artist from Cordoba, depicting Christ appearing to Mary Magdalen. Notice, too, a very interesting inscription over the door on the right which names the first six Indians brought back from the New World to Barcelona by Christopher Columbus in 1493 and baptised in this cathedral.

Continuing up the N aisle, the first chapel (with heavy Baroque retablo) is dedicated to *St. Severus*, one time Bishop of Barcelona and martyr. At the time of writing, the very beautiful crucifix known as *Christ of Lepanto* is placed here and a purple band of cloth had been tied around his ankle and extended through the railings of the chapel for people to touch. It comes from the flagship of Don John of Austria who defeated the Turks in the Gulf of Lepanto in 1571 (a replica of the ship can be seen in the Maritime Museum, see page 64). It is one of the most venerated objects in the cathedral and it appears to be moved around from time to time, as the religious calendar dictates, so as to form a real and tangible part of everyday worship.

The second chapel, dedicated to *St. Mark* and with late 17C retablo and scenes of the saint's life in relief sculpture, is also the *Chapel of the Association of Cobblers*. (This will explain to the sharp-eyed visitor why there is a stone carving of a boot high up on the *outside* wall of the cathedral at this point).

The third chapel, dedicated to *St Bernardinus of Siena*, has a simple retablo with the Sienese saint in the centre, flanked by St. Michael, the Archangel, and St. Anthony of Padua and with St. Jerome above. This chapel is connected with the *Association of Matmakers*.

The fourth chapel, to *Our Lady of the Rosary*, has a somewhat brighter retablo (by the early 17C artist *Agusti Pujol*); notice particularly the panel at bottom right showing the familiar scene of the birth of Christ in a quite delightful circular design, and with faces wreathed in smiles.

The fifth chapel, to *Mary Magdalen*, is in more sombre style and her image stands on the altar. The early 15C painted wood retablo is dedicated to Saints Bartholomew and Elizabeth.

The sixth chapel – to the *Immaculate Heart of Mary* – has a remarkable 15C painted wood retablo which completely fills the back wall and which is dedicated to Saints Sebastian and Thecla. Notice the kneeling figure of the donor (Canon Joan Sors) painted in to the lower central panel on the right of the figure of St. Sebastian. (Because of bad lighting it is quite easy to miss this charming touch).

The seventh chapel, to *Our Lady of Joy*, has a modern sandstone retablo with alabaster figure of Mary (looking slightly yellower than the sandstone) by the sculptor *J. M. Camps y Arnau* in 1945. The figure on the right hand wall is that of Pope Pious X.

The eighth chapel is dedicated to *Our Lady of Montserrat* and contains the familiar image of the black virgin and child, this one carved in 1945. The retablo dates from 1940 and has paintings of various saints associated with Montserrat.

You are now standing opposite the lovely staircase which leads to the pulpit inside the Choir (described earlier) and which was probably created by the same early 15C sculptor. The figures on the access jambs are those of Mary and the Angel Gabriel. The wrought-iron decoration on top of the balustrade is particularly striking. On your left is St. Ivo's door and above you is the 16C organ whose protective casing in the form of paintings on cloth can be seen in the cathedral museum. It is worth pausing a moment at this point for one of the most uninterrupted and breathtaking views of the whole cathedral.

You come now to the *Presbytery*, the oldest and most architecturally pure section of the cathedral. The round windows high in the cupola still contain some of the original 14C and 15C glasswork. The floor of the Presbytery is a metre higher than that of the rest of the building so as to make room for the crypt below. Dominating the Presbytery is a magnificent Episcopal Chair which was carved in alabaster in the 14C. Above the chair is the Holy Cross (*Santa Cruz*), held aloft by six angels to signify exaltation. This is a modern work – by the sculptor *Federico Mares* – and was installed in its present position in 1975. Until 1970 there had been a very gilded retablo but this was removed to another church and the nave of the cathedral acquired a lot more light as a result. The High Altar table below rests on sections of Visigothic (6C) columns; these were here originally, then removed to the Museum, then moved back again in 1970 when the retablo disappeared.

A flight of steps in front of the altar leads down to the *Crypt* wherein lies the *Sarcophagus of St. Eulalia*. Its position directly beneath the High Altar was carefully planned so that the congregation could see and pray to both the Holy Cross and St. Eulalia at the same time. The crypt is in the form of an apsidal chapel and was built in the 14C by *Jaume Fabré*. The vaulting is unusually flat (because of the presbytery floor above) and is divided by twelve arches which converge into an important keystone bearing a painting of the Virgin and St. Eulalia. The centrepiece (and some would say the heart and soul of the cathedral) is the huge alabaster sarcophagus completed in 1327 by an unknown Pisan artist. The delicate carving shows scenes in the life and martyrdom of the saint and on the front face of the lid is a procession of princes and bishops bringing the holy remains to the cathedral.

Angels with gilded wings guard the four corners of the sarcophagus and in the middle stands the Virgin with child in her arms. The heavy tomb stands on an assortment of fluted and twisted columns – an almost lighthearted touch, it seems, in the presence of so much solemnity. The whole imposing structure is admirably set off by the finely carved walls of the crypt with its gallery closed off by dark red curtains visible between short squat columns supporting the vaulted roof. All of this can only be peered at through the iron grille across the bottom of the stairway and it is worth putting 25 ptas in the box for the light to go on and every detail to become visible. The crypt was restored to its present immaculate condition in 1970. Before leaving, notice the entry arch covered with small carved heads which probably represent church dignitaries of that time. The heads are repeated up the walls of the stairway.

Behind the Presbytery are 10 chapels built in to the wall of the apse. The first, next to St. Ivo's door, is the *Chapel of the Souls*. Here, in a niche in the right-hand wall, is a very fine early 15C alabaster sarcophagus. The prone, be-robed figure is that of *Bishop Ramon d'Escales* who died in 1398. Notice the weeping figures below with very expressive faces. On the left of the chapel is a modern life-size figure of the crucified Christ, clearly much venerated by worshippers today.

The second chapel, dedicated to the *Heart of Jesus*, is by a modern sculptor and has little to commend it.

The third chapel – to *Our Lady of Ransom* – has a baroque altar in the central panel of which is a carving representing the founding of the Order of Ransom (in 1218) with a knight receiving the habit of the new Order from St. Raymond of Penyafort and with King James I looking on. Looking down on all this from above is the Virgin herself.

The fourth chapel is called *Holy Places in the Holy Land – the Holy Sepulchre*. It has a 15C painted wood retablo with scenes in the lives of the two saints to whom it was dedicated, St. Clare of Assisi and St. Catherine of Alexandria. On the walls are paintings of the martyrdom of St. Stephen to whom the chapel was originally dedicated and who was patron saint of bit-makers (as in horses' bits).

The fifth chapel contains a 15C painted wood retablo with scenes depicting the lives of St. Martin of Tours and St. Ambrose of Milan and on the walls are pictures of the life of St. Peter the Apostle. It is difficult to distinguish much of this because of bad lighting and poor state of repair.

The sixth chapel, dedicated to *St. Helen*, the mother of Constantine the Great, contains another painted retablo. Dating from the 14C it has 18 panels and is dominated by a very lovely, utterly simple scene of the Annunciation. It is one of the spiritual joys of the cathedral. Other scenes are less easily recognisable and include a charming cameo of 3 figures in bed at top right. St. Helen herself is represented by the modern figure on the altar.

The seventh chapel – to *St. John the Baptist* and to *Joseph*, husband of Mary, has a very fine 16C gilt and polychrome retablo with 12 reliefs showing events in St. John's life. Joseph, the patron saint of carpenters, appears in a niche and the chapel belongs now to the Association of Carpenters.

The eighth chapel, to *St. Benedict*, contains a wonderful painted wood retablo by the 15C artist *Bernat Martorell*. There are scenes of various miracles including that of the loaves and fishes and in the top centre is a simple and moving depiction of the crucifixion. This is another of the cathedral's treasures, of great artistic merit and in remarkably good condition. By contrast the ninth chapel, to *Our Lady of Fatima*, is of little merit and the retablo in the form of a tryptich is by an unknown artist.

The tenth chapel, to *St. Francis of Assisi and St. Anthony*, contains an unremarkable heavy baroque retablo in gilded wood. The chapel belonged formerly to the Association of Carters.

The *Sacristy*, alongside the last chapel, is entered through a small gothic door. As you enter, notice high on the wall the wooden sepulchres of the Count of Barcelona, Ramon Berenguer I, and his wife Almodis, who founded the Romanesque cathedral in the mid 11C. The Sacristy houses the Treasury and it is necessary to seek special permission to see this. It contains among other things a superb 14C *Processional Cross* of silver overlaid with gilt and bearing 10 beautifully worked blue enamels (5 on each side); in front is the crucified Christ and on the back is an image of St. Eulalia. Here, too, is the famous 14C *Monstrance* – a very strange affair to modern eyes. Heavily ornate and fashioned in silver and gold, it is encircled by a silk sash encrusted with jewels and stands on a throne, said to have belonged to King Martin the Humane. It has been admired and enriched throughout the ages, by kings and bishops, which probably accounts for its rather excessive ornamentation. Other items in the Treasury include a mitre belonging to the 12C bishop, St. Ollegarious and a charming Moorish chest in ivory – a reminder that Christianity did not always hold sway in Barcelona.

You enter the **Cloisters** through a Romanesque door which is a relic of the second cathedral. Best seen from the cloister side, it is splendidly carved in white marble and is believed to have been a gift of the first Count of Barcelona (which could explain why his sepulchre has been located close to it). The Gothic tympanum above was added at the time when the door was inserted into the present building.

The Cloisters were built over a period of 2 centuries, the side adjoining the cathedral being the oldest part. There are chapels on 3 sides, many of them empty now and most of them closed. The most noteworthy feature of the Cloisters is probably the wonderfully carved frieze which borders the interior above the multiple columns, many of which have intricately carved capitals. One could spend a long time identifying the various scenes from Old and New Testaments and not find a repetition anywhere. An amusing, and arguably intrusive, feature are the noisy geese which traditionally live in the central pool. Alongside the pool, is a temple, particularly remarkable for its lovely 15C central keystone showing St. George killing the dragon, watched by 8 angels.

Housed in the W side of the Cloisters is the **Cathedral Museum** (open only between 11 and 13 hours). The lower of the two rooms was once the Chapter Hall and is richly decorated and not therefore the best setting for some of the exhibits whose innate simplicity can cause them to pale before the heavy and richly painted walls and ceiling. However, some of the pieces do arrest the attention and none more so than the superb *Piedad* by the 15C Cordoban painter, *Bartolomé Bermejo*, in which Mary is holding the broken body of Jesus in her lap. There is also an assortment of panels from retablos, the painted cloth which rightly belongs with the great organ over St. Ivo's door and (inevitably) a tryptich with scenes from the martyrdom of St. Eulalia. Nothing is labelled in this museum and the atmosphere is slightly oppressive. To the right of the museum is the *Chapel of St. Lucia,* really a separate building joined onto the cloister by a short passageway, and with its own door on to the street. The door, Romanesque and probably surviving from the 11C cathedral, is the loveliest part of it; it is in local sandstone and has four finely carved archivolts resting on capitals showing scenes of the Annunciation. In the tympanum is a picture of St. Lucia who was martyred in Sicily in the early 4C for little more than refusing to marry a rich and influential suitor. At the time her eyes are reputed to have been torn out and then miraculously restored. Because of historical connections with Sicily in the Middle Ages she has always been venerated in Barcelona and particularly by people with sight problems. The belfry above the door was added in 1681. Inside the chapel behind a glass shield is the sepulchre of Bishop *Arnau de Gurb* who constructed the chapel in the mid 13C. It is a fine piece, raised up on 4 columns with the prone figure of the bishop in pontifical robes above. There are several other interesting tombs and the altar is modern, inserted in 1947 to replace one which was burnt during the civil war.

Leave the Cathedral now to explore the rest of the **Gothic Quarter**, pausing every now and then to look at the scores of antique shops tucked away in the narrow streets between the historic monuments.

The *Archdeacon's House* (*Casa de l'Ardiaca*) is to be found opposite the Chapel of St. Lucia; it combines Gothic and Renaissance styles, with graceful windows and a charming inner courtyard with fountain. The house is now used to store the archives of the city.

Next to the Archdeacon's House is the *Bishop's Palace* (*Palau del Bisbe*) which has a rather severe 18C façade but makes up for this with an original courtyard preserving a Romanesque gallery and some fine 13C triforium windows. The Palace faces on to *New Square* (*Plaça Nova*) – a market place in Roman times and the spot where began one of the two main Roman roads which criss-crossed the town – the *Cardo.* Overlooking the Plaça somewhat incongruously are huge drawings by Picasso on the façade of the College of Architects. As evidence of the Roman era there remains a pair of round towers which formed part of the Roman wall and which have now been fully restored. They marked one of the main gates to the town – the *Portal del Bisbe*).

On the far side of the Bishop's Palace is one of Barcelona's most romantic and unspoilt squares, that of *Felipe Neri,* presided over by its Baroque church. Peaceful and outside the general route of traffic and tourists, it is a pleasant spot to pause a while.

On the N side of the Cathedral Square (*Plaça de la Seu*) is the *House of Pious Almonry* (*Pia Almoina*), also known as the *Canonry House* (*la Canonja*). It was built in the 15C to house an institution of that name whose function was to provide free meals for 100 poor people each day. Close by is a significant section of Roman wall.

A little way up the street which skirts the N side of the cathedral (*Carrer dels Comtes*), in an old ecclesiastical building, is the *Federico Mares Museum* containing a vast assortment of Romanesque polychrome wood sculptures from all over Spain. There is an important collection of tiny Iberian figures including men on horseback, men wearing short skirts (like kilts) and women in capes, probably used as votive offerings to the gods; also some good Graeco-Roman terracotta figures and Roman stone carving. Upstairs there is a bit of modern light relief in the form of dolls' house furniture, model railways, cigarette cards and much else besides. The only way to avoid getting cultural indigestion in this museum is to walk fairly fast through it, or to discipline oneself to see only a small part of it.

Further up the street is the *Palace of the Viceroy of Catalonia* (*Palau de Lloctinent*) which houses the archives of the Crown of Aragon. The library contains a priceless collection of medieval documents and is not open to the public. It is however worth entering the courtyard and walking up the steps on the left of the entrance to study the remarkable bronze door at the top. This is a modern work (1975) by the sculptor *Josep Subirachs* (born in Barcelona in 1927 and currently working on the *Sagrada Familia Church* (see page 71)). At first sight, at least to the unaccustomed eye, this door appears to display a random selection of figures and maps; closer inspection reveals a carefully devised monument to Catalonia's eventful history and the key lies in the central panel which explains what everything is. Particularly interesting is the map of the Mediterranean showing Catalonia as the dominant power and Southern Italy and Sicily as colonies. Some of the figures are carved in reverse – looking like moulds from which the sculptures have been removed; this playful interchange of convex and concave is arresting and sometimes beautiful.

Behind the *Palau de Lloctinent* hides one of Barcelona's most evocative and distinguished historic sights – the *King's Square* (*Plaça del rei*), occupying the site of the former Royal Palace of the Counts of Barcelona. At the end of the Square – up an elegant stairway and through a Romanesque doorway – is the 14C *Tinell Hall*, famous for having been the place where the Catholic Kings – Ferdinand and Isabella – received the triumphant Columbus on his return from the New World in 1493. Although this immense room is now frequently occupied by modern art exhibitions, it is still possible to appreciate its fine proportions and the wood panelled ceiling supported by huge stone arches. Just visible are the remains of wall paintings and some of the windows are said to date back to the 11C. The hall was converted to a church in the 18C and then restored to its original function as place of assembly in 1940.

From outside it is interesting to notice that the original hall has been encased in a later framework of shallow arches and buttresses (which incidentally do not conform with the spacing of the original windows). This was undoubtedly done so as to reinforce the building to sustain the weight of the tower above, known as *King Martin's Look-out Tower* and added in the mid-16C. It comprises five storeys of porticoed galleries and adds distinction and grace to the Square.

Also in King's Square is the excellent **City Museum (Museu de la Ciutat)**, by far the most exciting museum in town because it guards within its subterranean depths the beginnings of Barcelona – Roman *Mons Taber* – in *situ*. The 16C *House of Clariana-Padellas* was originally sited on the *Carrer de Mercaders* nearby but was moved to its present site, stone by stone, in 1931, when the Roman discoveries were first made and the Municipality decided it should be the city museum. Because of the Civil War serious excavations did not begin until the early 1940s and the museum did not open till 1943. Excavating under the cathedral began in 1968.

Obviously much of what is tantalizingly there cannot be brought to light because of the danger of weakening foundations of what is above. As our guide said, "we have only part of a city here: the rest of the city is under the city". But there is enough to tell us a great deal about the inhabitants of *Colonia Julia Augusta Paterna Faventio Barcino*, the earliest of which were retired legionaries.

Inside the Museum, descend the stairway and you will find yourself standing in a street alongside the first, 1C, wall. In front of you are fragments of houses, and of houses built upon houses as the level of the city rose in time (it was anyway built on a hill). There are mosaics, public baths (with *frigidarium* intact), huge amphoras embedded in the floor for storing wine and oil, and countless streets including one leading to the Forum (which has not yet been excavated). Then there is the 4C wall which went up outside the earlier one and was defensive (deemed necessary after the invasions from the N). This wall used bigger boulders, and indeed anything the builders could lay their hands on as ballast – here and there an upside-down column or a plaque, and even coffins and tombstones from an earlier necropolis which was outside the original wall.

The visitor can walk freely around amongst all this and there are plenty of well-lit walk-ways, maps, plans and explanatory models to help. Let us hope that by the time this Guide is published, some of these at least will be labelled in one or two other languages besides Catalan (it will not be for want of asking if they are not!).

There was a 4C Paleo-Christian church under the Cathedral and you can stand in what was its nave. It faced N-S. It gives quite an eerie feeling to catch a glimpse of the foundations of today's massive church above you. The head of the early church is gone, (probably destroyed when the 11C Romanesque church was built), but there is a model to show how it would have been. A baptistry was later built on the other end, since total immersion was necessary before early Christians were allowed to enter the church. Later still, when people were automatically baptised as children, the baptistry was turned into a cemetery, which is how it appears today. There are amphoras lying about which seem to have been used as coffins for children, and several sections of coffins made of tiles.

At one point it is possible to go up some stairs to stand by the vault of the 11C church. This offers a lesson in how the 11C builders achieved the perfect curve (by using a wooden frame), and also gives a chance to appreciate by how much the level of the city had risen over the years. Here too one can see 16C houses, on top of Roman ones, the builders using Roman fragments just as their ancestors had.

This whole experience is unforgettable and one's excitement is heightened by the knowledge that there is so much still to find and that archaeologists – even perhaps as you stand there – are tunnelling under the heart of medieval Barcelona to discover more of its Roman origins.

The rest of the Museum, which occupies all of the house above ground, comes almost as an anti-climax but is nevertheless worth a visit for it takes you easily through the intervening years up to the present day. Notable are the splendid 17C and 18C maps and plans of the city. Many of these are French (as well they might be) and show sieges, battles, troop encampments, ruined forts etc drawn in the finest of detail, and looking a bit like expensive war games waiting to be played. There are also informative maps showing the various periods of expansion of the town over the centuries and some amusing pictures of the first factories and railways, belching huge clouds of smoke over the city.

Remarkable too is the unique clock, filling a whole room and said to weigh 5,512 kgs. It was built between 1575 and 1577 by Flemish clockmakers and has a single mechanism for timekeeping and for chiming, and no dial. It once lived in the cathedral belfry and was retired in 1864.

From Room XVI on the first floor you can pass out of *Clariana Padellas House* in to the *Chapel of St. Agatha (Capella de St. Agueda)*. This 14C church with its elegant and slender tower is all that remains of the royal palace and one of its sides rests on part of the 4C Roman wall. This is best observed from the *Plaça de Ramon Berenguer el Gran* outside – a kind of sunken garden right up against the wall which has the added attraction of a fine equestrian statue of its namesake by the modern sculptor, *Josep Llimona*. The interior of St. Agatha's Chapel is simple and has a fine painted wood retablo showing scenes in the life of Christ above, and of various saints below. This is a 15C masterpiece of Jaume Huguet. The Gothic windows all display heraldic shields and there is an explanation of these on the wall at the W end.

At the centre of the Gothic Quarter, marking the spot where the Romans had their forum and where the two main streets – *Cardo* and *Decumano* – intersected, is *St James' Square (Plaça de Sant Jaume)*. It can be reached from Placa del Rei by way of *Carrer de la Llibreteria*, or (from the W front of the cathedral) down *Carrer del Bisbe*. This huge open Square is still a lively centre of interest and activity and comes into its own every Saturday and Sunday

evening around 18.30 hours when Catalonia's stately national dance, the
Sardana, is performed by young and old holding hands in innumerable
circles. (This also happens outside the Cathedral on Sundays at noon). The
Square is dominated by two elegant buildings which stand opposite each
other: the *Palace of the Generalitat (Palau del Generalitat)* and the *City Hall
(Ajuntament)*, both of major significance in the city's history.

The **Palace of the Generalitat** was built as the first permanent seat of the
Catalan parliament at the beginning of the 15C. It has come through 5
centuries of troubled history and stands still a much loved and living symbol
of democracy. The façade overlooking Carrer del Bisbe is original and
includes what was once the main entrance. The medallion over the door is
famous and history relates that the sculptor was paid twice the agreed price
because the authorities were so delighted with his representation of St.
George killing the dragon. The gargoyle on the left represents the maiden
who was being rescued.

The main façade, overlooking the Square, was added in the 17C. It is
Greco-Roman in style and has a 19C equestrian statue of the patron saint in
the centre. The horizontal line of the windows, echoed by the elegant
balustrade and set off by classical columns at each end, is a particularly
harmonious feature.

Inside the main entrance is a truly magnificent courtyard with sweeping
staircase leading to a first-floor gallery of Gothic arches supported by slender
columns. Above this is a second gallery of much flatter arches, topped with
pinnacles and some remarkably fine gargoyles.

On the first floor, with its lovely wood ceilings painted in Mozarabic style,
is the much revered *St. George's Chapel,* instantly recognisable by its
flamboyant late Gothic door. Inside, the Chapel has two sections: the first is
15C, with a fine ribbed vault and central boss of the saint. It is lit by a rose
window (of rather unfortunate modern design) and contains a fine Catalan
tapestry which apparently took the 15C artist four years to complete, since
the relief effect is laboriously obtained by layers of stitching (in gold, silver
and silk thread) rather than by inserting stuffing. The altar front is a silver
reproduction of the tapestry. The second section, added in 1620, has a small
cupola beneath which are suspended four capitals without any columns,
evidence that the weight is perfectly carried by the arches and walls and
needs no further support (a form of architectural showing-off). Beneath is
yet another representation of St. George, this time an articulated silver
figure.

Alongside the Chapel is the 16C Courtyard of Oranges (*Pati dels
Tarongers*). This charming piece was the first extension to the Palace and the
galleries with pink marble columns are in Renaissance style; it is overlooked
by a small Gothic bell tower still holding its original bell which is rung on
special occasions and can be heard throughout the Gothic Quarter. The
quite remarkable gargoyles deserve a few moments of attention and include

such figures as the Mace-bearer who would have preceded officials on formal occasions.

Leading off the patio is the resplendent 16C *Council Chamber* with its heavy gilded and coffered ceiling (designed so as to avoid any echo) and walls thickly lined with Flemish tapestries. This rather overpowering room has seen the signing of many historic treaties and proclamations but today it is rarely used. Alongside it is the *Torres-Garcia Room*, so-called because it contains allegorical murals by the early 20C Catalan painter of that name. Leading off it is the 17C *Hall of Sessions* used by the present-day Cabinet when they do not prefer to meet a little less formally in the *House of Canons* (the official residence of the President) which is reached by way of the bridge spanning Carrer del Bisbe.

One more hall remains to be described in this remarkable building which also includes offices for at least 200 staff, and that is the 17C *St. George's Salon* (*Saló de Sant Jordi*). This was originally planned as a replacement to the Gothic chapel which was considered by some to be too small. Instead, and despite the provision of columns and side aisles, it was turned into a reception hall and the walls were covered with murals depicting some of the main events in Spanish history. The hall is dominated at each end by two vast frescoes, one depicting the black Virgin of Montserrat and the other showing the triumphant Columbus (Colon), with Indians in attendance, being greeted by the Catholic Monarchs, Ferdinand and Isabella, in Barcelona. Also represented on the walls are such events as the Battle of *Las Navas de Tolosa* (in which the Moors were decisively beaten by the Spaniards in 1212), the Battle of *Lepanto* (when Don John of Austria beat the Turks in 1571), the reconquest of Mallorca by King James I, and the intriguing story of the drummer boy – Isidro – who by his bravery brought about the retreat of the French from Montserrat without a shot being fired. Hanging from the dome and adding a touch of formality to all this colourful drama is a huge and elegant crystal chandelier said to weigh over a ton.

The City Hall (*Ajuntament*) is also magnificent and still retains vestiges of the original 14C building including the façade which overlooks *Carrer de la Ciutat* (on the left as you face the building from the Square). The main façade is neo-classical and the marble statues on either side of the entrance are of King James I on the left and Councillor Fivaller (a leading local politician) on the right. Inside, on the ground floor, is a rich scattering of works by Catalonia's leading contemporary sculptors including *Subirachs* and *Joan Miró*. Up the stairs are various rooms of great beauty including the famous *Hall of One Hundred* (*Sala de Cent*), a spacious and rich chamber built in 1370 for 100 elected councillors and entered through a splendid Renaissance doorway. It was restored in time for the Great Exhibition of 1929. There is also the *Hall of Chronicles* (*Sala de Croniques*) which was built at this time and has a black marble floor and paintings by the modern Catalan artist, *José Maria Sert* recalling the 14C Catalan expeditions to the Eastern Mediterranean. The dark decor sets off the artist's monochrome genius to perfection. Lastly, and visible from a balcony on the top floor of the building, there is a charming Gothic courtyard.

If you walk up the narrow medieval street, *Carrer del Paradis* (in the far right-hand corner of the Square as you face the Palace), you come to four Roman columns, all that remain of the *Temple of Augustus* erected here in 1C AD at the highest point of the Roman town. The columns are splendidly preserved within the courtyard of what is now the Catalan Excursion Centre and Alpine Club. It is worth climbing halfway up the stairs to appreciate the capitals and to become fully aware of the sheer scale of the columns. They stand three in a row and one behind, like some giant intruders from a bygone age, and there is a conveniently placed drawing nearby showing how the temple would have looked.

The little Gothic Church of *Sant Just y Pastor* is to be found a short way along *Carrer Hercules* (leaving the Square by the left-hand corner, facing the City Hall). This is believed to be the oldest church in the city, built in the 14C on foundations of an earlier church probably going back to 8C. Today there is not much to see. No longer in use, the church appears to have been locked up for many years and later buildings lean hard up against it. It is interesting however to know that any statement sworn at the altar of the San Felix chapel inside (which sadly now the visitor is unable to see) has the legal status of a sworn testament. This right was conferred in the 10C and was unique to this church, The square which it overlooks (*Plaça de San Just*) is peaceful and forgotten: a sense of sadness and neglect pervades the area which is but a 5-minute stroll from the vibrant Saint James Square. In just such contrasts of mood lie the intrinsic charm of Barcelona's Gothic Quarter.

The Ramblas and the Waterfront

If the Gothic Quarter is the heart of old Barcelona, then the *Rambla* is its main artery, descending for about a mile from the *Plaça de Catalunya* to the waterfront, skirting the western flank of the Gothic Quarter as it goes, and accessible from there by way of *Carrer Ferran* which leads out of St. James Square.

The Plaça de Catalunya claims to be as big as the Paris *Etoile*, and feels like it too if you happen to want to cross from one side to the other on foot. It is very much the hub of the city, and is the main link between the Extension and the old quarter; to the N are the prosperous shopping streets and impressive office blocks of cosmopolitan Barcelona, to the S the wild and wonderful Rambla usually known in the plural because it comprises five different streets.

Its main characteristic, and the reason for its international renown, is the vibrant and ever-changing pattern of life which packs every centimetre of its length, sometimes beautiful, sometimes squalid, never dull. Along its tree-shaded pedestrian precinct in the middle are cafés and restaurants galore and stalls selling animals, birds, tropical fish, second-hand books and masses of flowers; there are artists, acrobats, singers and magicians and some of the most outrageous whores in Europe who emerge at dusk and drape themselves around the lamp-posts.

There are also some modest and reasonably priced hotels here, a little shabby now and bearing only a few traces of a more prosperous era before the Extension was built, when this was the fashionable place to be. But they are clean and comfortable and hugely convenient for anyone wanting to live and breathe old Barcelona, and to explore the Gothic Quarter five minutes' walk away. A room at the back will assure a quiet night's sleep; a room at the front, on the other hand, assures a ring-side view of the action. The *Hotel Cuatro Naciones*, at no.40 and almost on the Waterfront, falls into this category. What is more, there is an underground garage right opposite it.

A leisurely walk down from Plaça de Catalunya to the Waterfront will reveal the following points of interest (all on the right unless otherwise specified): there is the grim unfriendly-looking Baroque building of the *Jesuit Church of Bethlehem* (just after *Pintor Fortuny street*) which is usually closed; shortly after comes the *Palace of the Vicereine* (*Palau de la Virreine*); it was commissioned in 1770 by the Viceroy of Peru, but he died before it was finished and it was named after his wife; it now contains a permanent collection of postage stamps (*Museu Gabinet Postal*) and is the headquarters of the Municipal Department of Culture.

A little further down is the *Market of St. Joseph* (*Mercat de Sant Josep*) also known as the *Boqueria*. It is a splendid colonnaded market with heavy roof typical of the 19C and imposing iron and glass entrance with Modernist decoration added in 1914. Inside is a mouthwatering display of local fruit, vegetables, fish and meat, all of very high quality.

Just behind the Market (off the Ramblas but worth the detour) is the *Hospital of the Holy Cross* (*Hopital de la Santa Creu*): a pilgrims' hospital in the 13C, it now houses the Library of Catalonia and the Royal Academy of Medicine and Surgery. The buildings date from many different periods and there are some peaceful courtyards through which to wander, some restored and some derelict. It is even possible to peer through a window at an old operating theatre with original table and huge chandelier above. It is interesting to note that Barcelona's most famous architect, Antoni Gaudi, died here in 1926 after being run over by a tram.

Back on the Rambla, at no.82 (on *Plaça de la Boqueria*) is a Modernist building known as *Casa Quadros* and designed by Josep Vilaseca in 1896. It is surprisingly decorated with umbrellas and fans and even a Chinese dragon, all left over from the time when it was an umbrella shop. At no.83 is the corner shop of *Casa Figueres* with striking Modernist façade complete with mosaic sign and relief of a female holding a sheaf of wheat. This was once a bakery and is one of the best preserved gems of Modernism anywhere in town.

The next building of interest is the 19C *Lyceum Theatre* (*Gran Teatre del Liceu*). Its unpromising and shabby façade hides one of Europe's most ostentatious opera houses which was once considered to be amongst the best.

The interior, which can accommodate 3,500 people, is certainly breathtaking and should be seen, either by taking a guided tour (possible around midday on weekdays), or by attending an opera during the season which lasts from November to March.

Cross the Rambla now for Barcelona's best proportioned square – *Royal Square (Plaça Reial)* which lies but a few yards up a narrow street and is worth a diversion. (It is also one way through to the Gothic Quarter). Plaça Reial is arcaded, lined with uniformly noble buildings mostly dating from the 19C, and nicely decorated with lamp posts by Gaudi. The architect won a competition with these as a young man in 1878 which explains their (for him) staid and traditional nature. Redolent of past grandeur, this square is now a rather sad place and springs to life only on Sunday mornings when it is invaded by stamp collectors and numismatists who set up their stalls and attract a steady following of serious visitors and eccentrics.

Back on the right-hand side of the Rambla and a little way along *Carrer Nou de la Rambla* which turns off it, there is the remarkable *Guell Palace (Palau de Guell)* designed by Gaudi as a town residence for the Guell family. A white building with parabolic arches and extraordinary excrescences on the roof, it is somehow the more striking for standing, as it does, tight- packed amidst traditional houses. It now contains a museum of theatrical art and is worth entering both for that and for the rich Gaudi interior. Carrer Nou de la Rambla marks the boundary of Barcelona's red light district known as *Chinatown,* or *Barrio Chino,* a particularly seedy area abutting on to the Rambla itself, but with one or two amusing and extremely cheap restaurants buried deep in its dark alleyways.

On the left, and with the end of the Rambla in sight, is the *Waxworks Museum (Museu de Cera)* with over 300 models. Here, to the strains of suitably atmospheric music, you will see a rather strange selection of world leaders, a bevy of Alice in Wonderland characters, the kings of Catalonia and some of the great Spanish explorers such as Pizarro. You end up being drawn inexorably towards the exit (*la Sortida*) in a pretty good imitation of a space ship. All in all, the Museum is good value. It offers a good mix of serious and not so serious and has less of an addiction to murderers and general horror than some better-known waxworks.

Finally, where the Rambla spills out on to the Waterfront by way of an extremely busy square known as the *Gate of Peace (Portal de la Pau)*, there stands a remarkable monument to Christopher Columbus (*Cristofal Colon*). The 8m bronze statue stands on an iron column 50ms high and was made by the architect *Gaieta Buigas* for the 1888 World Exhibition. It is possible to take a lift up to the top for an unforgettable view of the city. Far more relevant to the serious visitor however are the beautifully executed scenes carved into the base of the monument itself, depicting the various stages in the explorer's triumph: trying in the first place to convince a crowd of clerics and worthy citizens that the world is round and that his expedition could succeed; meeting with the Catholic Monarchs and receiving their blessing;

arriving in the New World on October 12, 1492; returning with token Indians; being greeted by the Catholic Monarchs in the Tinell Hall in Barcelona in April 1493 and created Admiral of the Fleet. Although Colombus was probably born in Genoa, Italy, and actually set sail for his first expedition from Palos in Huelva province, there is no doubt that Barcelona claims him for its very own.

Across a very busy thoroughfare to the right of the monument stand the superb medieval royal shipyards, called *Dressanes*, probably the best preserved of their kind in the world. In these gargantuan yards were created the mighty Catalan-Aragonese vessels which successfully roamed the Mediterranean and beyond for centuries. The scale and strength of the building is breathtaking. There are seven huge bays dating from the 14C and three more dating from the 17C. Very properly the restored part of building now houses the **Maritime Museum**. This is rightly dedicated to Spain's two greatest heroes of the sea – Columbus (the first floor) and Don Juan (ground floor) and quite the most exciting exhibit of all is the life-size replica of Don Juan's galleon in which he won the crucial battle of Lepanto against the Turks on 7 October 1571. It is possible to climb up steps to look right down into the vastness of the ship, to marvel at its length and admire the superb workmanship. The king's quarters are at the prow. There would have been 30 oars on each side, each requiring 3 oarsman. Walk round the outside of the ship to admire the detailed craftsmanship and rich decoration which could only have been entertained in the unshakeable belief that the ship was unsinkable. There are many helpful charts and maps from which one learns that 207 Spanish galleons were ranged against 208 Turkish ships and that the Spaniards had 84,420 men altogether. Lepanto is in the Gulf of Corinth and there is a painting of the battle on the first floor.

Other treasures in the Museum include a collection of priceless navigational charts and maps of the Mediterranean – some in reproduction and some original with the oldest of all dated 1375; a fine collection of memorabilia from the first passenger steam ships; lists of men and equipment from the 16C ships going to Cuba and the Philippines; fishing boats and artefacts brought back from the early colonies and a vast assortment of charts and paintings. Here and there through a window you catch a glimpse of the extent of the huge complex, with much of it still unrestored. There is no mention anywhere of the defeat of Philip II's Armada in the English Channel (not surprisingly perhaps).

A worthwhile bonus, and included in the price of your ticket, is a chance to board the replica of Colombus' flagship, the *Santa Maria*, which is permanently berthed on the far side of the road. The replica was constructed in Valencia for a film about the explorer's life in 1951. It is authentically fitted out and said to be exactly the same size as the original which is surprisingly small. Go below deck and see how cramped and dark conditions must have been; you can even go in to the hold where you feel the movement of the hull in the water and hear the grating of the woodwork; it is all very evocative.

The original Santa Maria was wrecked off the reef of Hispaniola Island (Haiti) on December 25, 1492.

A half-hour trip around the busy port in one of the many waiting sightseeing boats is recommended, and the small boats, known as *golondrinas* – (swallows) are preferable to the bigger tourist vessels. A ride in a cable car is also possible from the quay close to the Santa Maria all the way to Montjuich.

Just outside the Dressanes along the *Avinguda de Paral-lel* is a fine example of medieval city wall. For a change of mood, walk a little way up the Avinguda and turn right into *Carrer de Sant Pau* to discover a hidden treasure of a Romanesque church – *Sant Pau del Camp*. It was built in the early 10C outside the city wall which is the reason for its name which means Saint Paul *in the fields*. Destroyed by El Mansour in 985, it was restored three centuries later when the present façade with fine portal were added. The church has been closed now for many years but it is said to contain a tiny cloister with paired columns and lobular arches, as well as one or two features which predate the Moorish attack. Its three apses, clearly visible from outside with their Lombard arches, are typical of the Romanesque period, hallmark of hundreds of similar churches throughout the Catalan countryside.

Behind the Waterfront: Santa Maria del Mar and Carrer de Montcada

At the far end of the *Passeig de Colom,* which extends the length of the Waterfront is the *Stock Exchange* (*La Llotja*) where a neo-classical façade hides a fine hall of pure Catalan Gothic style. Built as a market and customs office in the 14C, when Catalonia's Mediterranean trade was at its height, the hall consists of a series of large rounded arches and has a fine wooden ceiling.

Behind the Llotja (five minutes' walk) is one of Barcelona's treasures, the very elegant and unspoilt Church of *St. Mary of the Sea* – *Santa Maria del Mar,* built in the early 14C on the site of an earlier church (919) which in turn stood on the site of a Roman necropolis. It has always been called "of the Sea" because it stood on the road between the medieval city (the Gothic Quarter) and the port, and would have had a congregation consisting largely of merchants and seafarers with a sprinkling of nobles from *Carrer de Montcada,* and of craftsmen (after whom many of the local streets are named). When the town was first extended beyond the city walls during the reign of James I, the original church of the *Barrio de Santa Maria del Mar* was deemed too small; the foundation stone of the present building was laid in 1329 by King Alfonso I who had captured Sardinia the same year and saw this act as a thanksgiving for his victory. It was completed in 1383.

In medieval times the area in front of the church was a place of public entertainment, processions and executions. Now it seems that there is considerable poverty and neglect in the quarter as prosperity and public attention have moved elsewhere. But the church itself is well kept and has recently undergone major restorations. It is remarkable for being one of the purest examples of Catalan Gothic still surviving. Completed as it was in a mere sixty-one years, it suffered no deviations from the original architect's plan and any restorations since then have been carried out in the strictest conformity and control. The massive exterior is given added lightness by two octagonal towers, each having three storeys and eight windows per storey. The pure Gothic W door has a magnificent statue in the tympanum of the risen Christ holding up nail-scarred hands. An ornate Gothic rose window above is flanked by two sombre buttresses. The window was shattered by an earthquake in 1428 but much of the original glass was later reincorporated.

Inside one is stuck by the immensity of space, and the uncluttered simplicity of the soaring arches with no intruding horizontals to spoil the Gothic line. The high altar, framed with a semi-circle of eight graceful octagonal columns reaching to the roof and echoing the line of the apse behind, is gloriously visible from the whole of the church. The lines of columns follow down the single nave, creating two side aisles, but they are so far apart that the effect of lightness and space is not lost. Moreover the church is illuminated simply by natural light filtering through its own stained glass windows and no artificial lighting is necessary. Many of the windows are exceptional, especially the 15C 'Last Supper' in the left aisle.

There is much original carving to be seen, both on walls and tombstones: the tablets either side of the altar steps are particularly striking and represent 14C labourers cutting and carrying stone for the new church, all the way from Montjuich where it was quarried. There are similar scenes, though rather more weathered, on the capitals at the W door. On the modern high altar (the original was destroyed during 1936) stands a 14C figure of the *Virgin and Child,* preserving still some of the original colour in the folds of the gown. Beneath stands a somewhat incongruous wooden model of a medieval ship, presented by the School of Arts of Barcelona. Many of the capitals and bosses within the church are currently being restored to their full colour glory. The work is being faithfully carried out according to pure Gothic principles, but the untrained eye finds the contrast with the all-pervading grey stone somewhat stark.

Just beyond the church is *Carrer de Montcada,* built in the 12C by the noble family of that name. It is an unusually (for those days) straight street and is lined with aristocratic mansions, many of which have their courtyards open to view. The nobility who witnessed the construction of Santa Maria del Mar in the 14C would have lived here and one has a feeling that some of their descendents still do, though many of the palaces – in both Gothic and Renaissance style – have now been converted to museums and galleries. A slow and thoughtful wander down this fascinating street (and perhaps into some of the similarly evocative lanes which join it, such as *la Barra de Foro*), spotting family coats- of-arms carved above elegant portals, and visiting some of the many galleries and craft shops, is time well spent. It is a special pleasure to see the hot colours of modern artists displayed against the cool background of a Gothic wall or a Renaissance arch.

There is a *Museum of Textiles* with some wonderful lace in the 13C *Palau dels Marquesos de Llio* at no.12. But the main attraction is the excellent *Picasso Museum*, occupying two adjacent palaces (nos.15 and 17) and presenting much of the artist's earliest work. Picasso was born in Malaga in 1881. He came to Barcelona at the age of 14 to study art and many of the paintings and drawings on display here reveal the early experimental stages of creative genius. Particularly intriguing are the many variations on the theme of Velázquez' painting, *Las Meninas*, which is permanently on display at the Prado in Madrid.

The Extension and Modernism, Ciutadella Park; Pedralbes

L'Eixample (Catalan) or *l'Ensanche* (Spanish) means Extension and refers to the development of Barcelona beyond its medieval walls which took place in the second half of the 19C. This was no haphazard urban sprawl but a carefully planned and architect-designed new city, reflecting the prosperity and high expectations of Barcelona's growing bourgeoisie at that time. Conceived by *Ildefons Cerda*, it consists of a grid of horizontal and vertical streets, theoretically equidistant and crossing each other at right angles. It is several times larger than the medieval city which it envelops on three sides; it incorporated several outlying districts into the one mega city and it now neatly fills the space between coast and mountains behind.

The Extension is strategically dissected by several wide avenues intended to speed you from one side of town to the other: the *Diagonal*, the *Paral-lel* and the *Meridiana* cut diagonally across the grid of little squares; the noblest and widest of all is the *Gran Via de les Corts Catalanes* which passes through (or near) the three main road junctions – *Plaça d'Espanya, Plaça de Catalunya* and *Plaça de les Glories Catalanes*, and behaves like an extension of the motorway from the airport and the south. The main vertical axis is the *Passeig de Gracia* which once led from the walled city to the then suburb of *Gracia*.

The Extension offered the perfect stage for the architectural development of Modernism (or *Art Nouveau*) – the exuberant expression of prosperity and confidence experienced throughout Europe before World War I. For Catalans, Modernism was also a celebration of the rebirth of their own culture and pride and Barcelona is renowned for having the largest and most exciting collection of Modernist buildings anywhere in Europe. These range from palaces and prestigious exhibition halls to small private houses and shops. So fashionable did the style become that even some buildings in the old city (the Ramblas for example) were given Modernist façades.

The city is considered to have given birth to its own brand of Modernism on the occasion of the International Exhibition of 1888 held in the *Ciutadella Park*. This is therefore the proper place for visitors to start their education. It is but a few minutes' walk from *Carrer de Montcada* (along *Carrer Princesa* which crosses Montcada).

The significance of the choice of this Park for Barcelona's first 'At Home' to over half a million people needs explaining. The Park was named after the citadel which the Bourbon King Philip V commanded to be built on that very spot in 1714, having first razed to the ground the pleasant residential suburb of *La Ribera* which had stood there before. This was to enable his soldiers to quell any sign of trouble on the part of the rebellious Catalans, and came in the wake of the War of Succession in which Catalonia had fought on the losing side in support of the Archduke Charles of Austria. After a heroic struggle the Catalans were decisively defeated by the superior Castilian army which was reinforced by French troops. The angry king then imposed a programme of drastic punishment and pacification of which the Ciutadella was the most visible and hated symbol. It was eventually demolished in 1868 and replaced by the present delightful park, intended to erase bitter memories of shame and repression.

The entrance is marked by a *Triumphal Arch* which stands on the broad *Passeig de Lluis Companys* and was built for the occasion by *Josep Vilaseca* in uncovered red brick with some ceramic decoration. It has the same proportions as a classical triumphal arch. More interesting examples of early Modernism await inside the Park, notably the Restaurant of the Exhibition, known as the *Castell dels Tres Dragons*, by *Domenech i Montaner*. Now housing a Zoology Museum, it experiments with new construction techniques and materials such as rolled iron and uncovered brick and yet has a distinctly medieval flavour.

The Park is a favourite place for peaceful recreation for young and old alike. One of the focal points is the monumental fountain. Several artists, including the young Gaudi, participated in the creation of this huge ungainly affair which does, however, have one or two redeeming features such as the griffons on the front. All around are sub-tropical gardens with green parakeets in the trees and a large lake, in the middle of which is a simple marble sculpture of an inconsolable woman (*La Desconsol*) by J. Llimona.

All that remain of the Bourbon citadel are the chapel, the governor's palace and the arsenal. This last has been completely rebuilt inside and now houses the Catalan Parliament and the *Museum of Modern Art*. The former is not open to the public, but the latter is worth a visit for it contains a distinguished array of Modernist art – paintings, sculptures, and furniture, and a very singular collection of tree trunk sculptures displayed against mirrors on a patio. There are also one or two good examples of pre-Modernist art such as the remarkably detailed painting of the *Battle of Tetuan* by Fortuny (born in Reus in 1838) which occupies an entire wall. Worth a visit, too, is Barcelona's Zoo which occupies about a third of the Park. It includes African animals, monkeys, reptiles, birds and an aquarium.

It would take many pages to describe every Modernist building in the Extension. The observant visitor will anyway get used to spotting examples as he goes. They are all different: many are witty, a few outrageous, some strikingly beautiful, and all instantly recognisable as 'different'. We describe here only the most notable representatives, many of which are concentrated in the area around the *Passeig de Gracia* (once a kind of millionaires' row).

A personalised residence designed by one of the leading exponents of Modernism – Antonio Gaudi, Josep Puig i Cadafalch and Lluis Domenech i Montaner – must have been the ultimate in one-upmanship.

Starting at the *Plaça de Catalunya* end of *Passeig de Gracia* you come first to *Casa Lleo Morera* (at no.35) by Domenech i Montaner (1905) in exuberant floral style. Next, at numbers 41 and 43 is a rather uneasy juxtaposition of two totally dissimilar styles: *Casa Amatller* (Puig i Cadafalch, 1900) comprises an angular façade which was added on to an existing house. It has a Flemish-style stepped gable and a floral Gothic main gallery. The nationalist theme of St. George fighting the dragon is also there. Next to it is *Casa Battlo* (Gaudi, 1907). The Battlo family were wealthy textile manufacturers who commissioned Gaudi to rebuild their house. Its sensuous curves and distinctive upturned roof, with tiles imitating a dragon's skin, make it look like a piece of theatrical scenery from some central European romance. Most notable is the casual scattering of tiny ceramic tiles in blue, purple and green across the whole of the front which, on rainy days, gives the building a distinctive translucent sheen. The block containing these two buildings is known as the *Mançana de la Discordia* (Block of Discord). Gaudi also designed furniture for the Battlo family, much of which can be seen in the Gaudi Museum in Park Guell. Notice, incidentally, the unusual iron lamp posts along Passeig de Gracia with mosaic seats. These are known as *fanalsbancs* and were designed by P. Falques in 1900.

At no.92 stands *Casa Mila* (also known as *La Pedrera*) which is the best known and most widely acclaimed of Gaudi's secular buildings, completed in 1907. Looking, at first sight, rather like a child's freehand drawing, this 5-storey block of flats has no straight horizontals whatsoever: all its lines undulate like waves. Moreover the building occupies a corner site so there is nothing to arrest the sense of continuous fluid movement. Notice particularly the heavy wrought iron balconies whose tortured shapes on closer inspection turn out to represent fronds of seaweed, rocks and other seaside objects. On top of the wavy penthouse is a collection of extraordinary abstract forms, surely the most absurd collection of chimneys and ventilators anywhere in the world. It is necessary to stand some way back in order to see them all (or hire a helicopter). The building, way before its time, has a rhythmic beauty all its own. It takes to the very limits the plastic possibilities of stone and injects a healthy element of fun into the heart of what is, undeniably, a serious and business-like city.

Arriving at La Diagonal and turning right into it, you will see (at no.373) the *Palau Quadras* by Puig i Cadafalch with naturalist decoration and interesting indigenous and exotic elements. Today it houses the city's *Museum of Music*. A little way along is the *Casa Terrades*, occupying a triangular block between two streets and instantly recognisable for being so totally different from anything else around. It too is by Puig i Cadafalch; it is surmounted by triangular spikes, and has slender conical spires at the corners. If you walk down the Diagonal as far as *Plaça Mossene Jacint Verdageur*

Barcelona. Casa Battlo by Antoni Gaudi

and look right, you will have a splendid view down towards Ciutadella Park by way of the eye-catching Triumphal Arch which marked the entrance to the 1888 Exhibition.

You are very close now to Gaudi's sacred master work – the controversial and still unfinished **Church of the Holy Family (el Templo Expiatorio de la Sagrada Familia)**. There is so much to see here that it is essential to arrive fresh, rather than at the end of a long day of sight-seeing. There is, conveniently, a metro station (Sagrada Familia) right alongside.

With so much expansion and increase in population, it is not surprising that Barcelona felt the need of a new Church. A local religious group, the Spiritual Association of St. Joseph, acquired the site and then applied to the Pope for support. The Pope agreed to return to them half the money they had collected each year and paid to the Vatican. With some degree of financial security therefore, the Association commissioned the Diocesan architect, *Francisco de Villar*, to carry out the work. The foundation stone of the Church of Atonement of the Holy Family (*Templo Expiatorio de la Sagrada Familia*) was laid on St. Joseph's Day, October 1882. Villar's designs were strictly Neo-Gothic. For some reason he withdrew from the commission and was replaced the following year by the young Catalan architect, Antoni Gaudi, who was to dedicate the rest of his life to it. Gaudi duly completed the crypt and the outer walls of the presbytery according to Villar's plans; then, in 1893, he produced new designs based on his own unique and inspired interpretation of traditional Gothic styles.

Gaudi conceived the idea of a symbolic church with three façades: one dedicated to the Nativity, one to the Passion and Death, and one to the Ascension of Christ. Each façade would have four towers and the sum of the twelve would represent the twelve apostles, the top of each spire being crowned with polychromed pinnacles representing a bishop's crozier, mitre, cross and ring (the apostles being seen as the first bishops of the Church). A central tower, taller than all the rest (560 ft) would rise from the central cimborium and be finished with a cross and a lamb symbolising Christ. This would be surrounded by four lower towers carrying the symbols of the Evangelists: the eagle, the ox, the lion and the angel.

Tragically Gaudi was run over and killed by a tram in 1926 (his body lies in the crypt). He had completed only one of his monumental façades – that of the Nativity – together with the crypt and the presbytery. Work stopped after his death and did not resume again until 1944. Construction of the second façade – that of the Passion – for which he left no detailed drawings – has only just been completed.

The awesome task of finishing the whole church proceeds in fits and starts, for it depends solely on donations and the entrance fees paid by thousands of tourists who come to see it every year. As Gaudi did not leave complete plans, there have at times been doubts as to the wisdom of continuing the project at all. Can there be any justification today for a church on this scale, greater in size and height than any other European church and with a capacity for over 5,000 people? The answer, at least to most Catalans, is most fervently affirmative. They see this amazing building as an extension of their own faith and an expression of deeply felt pride in their heritage. The world, on the whole, regards it now as a magnificent example of Catalan modernism, the unfinished masterpiece of an inspired genius, perhaps even the finest ecclesiastical building of modern times.

The Exterior: The visitor is struck first of all by the sheer size and scale of the building. It is a good idea to take a few minutes to sit in the park opposite the E façade of the Nativity, from which point there is a good view of the whole, which gives credence to the popular belief that Gaudi allowed himself to be inspired by the vertical columns of the Montserrat mountains, where he had previously worked for a while, restoring the Monastery. A concentrated look at the individual towers suggests that, at the same time, the architect was also echoing the filigree forms of the traditional cathedral in the Gothic Quarter, albeit with some artistic licence.

Approach now for a closer inspection of the great Nativity porch which is the architect's most personal and characteristic creation. The stone framework of the three portals looks almost as if it is melting away in the sun. And all the richly sculpted figures beneath seem to be engaged in *doing* something: the sense of momentarily arrested movement is quite startling. Alongside various renditions of the birth of Jesus are a whole lot of perfectly ordinary people doing everyday things – shoemakers, peasants taking animals to market etc – which immediately brings the familiar story on to a level where we can all participate.

Specifically, and going from left to right, the three portals are dedicated to *Hope, Charity* and *Faith*. In the first, notice the scene of the child Jesus in Joseph's carpenter's shop, with various tools around; on the left is the Flight to Egypt and, on the right, the Massacre of the Innocents. A stone from the Montserrat mountain appears in the upper section. The central and biggest portal of Charity has at its centre the nativity scene and all around it are symbols of the cosmic world as well as those of the living world of mankind; alongside are angels, announcing the joyful news on long thin metal trumpets. On the pinnacle of this porch is the green form of a cypress tree, said to be 'eternal and incorruptible' and a refuge for birds in a storm. The third portal – Faith – shows amongst other things St. John preaching the arrival of the Messiah and, on the left, St. Elizabeth visiting the Virgin Mary.

Walk around the church to see the other façade, that of the Passion and Death, which also has three portals. But there the resemblance ends. This porch is grim and hard-outlined by comparison, with angles and straight lines rather than curves. The mood is one of desolation, the outer framework suggestive of prison bars. The portal of Faith (on the left this time) shows Christ's entry into Jerusalem as king and prophet, and various scenes of Him being questioned and insulted. The portal of Hope on the right shows acts of flagellation and of crowning with thorns and Christ's progress towards

Calvary carrying the cross. In the centre, the portal of Charity displays the crucified Christ with Mary and Peter at His feet, and with the crucified thieves on either side. Above is a scene of Christ washing the disciples' feet and, above that, the last Supper. In the tympanum Christ is depicted kneeling and full of anguish in the Garden of Olives.

Suspended from a steel girder above all this is a powerful figure of the crucified Christ with three weeping figures alongside. Beneath it, on a kind of platform, is a strange group of figures including two Roman guards wearing horrendous death masks and looking as if they have just walked off the set of *Dr Who*. This is the work of its contemporary sculptor *Josep Subirachs* – and the central figure of the Virgin is certainly typical of his clean and powerful style. Only recently revealed, this section of the façade is causing deep affront and passionate debate within the city, on the grounds that the sculptures are right out of keeping with Gaudi's own naturalistic style. It is condemned as 'bad taste' and 'degenerate modernism', even 'a betrayal of Gaudi'. No doubt the fury will die down. Lifelong supporters of the church have been here before. Almost every new relevation has caused controversy, they say, and the impetus to complete the work is, if anything, strengthened rather than discouraged.

The presbytery, or apse, which faces N, with its seven chapels, is more traditionally neo-gothic in design but close examination will reveal some typically Gaudi-esque forms on the pinnacles and one or two most unusual gargoyles.

The Interior: It is imperative to go inside to receive the full impact of the work. Where else in the world can one stand in the middle of a vast church which is still being built? One is astonished first of all by the enormity of the job which still has to be done: the nave, the S transept with its façade dedicated to the Ascension (and its four towers), the roof with the central cimborium which will carry the central tower – all these have yet to be built. Piles of stone lie around waiting to be hoisted aloft by huge cranes, or fashioned into some sublime shape by craftsmen.

Besides generally appreciating this unique textbook of church architecture laid out before you, there are three specific things you can do, all of them worthwhile: firstly you should study the very complete model of the finished work; it shows there will be five naves and that the weight of the roof is to be carried by parabolic arches of great height formed by columns which branch like trees, thus eliminating the need for buttresses; all around the walls of the nave and presbytery, about halfway up, is a gallery or triforium, designed to hold massed choirs of 1,500 people. Secondly, you can visit the *museum* which is housed in a chapel below ground level. This contains, amongst other things, photographs showing the various stages of construction since 1882, and a blown-up one of the Nativity façade with all the detail explained and statues named. Thirdly (but only for those with a head for heights) you can take a lift up inside the wall of the Nativity façade and walk along some of the upper galleries to have a closer view of the fine sculpted detail.

The building is open from 9 to 19 hours every day and the visit costs 250 pesetas.

There are three more expressions of Modernism which should not be missed. The first, *Hospital de la Santa Creu i de Sant Pau,* is quite close to the Sagrada Familia church, connected by the *Avinguda de Gaudi.* The work of Domenech i Montaner and covering an area of some 100,000 square metres, the Hospital consists of half a dozen tiled pavilions set in lush gardens and connected by underground corridors. The entrance building is distinguished by an ornately vaulted ceiling and has an elegant tower. An unclad brick structure is charmingly decorated with statues and ceramic mosaics and the whole is calculated, surely, to lift the spirits of the sickest of patients, or at least those who come to visit them.

Secondly, and by the same architect, there is the unforgettable concert hall known as *Palau de la Musica Catalana,* on the corner of *Carrer de Sant Pere mes Alt* and *Carrer Amadeu Vives.* It is five minutes' walk from *Plaça de Catalunya* (on the edge of the Gothic Quarter), or two minutes' walk from the metro station of *Urquinaona.* There is no other concert hall quite like this one with its audacious inverted cupola of multi-coloured glass and its wildly romantic decor rich with mosaics and sculptures of muses all around the stage. Whether or not this extraordinary flight of fancy is to your taste, it is a worthy example of the sheer exuberance of its period and still plays an important part in the city's musical life.

The third Modernist extravaganza – once seen never forgotten – is the absurdly Disney-esque *Parc Guell,* inspired by Gaudi. It is located N of the city and it is necessary to drive, or take a taxi, or take the metro as far as *Lesseps* and walk ten minutes or so from there. It was originally conceived as a garden city for sixty houses and was commissioned by Gaudi's wealthy patron, the banker Eusebio Guell, in 1910. Gaudi only succeeded in laying out the main city centre – specifically, the market place and the entrances, streets and pedestrian ways leading to it – before the project ran out of money. In 1922 the Municipality converted what had been done so far into a public park, which is what it is today.

The park is surrounded by a high wall and the main entrance is marked by two pavilions, each with a roof made of multicoloured broken tiles. The one on the right was to have been the porter's lodge, whilst that on the left would have been an administrative building and telephone exchange. The park's dominant feature is the market place, approached by a broad stairway with central dragon sculpture. It is in the form of colonnades between no-nonsense Doric columns supporting a flat roof. Go up on to the roof which supports a square surrounded by a delicious undulating bench made of every kind of ceramic shape and colour, including bits of tile (?left over from some grander building), bottles, saucers and even cups. Everyone loves this place, from the very old who tuck into a hollow which turns out to be just the right shape for a siesta, to the very young for whom it represents the ultimate wonderland. This, and other ceramic creations in the park, is the work of *J. M. Jujol* who was a pupil of Gaudi.

Gaudi's garden city was to have had separate routes for traffic and for pedestrians, the latter being steep and often stepped so that cars could not have used them. Sometimes the two were superimposed, with ramp above for traffic and covered arcade beneath offering shade and shelter to those on foot. A wander through the trees along these various ways can be a delightful experience. The path known as *La Lavandera* (left of the market place) is particularly enchanting. It is so-called because there is the figure of a washerwoman alongside one of the columns. It has leaning shapes, glorious rounded arches and panoramic views over Barcelona. The whole crazily inclined structure is faced with stone so as to look natural but in fact much of it is reinforced concrete (Gaudi was the first to use this in Spain).

The one real house in the park is now the Gaudi museum and was the home of the architect for 20 years until his death in 1924. It contains some very interesting pieces of furniture which he designed for some of his masterpieces in the city such as *Casa Battlo.*

On the very edge of the Extension, at the W end of the *Diagonal,* is the prosperous residential area of *Pedralbes.* As well as being home to Barcelona's magnificent football stadium – *Camp Nou* – it contains an Italian-Renaissance-style *Palace* set in gardens which face on to the Diagonal (metro: *Palau Reial*). The palace was built by the Municipality for King Alfonso XIII in the early 1920s and he lived there until 1931 when the electorate voted for a republic and he was forced into exile. This grandiose building in several shades of yellow is still stuffed full of ornate furniture, chandeliers and tapestries, mainly from Italy, and it can be visited each day during the hours 11-12 and 17-18. It is quite often used for art exhibitions when the visiting hours are extended.

The gardens are an attractive mix of conifers, palm trees and bamboos. There is even a fountain by Gaudi (*Font Gaudi*) approached through a bamboo plantation. It is in the form of a dragon with its tail neatly wrapped around the water pipe.

Of considerably more historic interest is the **Monastery/Museum of Pedralbes** which is higher up the hill and is approached by way of the *Avenida de Pedralbes* which is lined on either side by expensive apartment blocks. There is a car park in the *Plaça del Monestir* (metro: *Reina Elisenda*).

The Monastery was founded in 1325 by King James II's queen, Elisenda de Montcada, and is still inhabited by a small community of nuns. The Church is typical, austere, 14C Catalan Gothic with buttresses and chapels between them, and a polygonal apse. It has a large 3-storey cloister (top one added later) with poplars and orange trees, and the tomb of Queen Elisenda is located between church and cloister.

The Museum is housed in the many dependencies: chapels, cells, dormitories and so on, and contains a significant collection of religious art and ceramics from 14C to 17C. Not to be missed are the remarkable frescoes (dated c.1346) by the Catalan painter, *Ferrer Bassa*, in the *Cell of St. Michael*. He travelled to Italy to learn new techniques and his work reflects many Italian Gothic characteristics including very expressive faces and an abundance of space in the pictures. These are the only documented paintings by this short-lived artist who died of the Black Death in Barcelona in 1348.

There are many distinguished old buildings in the vicinity of the Monastery including a particularly charming house immediately opposite the Museum exit with Romanesque doorways and carved capitals. It all used to be the separate village of *Sarria* and was only integrated into Barcelona in 1921.

Montjuich

Montjuich, with its gardens, historic monuments, fun fairs and culture ancient and modern, is a total experience. Whatever your mood, or age, or background, there is bound to be something to suit your taste. And now, with preparations in full swing for the 1992 Olympic Games, Montjuich is about to become the centre of the world. There can be few great cities with so suitable and accessible a venue for an international event. Jutting out into the sea and forming the S arm of the Port of Barcelona, the hill is a mere 2 minutes drive (ten minutes' walk) from *Plaça d'Espanya*. It is also easily accessible from the *Gothic Quarter*.

Significant Iberian finds on the hill tell us that Montjuich was inhabited long before the Carthaginians and Romans arrived. The Romans called it '*Mons Jovis*' (mountain of Jupiter) but it is generally accepted today that the name means '*Hill of the Jews*' since a Jewish cemetery was discovered there. The Counts of Barcelona built an important castle there in 11C to discourage the Moors from returning. But the castle which today houses a military museum and also serves as a mirador for tourists dates from 1640. 54 years later it became a fortress from which the defeated Barcelonese were controlled by Castilian forces after the War of Succession.

Montjuich really came into its own in modern times when it was chosen as the site for the 1929 Barcelona World Fair by the first Spanish dictator, Miguel Primo de Rivera. The entire hillside facing the city was laid out with gardens and sprinkled abundantly with palaces and pavilions, many of them in Italian Renaissance style and now housing museums.

The most straightforward approach is from Plaça d'Espanya along the opulent *Reina Maria Christina Avenue*, the entrance of which is marked by two imposing towers left over from 1929. On either side of this Avenue there are permanent exhibition halls. (Sometimes the avenue is closed off and it is necessary to turn left and enter Montjuich from the side). Because the park is extensive and the attractions fairly widespread, some form of transport is desirable here. On ordinary days, at least, one can park with ease outside any of the monuments; taxis are also usually available and frequent buses make the circuit. A novel way of arriving is by cable car – from *Barceloneta* or the quay near the *Santa Maria* – which, after a dizzy spin over the port, deposits you outside a restaurant by the Castle. There is also a funicular between this restaurant and the road far below. Both cable car and funicular function somewhat sporadically, and not at all in the winter.

If you enter from the Reina Maria Christina area you will pass through the main gardens, resplendent with fountains and manicured flower beds, and come first to the *National Palace (Palau Nacional)* which looms over all and houses the **Museum of Catalan Art**. The dome of this somewhat pretentious neo-classical building is sometimes compared with that of the Capitol in Washington. Its medieval art collection is outstanding and should not be missed.

The Romanesque section has good 11C and 12C wood carvings and altar frontals but the most memorable exhibits are the gloriously rich and imaginative frescoes, skillfully transferred from their original church walls by an ancient Italian process known as *Strappo* (described on page 19) and displayed here alongside pictures of their mother churches, many of them in the Pyrenees.

The Gothic section is no less interesting. Its paintings reflect the Catalan expansionism and religious intolerance of the period with scenes of battles and the burning of martyrs. The mood is grim and cruel and the earthy humour and exuberance of the Romanesque artists has quite gone. Nevertheless there is pure beauty in some of the alabaster statues, retablos and altar frontals.

Off to the right (everything is clearly signposted) is the *Spanish Village* (*Pobla Espanyol*) which scores full marks for originality. It consists of houses from Spain's many and varied regions with architecture faithfully reproduced, erected in their regional groups over a 5-acre site. Many of the houses contain craft workshops showing local skills such as pottery and glass-blowing, and exhibiting goods for sale. The village is an undoubted success for all the family, and there is a certain inevitability about the junk shops and cafés which are beginning to creep in.

On the other side of the Palau Nacional are many more points of interest. Firstly there is Barcelona's main *Archaeological Museum* with Greek and Roman finds from Empurias and relics from Roman Barcelona as well as Iberian remains from Montjuich itself. This Museum is currently being renovated but it is hoped to have all the exhibits once more in place by early 1992. Close by there is an *Ethnology Museum.*

Of great interest, and very popular with the Barcelonese, is the *Contemporary Art Centre – Centre d'Estudis d'Art Contemporani* (CEAC) created by the artist, Joan Miró. It houses a permanent exhibition of over two hundred Miró paintings, plus sculptures and tapestries, and there is also a sequence of his drawings which enables one to trace development from the first childlike attempts to more recent work. There are also constantly changing exhibitions of contemporary work from all over the world with particular attention paid to young artists struggling to make a name. A library of some ten thousand volumes, and facilities for concerts, lectures and films complete the Centre. The building is as exciting as the work it contains, created all in white by Miró's friend, the architect *Josep Sert* in 1974. A symphony of harmonious shapes in concrete and glass, it creates an environment of pure light which suffuses all it touches with an unusual vigour and sense of joy. Quite close to the Centre, in a former quarry, is a reproduction 'ancient' *Greek Theatre* which is occasionally used for performances and can hold two thousand people.

There is also of course the great *Olympic Stadium*. Originally built for the 1929 World Fair, the hope was that it would be used in the 1936 Olympics. This was not to be and the Stadium fell gradually into disrepair, so much so that by the time the bid for the 1992 Games was accepted, only the exterior walls were deemed worth retaining. The interior was blown up and then completely rebuilt into today's show piece which seats 80,000 without a single pillar or post to obscure the view. In the vicinity too is a swimming pool, a sports palace which doubles as a concert hall, a show jumping area and a fabulous fun fair complete with roller coaster.

Lastly there remains the moated *Castle* which crowns the highest point of Montjuich. The moat is now a garden and one can drive or walk over the drawbridge to visit the Military Museum inside or simply to walk about and enjoy the fabulous views of the coast, the city, and of *Tibidabo*, the corresponding high point on the opposite side. The castle is surrounded by gardens and a terrace from which the cannons of many ages guard it still.

Environs of Barcelona

The heavily industrialised and congested environs of Barcelona are best avoided or, at the very least, crossed as quickly as possible, preferably by motorway. The exception to this rule, is the range of mountains which forms a natural boundary to the N and over which a scenic road leads, from the Pedralbes area, to the small town of *Sant Cugat del Valles* and its famous monastery.

First however comes *Tibidabo*, the viewpoint *par excellence* and a wonderful spot from which to bid farewell to Barcelona and to appreciate the straight lines of the Extension and the distinguished jumble of the Gothic Quarter squeezed in around the Columbus monument. Apart from its undeniable value as a viewpoint Tibidabo is frankly a disappointment. The neo-Gothic *Church of the Sacred Heart* (*Templo Expiatorio de Sagrado Corozon*) is unusually ugly and gains nothing from either the over-large figure of Christ with arms outstretched (a well-known landmark) or the TV mast right up against it. Perhaps the best thing about Tibidabo, with its cluster of candy-floss stalls and tourist junk, is the amusement park; it must be fun to catch glimpses of the city below from the top of the Big Wheel. (Tibidabo is accessible by road or by funicular from the *Peu de Funicular* metro station in town).

The road now winds its way through pine woods for a further 7km to *Sant Cugat del Valles*, named after the Benedictine *Monastery* at its heart. The town itself looks unpromising but a degree of good faith and attention to signposts will get you there. It was founded in 9C over a Visigothic Mausoleum built to contain the relics of *Sant Cucufas* who was martyred in 303 by order of the Roman Emperor Diocletian. Today's church was started in 11C and the lovely bell tower with Lombard bands is the oldest part. The façade with crenellated wall and outsize rose window was added in 14C. Inside, the nave and two aisles have pointed arches and there is an octagonal cimborium. The three apses are semi-circular inside and polygonal outside.

But it is the Romanesque *Cloister* which draws people here from far and wide. It is one of the biggest in Catalonia and the lower gallery has a double row of columns with exceptionally fine carved capitals (144 altogether) ranging from simple strapwork patterns to the most detailed biblical scenes, the best of which are in the wing alongside the church wall. Much of this was the work of the 12C sculptor, *Arnau Cadell*, who has left for posterity a self-portrait with his name on the capital at the NE corner (unfortunately badly mutilated). Above the arches there is a row of blind arcading with medallions which also merit a detailed look. The Cloister's upper storey was added in the 16C. For some time now work has been going on to excavate the Visigothic mausoleum of the martyr which lies under the E wing.

There is a sense of timelessness and peace about this monastery, and particularly the cloister, which justifies the time spent finding it and can make one oblivious of the modern bustle just over the wall.

For those who wish to make a more extensive tour from Barcelona, the road continues from Sant Cugat to Rubi and on to *Terrassa* (15km), and thence to the famous *Monastery of Montserrat* (see Route 9). Montserrat is also accessible by train from Barcelona (*Estació Plaça Espanya*).

BARCELONA TO TARRAGONA

A. Inland route via Vilafranca del Penedes

Leave Barcelona on the N340 from *Plaça d'Espanya* and pass as quickly as possible through the anonymous suburbs of *Sant Feliu de Llobregat* and *Sant Vicenc dels Horts*. Once through the latter the road becomes attractive and mountainous and continues that way as far as *Vilafranca* (31km from Barcelona). Just before arriving, 7km off the main road on the right, is the former Benedictine *Monastery of Sant Sebastiá dels Gorgs*. It was founded in 1029 and has a good door with well-preserved tympanum showing Christ surrounded by angels. Also worth noticing are the charming bell tower with paired windows, and the remains of a cloister thought to be two centuries

BARCELONA - TARRAGONA

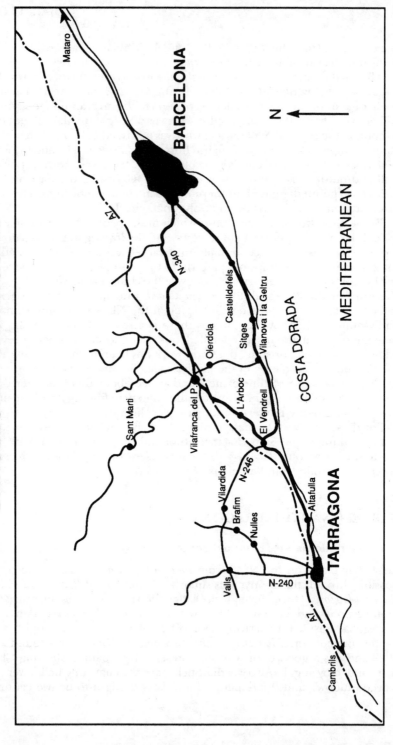

later than the rest of the building and containing elements obviously brought in from elsewhere such as a marble Visigothic capital.

Vilafranca del Penedes is Catalonia's leading wine town and is justly famous for its wine museum which occupies a former royal palace. The foundation of the town in the 12C coincided with – and was probably caused by – the gradual abandonment of the fortified hilltop town of *Olerdola* (see Excursion). The Moors had been driven out of Tarragona and Tortosa and so people felt safe to come down from the hills and live and farm on the fertile plain. Vilafranca – 'free town' – was built to attract settlers. It was soon a thriving market centre with a university and a royal palace in which, it is said, Peter the Great died in 1289. Shortly after this event, the palace was presented to the nearby *Monastery of Santes Creus* and, in 1503, a new palace was built next to the church for visiting royalty (*Palau Balta*). The older palace, which stands opposite the church, was retrieved from the monks in 1835 and a century later was converted to house both city and wine museum.

Vines have probably been grown in the Penedes region since the Iberians first learned the skill from Greek traders. But it was not until the end of the 18C that wine began to be produced here on an industrial scale, and exported to markets in Europe and America. The **Museum** (open 10-14 and 16-19 hours daily) tells the story from its prehistoric beginnings to the present day by way of excellent dioramas which illustrate the various processes from grape-picking to consumption by Greeks, Romans, Egyptians and so on. There is also a splendid collection of wine presses, giant barrels and all the paraphernalia of wine making and wine drinking then and now. The visit ends with a free tasting session.

The City Museum (on the first floor of the same building) contains the city archives and also collections of ceramics, paintings and archaeological finds donated by local people. Exhibits are interesting rather than spectacular or unique, and collections are named after the donors. There is, for example, the *Trens* collection of Catalan paintings, including a possible Picasso, donated by a Vilafrancan priest of that name in 1976; and there are some 480 pieces of 15C and 16C ceramics donated by *Monseigneur Joan Bonnet* in 1978 who paid for the museum to be enlarged so as to accommodate his collection. There is even an exhibition of local birds.

Opposite the Museum building and dominating the square is the huge and unlovely *Parish Church of Santa Maria*. Its neo-Gothic façade was added in 1903 but the main body – single nave with polygonal apse – is 15C. Inside there is a single object of beauty and that is the outstanding group of figures carved in marble by the Modernist sculptor, *Josep Llimona*, which stands in the crypt.

Before leaving the square, notice the *monument to the 'castellers'* said to be one of the tallest modern sculptures in Spain. It represents a very favourite pastime of the local people in this region – the formation of human pyramids. Vilafrancans pride themselves on being able to achieve five 'layers' and the monument is a fitting recognition of their superior skills.

Five minutes walk from the square, in a SW direction, is the ancient *Convent of San Francisco* whose cloister contains some Roman stones and architectural pieces and some good Gothic carved tombs.

Two excursions from Vilafranca del Penedes

1. (10km) The Romanesque church of *Sant Marti Sarroca* overlooks a village of the same name (on the road to *La Llacuna*). It has a particularly fine apse, lavishly decorated inside with semi-circular arches atop slim columns and capitals carved with animals and plants. Outside, the W front is also highly ornate, scattered with a series of stone heads and comic figures such as a man doing a somersault and a cat with crossed legs. There is also a bell tower and the whole building is in a soft, creamy yellow stone: a veritable delight and well restored in 1906.

2. (6km) South of Vilafranca (along the 244 road to *Vilanova i la Geltru*) is *Olerdola*, where a medieval fortress ruin contains elements of much earlier fortifications built on the same spot. The oldest part of the surrounding wall is the lowest section nearest to the car park from where there is an excellent view of huge cyclopean stones erected by the Iberians and built on to by both Carthaginians and Romans.

Inside this section of the wall is a small museum with explanations and pictures of recent excavations. From here a path takes you up past a *Roman water cistern* with feeder canals, remains of granaries and other traces of Roman occupation, to the 12C *Church of Sant Miquel*. The church was built on the foundations of an earlier one possibly dating from the 10C and a Mozarabic horseshoe arch (in the NE chapel) still remains from this early period. The rebuilt church which stands today has a single nave, two square apses, an octagonal lantern and a fine W door. Inside, the plain and simple semi-circular vault, and the total lack of any adornment whatsoever, gives an air of quiet nobility.

Outside the church, cut into the rock right up against the SE wall, are one or two tombs. But these are just a foretaste of the *Necropolis at Pla de Albats* (4 minutes walk from the car-park in an E direction, outside the fortress walls) where there is an astonishing collection of forty-five tombs (probably Iberian). The tombs, empty now and eerily shaped to the bodies they once contained, are carved in many different sizes and include some incredibly small ones, suggesting that these were family groups. They all point E-wards and such is their fame and abundance that the name *Olerdolana* is used countrywide to describe prehistoric tombs of this type.

Much of the very beginning of Catalonia is encapsulated in the Olerdola complex, ranging as it does from mysterious prehistory, through the Roman and Moorish invasions, to the relative security of the medieval period when it was abandoned for the fertile plain below. Olerdola is an evocative and rewarding site and should not be missed.

Back on the main road, the little town of *L'Arboc* (10km W of Vilafranca) retains vestiges of former prosperity including an immense 17C fortified church which was built over the foundations of a Romanesque one. Only the chapel remains of the earlier building which is on a much smaller scale and has a particularly charming window with a pair of noble escutcheons on each side.

You now pass through a rather ugly industrialised stretch for 8km to **El Vendrell**, a town which on first sight appears to have little character. It is somewhat redeemed however by the splendid Baroque façade and 18C bell tower (*El Angel*) of its *Parish Church of Sant Salvador*, and by the *Pablo (Pau) Casals Museum*. The famous cellist was born here (1876-1973) and his father was organist in the church. The Museum contains not just personal memorabilia but the cellist's own distinguished collection of paintings by Catalan artists.

El Vendrell really springs into life for its Fiesta (usually on 24/25/26 July each year) when the local *castellers,* known as '*Los Nens del Vendrell*', rival those of Vilafranca and Valls with the height and splendour of their human pyramids. The town is also proud of its 'giants' who emerge from their usual quarters in the Town Hall and are processed around the town, much to the delight of locals and tourists alike.

At El Vendrell there is a choice of joining the *Coastal Route* or continuing inland by taking the slightly longer but much more peaceful and rural road (246) by way of some fairly unremarkable villages. Pass through *Redonya* and *Vilardida* and then turn left after 2km towards *Brafim* (or continue 8km W-wards to join the main N240 road at Valls). Brafim is a simple and unspoilt village with some charming old streets and good Gothic and Baroque façades. From Brafim continue S-wards through Nulles, picturesque from a distance with its Swiss-style onion-dome church but disappointing on closer acquaintance. Continue through l'Argilaga and l'Oliva, passing under the motorway to arrive at Tarragona's northern ring road.

Anyone wanting to include the Roman *Aquaduct* (see page 97) on the way in to Tarragona can join the N240 from Valls by turning right to *la Secuita* (S of Nulls).

B. Coastal route

Leave Barcelona by the *Gran Via de les Corts Catalanes* which soon becomes the 246 dual carriageway (passing the turn-off to Barcelona International Airport). This stretch of the *Costa Dorada* is aptly named and its spectacular stretches of fine golden sand are legendary. Would that it were possible to see more of it amongst the uncontrolled and frequently tasteless development which has taken place during the last three decades as more and more international sun-seekers descend on Catalonia's coast. Nevertheless the corniche road, often snaking dramatically high above the sea, affords some glorious views of what must once have been a paradise. It is best avoided at week-ends during the high season when it becomes very congested indeed.

Castelldefels has one or two interesting sights in the upper part of town, notably its *castle*, after which it was named and which was first documented in the year 970. The castle was extensively rebuilt at the beginning of this century but retains some of its original stone. Alongside the castle is the Romanesque *Church of Santa Maria* which was completely rebuilt in the 18C. Also remaining from the past are five defensive towers built above the beach during the 16C as a safeguard against pirates. The best preserved towers are *Can Ballester* (circular and housing an archeological collection) and *Torrico* (square and used now as a studio by a local artist). There is no doubt that both castle and towers add dignity and historic perspective to a town which would otherwise be in danger of becoming just one more shining white blob on the Mediterranean coastline.

The road narrows and climbs to over 300m above the very lovely Garraf coves.

Sitges is a town with style and pedigree. Its old quarter is full of elegant houses which have been preserved by wealthy Catalan families. They started coming to this place at the end of the last century, attracted by Modernist painters who had taken up residence there and turned Sitges into a fashionable centre for the arts. It has now been designated a historic site which accounts for its successful preservation from mindless despoliation in the name of tourism.

Sitges is frequently referred to as *"la blanca Subur"* since it is believed to have been built on an Iberian settlement of that name. The medieval walled town of Sitges was first documented in 982. Today the most impressive (though not the most beautiful) building is the 17C *Parish Church of Sant Bartomeu i Santa Tecla* which overlooks the beach. Its distinctive shape with large 19C bell tower on one side and much smaller clock tower on the other is frequently used by local artists as a convenient emblem and no painting of the town seems to be complete without it.

Behind the church is the unusual *Museum Mar i Cel del Mar* built in 1913 over the ruins of the 14C town hospital by an American, Charles Deering, for his own substantial art collection. Undoubtedly stones, columns and even windows from the older building were used and mixed in with neo-classical imitations. The effect is on the whole pleasing and spacious and the museum today houses several collections, including some fine murals by J. M. Sert. Most of the original Deering collection has been removed to other museums.

Next door is the fascinating *Cau Ferrat Museum*. Originally a pair of 16C fishermen's cottages, the buildings were converted in 1892 by the local artist Rusinol and turned into a meeting place for fellow painters and friends, with Gothic doors and windows added, One of his friends was Miguel Utrillo, father of the famous Impressionist painter, Maurice, and both were leading figures in the artists' community. Today it is a museum notable for a very fine display of local wrought iron work dating from 10C to 20C. There is also a worthwhile collection of paintings and drawings by Catalan artists, including Rusinol himself and Miguel Utrillo; and there are two paintings by El Greco.

One further museum deserves mention and that is the one called 'Romantic' in the neo-classical late 18C, house of *Casa Llopis*. It contains furniture of the period and a nice collection of dolls and musical boxes dating from the 17-19C. There are also some admirable dioramas depicting life as it was lived by the bourgeois classes in the 19C.

Vilanova i la Geltru comprises two medieval towns which were joined together and extended in the 19C at a time when successful export of wines from the Penedes region and the installation of several cotton factories were bringing considerable prosperity to the area.

The most distinguished feature of the small extension ('eixample') is the huge arcaded square with palm trees and a definite Latin American flavour. This is not surprising since it was designed by a nobleman returning from Cuba. Close by is the library and *Museum Victor Balaguer* founded by the poet and politician of that name in 1882. There are said to be over 30,000 historic volumes and manuscripts in the archive. More relevant to the visitor is a fascinating art collection, mostly amassed by Balaguer himself and including '*The Annunciation*' by El Greco. There are also some Egyptian and Chinese artefacts.

The most historic building in the old quarter of *La Geltru* is the 12C castle itself. It is said that this was abandoned by many of its inhabitants in 1274 because of high seigneurial taxes and that they then proceeded to build the 'new' town of Vilanova alongside. The castle was restored at the beginning of this century and now houses a good collection of Catalan paintings and ceramics and some archaeological exhibits. The building itself retains several Romanesque walls and some lovely paired windows. Also in old La Geltru is the 18C parish *Church of Santa Maria* which is unremarkable and has only one good Baroque retablo to recommend it. The other parish church – of Vilanova – has a rather overpowering neo-classical W front complete with Corinthian columns and pediment. The neo-Florentine E façade was built in 1976 and has a little more charm, as does the bell tower.

Another museum deserves mention and that is the 'Romantic' one, housed in the *Can Papiol* at the N end of town and built by a rich landowner of that name in the late 18C. More stately home than museum, it is very similar in concept to the '*Romantic*' Museum in Sitges (and one ticket will allow entry to both). It presents a vivid picture of how life was lived by the fortunate at the turn of the last century with drawing rooms and music rooms filled with sumptuous furniture, and bedrooms decorated in varying styles ranging from Roman Empire to Louis XVI. The French general, Suchet, used to stay here during his campaigns on behalf of Napoleon and one of the apartments is named after him.

The fishing quarter at the S end of town (the other side of the railway line) is a delightful spot for a wander, with a sea front (*paseo maritimo*) and a lively fish market.

Continue 18km to *El Vendrell* (described in the Inland Route) and then join the N340 which runs for 28km along the coast to Tarragona and follows the route of the Roman *Via Augusta*. There is much to see along the way which will nicely prepare you for the intrinsic Roman character of Tarragona itself. First, about 8km out of El Vendrell, look out for the 2C **Arch of Bara** which stands somewhat incongruously on an island in the middle of the road, in commemoration of a Roman Consul who died in the year 110. This is one of the best preserved triumphal arches in Spain with four fluted Corinthian pilasters on each side. It rises to a height of over twelve metres and lacks only the Via Augusta which once passed beneath its feet.

Notice the imposing (but dilapidated) Renaissance castle at *Torredembara* as you proceed to *Altafulla*. Here, on a hill facing the sea, are the remains of what must have been a large Roman country house, known as **Els Munts**, one of several villas which are known to have existed in a rough semi-circle around *Tarraco* (Tarragona), providing its citizens with farm produce. It was built during the 1C AD and was probably occupied intermittently up to 5C when it was finally abandoned to the ravages of Visigoths and Moors. Excavations started in 1967 and revealed foundations of a large central L-shaped house with smaller buildings grouped around it. There were three thermal installations, one of which (S of the house) has been fully revealed and consists of a series of bathing pools plus *frigidarium* and *caldarium*, and with much of the hypocaust still in place. Well preserved to the NE of the villa is a large water reservoir with eight compartments. Mosaics, marble columns, and even some statues, demonstrate that Els Munts was once a very prosperous establishment indeed.

The little seaside town of *Tamarit* is worth a short detour; it has a noble castle dating from the Christian Reconquest period which stands in a glorious setting with gardens reaching down to the sea. A little further on, and accessible by a side road which crosses over the motorway (autopista) is the *Quarry of Medol*. Much of the stone used by the Romans for their immense building programme came from here and the monolith in the centre has been left to mark the original ground level and to show the depth to which the Romans excavated.

Finally, about 6km short of Tarragona, is the **Tower of the Scipios**. This is a simple funerary monument of three layers of dressed stone. It has two carved figures in the central section wearing military capes and thought at one time to have been the Scipio brothers, whose tombs were assumed to lie within. The name of the monument has remained, but it is now considered by experts that the figures are those of *Atis*, a pagan god associated with funerary rites. (It is unfortunate that the inscription above the figures has been so desecrated as to be illegible); the very faint traces of figures within the arch on the top layer are assumed to have represented the people who were really buried within, about whom nothing is known at all. The monument dates from the first half of 1C AD and probably once had a pyramidal top. It is not known when it was reduced to a ruin but it does appear in a drawing by Swinburne (18C) in its present form.

ROUTE 2

TARRAGONA

History   Huge cyclopean chunks of stone at the base of the city walls betray the prehistoric origins of Tarragona. The first invaders were the Greeks, who were expanding along both N and S coasts of the Mediterranean during the first millenium BC, establishing simple enclaves and trading posts as they went. It is likely that they discovered an already established Iberian settlement at this very strategic point along the coast.

Around 300 BC the Carthaginians arrived, integrated with the Iberians, founded Barcelona and Cartagena, or New Carthage (in the Province of Murcia to the S) and built a fortress on top of the Ibero-Greek site. They called it *Tarakon*. The Carthaginians' main purpose was a military one; they needed fresh conscripts for their armies who were fighting the Romans in the Punic war and they wanted to build up military bases from which to launch their attacks. (It was from Cartagena that Hannibal set off for Rome). The Romans meanwhile were aware of the growing military strength of their arch-enemies and, in 218BC, sent legions to the Catalan coast, under the command of *Publius Cornelius Scipio*, to chase them out of what had become a potentially devastating line of bases.

Tarraco (as the Romans named *Tarakon*) was the first stronghold to be liberated and the victorious Scipio turned it into a garrison town for his legions. His first act was to build a wall, following the traces of the original Ibero-Greek wall. That done, he led his legions inland and began the long task of subduing the Iberians and chasing out the last of the Carthaginians. Pliny was later to refer to the town as *Tarraco Scipionum Opus* in his *Naturalis Historia*, thus firmly fixing for posterity Scipio's claim to have founded it.

Tarraco prospered as port, as fortress and as city: in 45BC Caesar pronounced it a Roman colony and renamed it '*Colonia Julia Urbs Triumphalis Tarraconensis*' and in 27BC the Emperor Augustus made it capital of the province of *Hispania Citerior* or *Tarraconensis* which extended over the whole of the northern half of the peninsula. Augustus even lived there himself for a time (as did the Emperor Hadrian) and no expense was spared to make the town worthy of such distinction.

The most prestigious quarter contained the provincial forum, temples and important public buildings and was sited on the highest part (roughly where the cathedral is now). Below this was a circus, a theatre and residential

Tarragona. Roman Arch of Bara. 2C.

area with the most sumptuous mansions located nearest the centre. An amphitheatre was built beside the sea, a necropolis was placed outside the town on the banks of the river Francoli, the existing port installation was greatly modernised, and an aqueduct was constructed to bring water from the hills to the burgeoning population which, during Augustus' time is thought to have numbered 30,000. Arranged in a rough semi-circle around the town were agricultural settlements growing food and often containing villas which served as country residences for the rich citizens of Tarraco.

By the end of the 3C AD Roman interest in the Hispanic peninsula was diminishing partly because of a growing involvement in Gaul and Britain, and partly because the administration was beginning to lose patience with the rebellious indigenous tribes inland who still caused trouble over hugely dispersed areas, requiring a disproportionate amount of time and expense to control them. In short, the Romans were over-extended and Hispania was becoming a low priority.

Tarraco began to fall in to decay and was no match for the Visigothic invaders who poured in from the N in the early 5C and destroyed all but the highest section of the city. Little is known about the dark centuries which followed except that the Moors sacked it again in the early 8C, along with so much of Spain, and it remained in a state of mere survival until it was reconquered in the 9C; what is now Catalonia became part of an independent Christian state (known as the *Spanish March*) and Tarraco, now Tarragona, lost pride of place to Barcelona which was made capital of the new kingdom of Catalonia in 988. In 1118 Tarragona was granted by Ramon Berenguer III to the Norman adventurer Robert Burdet and it was he who began construction of the great cathedral, a symbolic act which must greatly have restored the pride and self-respect of this beleaguered city.

Throughout the centuries of Spain's history up to the present day Tarragona has suffered probably no more, and certainly no less, than most major centres: it was ruthlessly sacked by the British in 1705 for backing the Archduke Charles of Austria in the War of Succession, and again by the French in 1811 during the War of Independence because it resisted the army of General Suchet. Despite all this, Tarragona has managed to retain much of its treasured past in a walled section known as *Ciutat Antic*, corresponding to the Roman city later overlaid by the cathedral and principal medieval buildings. All of this relatively small area, plus the 19C extension where the newly rich bourgeoisie chose to live (and incidentally turned up more Roman remains) is worth visiting.

Sight-seeing On arrival you are advised to pass quickly through the industrial belt and follow signs to *Centro Ciutat* which will eventually lead to the great central junction of *Plaça Imperial Tarraco*. From here take either the *Rambla Nova*, or the quieter *Carrer Estanislau Figueras*, looking out for any left-hand turn signposted '*Ciutat Antic*'.

The old city still retains a very distinctive Roman flavour and the logical place to begin your tour is the *Archaeological Walk* (Passeig Arqueologic) which extends for about a kilometre between the original wall with its cylopean base and the much later perimeter wall built by English soldiers after they had captured the town in 1705. The entrance is situated at the end of the *Via de l'Imperi Roma*, (which turns left off Carrer Estanislau Figueras).

There are three theories as to the origins of the older wall, which once extended for over 3km around three sides of the old city. Some historians believe the massive boulders were placed in position very early by the indigenous Iberians, a theory borne out by the quantity of strange markings cut into the stone, said to resemble others found in known Iberian settlements throughout the land; others think the Carthaginians put them there, as part of a rampart to keep the Romans out; a third theory holds that the Romans themselves were responsible during the early period of their occupation, when they could well have used Iberian labour. Whichever is true, the great undressed stones are an extraordinary sight, held together simply by their own weight, and strongly reminiscent of the work of other indigenous peoples such as the Incas of Peru. At intervals along the wall are primitive 'gates', one of which is very close to the entrance to the walk. On top lie the smaller Roman ashlars, looking very regular and modern by contrast, placed by Scipio's legions and reassembled several times during the medieval years.

Along the length of the wall are three towers, the most important of which is the *Tower of the Archbishop* (*Torre del Arzobispo*), which manifests several periods of construction including a cyclopean gate as its base, and was completed in the 14C. The number of empty plinths along the way betokens the one-time rich array of statues, most of which have been removed to museums, and only the bronze figures of Romulus and Remus have been allowed to remain as a reminder of how Rome began. The huge figure of Augustus is a reproduction and was donated by the Italians in 1934. Cannons add a potent reminder of the war during which the outer wall was built and below this a pleasant garden has been laid out – *El Campo de Marte* – which provides a soft foil to the whole impregnable structure above it. It is worth noting that the *Passeig Arqueologic* has opening hours like a museum (viz 10-13.30 and 17-19 hours) and that it is necessary to retrace one's steps because the northern entrance – at time of writing – is closed off.

After completing the walk, pass through the Roman *Rosario Gate* and you stand in what was the highest and most important part of the Roman city. To the left, where once stood a temple to Jupiter, is the great medieval cathedral (described on page 93). Ahead lies *Forum Square* (*Plaça del Foro*). This is reached by way of the delightful cobbled *Carrer Merceria* (silk merchants' street) with its picturesque gothic arches. The Provincial Forum once stood where the Square is today, and is thought to have measured 300 x 200 metres. One or two remnants can be seen, including a section of the NE corner.

TARRAGONA

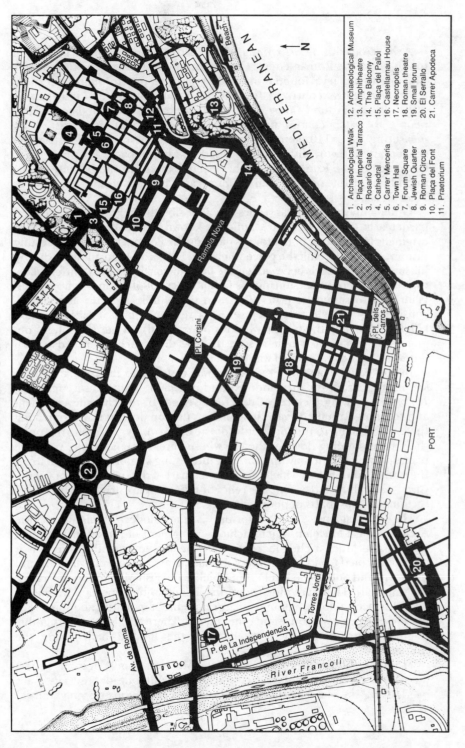

1. Archaeological Walk
2. Plaça Imperial Tarraco
3. Rosario Gate
4. Cathedral
5. Carrer Merceria
6. Town Hall
7. Forum Square
8. Jewish Quarter
9. Roman Circus
10. Plaça del Font
11. Praetorium
12. Archaeological Museum
13. Amphitheatre
14. The Balcony
15. Plaça del Pallol
16. Castellarnau House
17. Necropolis
18. Roman theatre
19. Small forum
20. El Serrallo
21. Carrer Apodeca

MEDITERRANEAN

Beach

Rambla Nova

Pl. Corsini

Pl. dels Carros

PORT

Av. de Roma

C. Torres Jordi

P. de La Independencia

River Francoli

A short walk down *Carrer Mayor*, which leads off *Carrer Merceria*, brings you to the site of the Roman circus. On the way notice the town hall (*Casa de la Ciutat*) with medieval foundations and a very lovely interior staircase leading up from a central courtyard (usually open, with a municipal information office on the ground floor). The circus probably accommodated 23,000 people to watch chariot races and other excitements in a vast arena measuring 347 x 110 metres. Some remnants of the original construction remain and are currently being cleaned up and prepared for public view. But much of the Roman flavour has been lost on this site because of the imposition of 19C neo-classical buildings and a tree-lined square known as *Plaça del Font.*

Other important Roman relics are accessible from Forum Square, and particularly the stark, square building known as the **Praetorium**, which originally formed one of the towers flanking the Forum. It has an interesting history: as well as being the place where the Emperor Augustus lived during his stay in Tarraco, it is believed to have been the birthplace of Pontius Pilate, future praetor of Judea, during his father's term of office in Tarraconensis. Hadrian also stayed here in 121AD. In the Middle Ages it was restored, considerably embellished and used as a residence by Catalan-Aragonese kings (at this time the Gothic windows were added). In the 17C it fell from grace and was used as a military store. In 1813 the French attempted to burn it down and the empty shell was later used as a prison.

In the early 1960s the Praetorium was restored to its original Roman simplicity (except for the windows) and in 1986 it opened as a *Museum of History*, containing pictures of different periods of the city's development and finishing with medieval Tarragona on the top floor. It is worth making the long climb up to the top if only for the opportunity of coming out on to the roof and gazing down at the city whose developmental stages you have been studying on the way up. Another interesting section of the museum is the tunnel down below, which once formed part of the support system of the Circus and which today contains relics of that complex structure, including sections of steps, parts of doors etc.

Hard up against the Praetorium is the modern building of the **Archaeological Museum** which includes a fragment of the original Roman wall *in situ*. Much richer in *objets* than the Praetorium, this Museum is especially noted for its collection of mosaics, many taken from villas around the town, and one of the loveliest of which is the Fish Mosaic (on the wall of the stairwell). There are nine rooms in all containing important fragments from Tarraco's public buildings, a large amount of sculpture and some nice bits of pottery, glass, bronze and other metals. There are also some Visigothic fragments including a few taken from the Basilica built inside the Amphitheatre.

From the *Placa del Rey* (upon which the Museum stands), it is but a short way down to the **Amphitheatre** which was built outside the city walls overlooking the sea. The Romans constructed amphitheatres only in their most favoured and prestigious towns and Tarraco/Tarragona is one of the few in Spain (and one of only two in Catalonia) to have received such a mark of honour. It is thought to have been built during the second half of the first century AD and probably seated some 12,000 spectators in three main tiers with the front seats reserved for the nobility and with a podium, or wall, below acting as a barrier between them and the performers. The spectacle itself would have been either a gladiatorial contest or a wild beast hunt and the Latin word for sand – 'harena' – was used for the central elliptical area which was thickly strewn with sand to absorb the blood. Gladiators were usually slaves or criminals, or they could be free men from all classes of society in search of honour and glory.

In the year 259AD a different kind of spectacle took place when *Bishop Fructuoso* of Tarragona and his two deacons were burned to death by the still violently anti-Christian Romans. In commemoration of their martyrdom the Christian Visigoths built a basilica on the site of the fire in the 6C; in the 12C a Romanesque church known as *Santa Maria del Milagro* was superimposed on the same spot and the ruins of this, embodying traces of the earlier Visigothic structure, still stand today, looking somewhat incongruous within the pagan splendour of the amphitheatre remains.

It has to be said that the whole site is at time of writing in a very sorry state of neglect; strewn with litter and daubed with graffiti, it provides an irresistible adventure playground for the local children. Since becoming a national monument in 1924, the amphitheatre has suffered from both wilful destruction and casual vandalism and it is to be hoped that restoration measures (which have now started) will quickly reverse the downward trend for this rare and remarkable reminder of Roman culture. Above the Amphitheatre, running parallel with the beach, is the well-known viewpoint known as *the Balcony* – a once palm-lined road which joins the end of the *Rambla Nova.*

The most important medieval site in Tarragona is of course the **Cathedral** which stands on the highest point of the city and is best approached by way of *Carrer Mayor.* Construction of the cathedral began in 1171, 53 years after the city had been handed over by Roman Berenguer III to Robert Burdet. It was built on the site of a mosque which itself had been erected over the remains of the Roman Temple to Jupiter. It took 150 years to complete and forms a fascinating text-book on the period of transition between late Romanesque and early Gothic architecture, offering examples of both styles, often in close juxtaposition.

Like so many of Spain's great cathedrals, this one is now severely hemmed in by later buildings and it is therefore quite difficult to gain a total impression of the exterior and the complexity of its structure. Carrer Mayor, however, affords a concentrated view of the west front with its ungainly silhouette caused by the broken gable and striking lack of pinnacles on top of the buttresses. But there is within this unsatisfactory setting a fine rose window, and also a superb *Gothic Door* which deserves a careful look. The door is divided in two by a central column carrying a delightful image of Virgin and Child and on either side is a row of apostles and prophets. The tympanum contains some geometric tracery (rather Moorish in style) and has a bottom layer of grotesque figures looking like souls in torment. The door is flanked by buttresses and two rounded Romanesque doors, each corresponding to a side aisle. That on the N side has a very early Christian carving in the tympanum and the other is surmounted by a relief of the Passion.

It is usual for visitors to enter by way of the Cloister on the N side which is all to the good because it offers probably the best view of the apse, and the great fortress-like bulk of the Cathedral surmounted by tower and octagonal plantera. The apse, the oldest part of the building is simple to the point of severity and has a quality of stern impregnability which suggests that the early builders were still afraid that the Moors might return.

The unusually large **Cloister** is made up of a series of pointed arches each containing three simple rounded ones supported by delicate columns. It was probably started about the same time as the main building. Many of the capitals are carved with typical earthy 12C humour and that of the procession of rats, carrying a cat on a stretcher and walking on their hindlegs is justly famous (it is to be found on the S side in the second bay walking eastwards). The animal theme crops up again and again and in many places the vault is supported by a boar or some mythical beast, especially on the S side. Notice also – on the W wall – a Moorish arch with Kufic inscription above, perhaps left over from the mosque which was here before.

The door into the main body of the cathedral is a particularly good example of late Romanesque with God the Father and the symbols of the Evangelists in the tympanum. Before passing through it notice the grotesque faces on the wall to the right – ram, dog, and a monkey wearing glasses – in naughty but delightful contrast with the dignified portal beneath.

Inside, the ground plan is essentially Romanesque with nave, transept and side aisles. The heavy columns are also Romanesque but the rib vault is Gothic. One of the most remarkable features is the main retablo in the central apse, carved in alabaster by *Pere Johan* between 1426 and 1433 and showing scenes in the life of *Santa Tecla*, patron saint of the city, said to have been converted by the teachings of St. Paul. For this she was cruelly tormented but survived both flames and hungry lions with the help of divine intervention. When viewed from the W end of the building, this lovely piece glows quietly out of the darkness, its golden pinnacles pointing delicately upwards towards the gentle curve of the grey stone apse. It fits very perfectly into its framework, neither dominating it, nor overwhelmed by it.

There are altogether twenty interior chapels varying greatly in period, in quality of workmanship and in beauty. On the N aisle, look out for the *Holy Sepulchre* (opposite the *Chapel of San Fructuoso*), containing an immensely powerful Christ figure surrounded at the tomb by five women and two men.

At the end of the N aisle, in the fourth apse, is the very lovely *Chapel of St. Mary of the Tailors* (*Santa Maria de los Sastres*). Quite different from anything else in the cathedral, it is one of the earliest examples of late Gothic style in Catalonia and is richly decorated. One of the most delightful touches is the series of 12 little carvings of tailors sitting sewing all around the walls. There is also a delicate arcading halfway up and a fine retablo with scenes from the life of the Virgin, carved in grey stone.

On the S aisle notice the Baroque *Chapel of Santa Tecla* (third along when walking E-wards), probably as elaborate as anything in the church and made of Tarragona marble. A little way along from here (behind the Choir) are some faded wall paintings dated from the 14C.

The *Choir* contains some good late 15C wooden stalls. The carving, at first sight, appears very formal and dull but a closer look at the wooden discs on either side of the seats reveals some deliciously funny medieval figures, both human and animal. Alas it is not possible to lift the seats to see if the misericords also contain revelations (as is so often the case).

It remains to mention the **Diocesan Museum** which opens off the Cloister and occupies the *Chapel of Corpus Christi* and the *Chapter House*. Remarkable amongst its good collection of sculpture, paintings, manuscripts and so on is a collection of some 50 tapestries dating from 14 to 17C and a fine retablo painted by *Jaime Huguet* (Catalonia's foremost Gothic painter).

One or two interesting buildings cluster around the outside of the cathedral and its cloister: these are (moving clockwise) the *Canon's House* with its pure Renaissance façade and, opposite it, the *Bishop's Palace* with heavy neo-Gothic façade. A little further on is the early 13C *Chapel of St. Paul* (*Sant Pau*) which stands protected inside a courtyard of a 19C Seminary. The chapel is said to mark the spot where St. Paul stood and preached to the citizens of Tarraco in AD60. Finally there is the old city *Hospital of Santa Tecla* conserving a splendid Romanesque door. Most of the earliest part of this building is in dire need of repair and its lovely soft façade looks as if it will soon crumble away completely.

There are two more medieval sites in the vicinity of the Rosario Gate which deserve mention. One is the *Plaça del Pallol* (just inside the gate) – a picturesque square of many styles, built on a base of solid Roman stone work which includes one splendid archway. A little further on, in the Street of the Cavaliers (*Carrer dels Çavellers*) is *Castellarnau House*, a stylish 14C mansion which is known to have housed many noble families, the most illustrious inhabitant being the Emperor Charles I himself in 1542. The house was remodelled by the Castellarnau family in the 18C but still preserves some fragments of the original structure in the basement, including some pointed arches. It is now open to the public as a museum.

Much of Tarragona beyond the Roman walls dates from the 19C. After widespread devastation caused mainly by Napoleon's armies at the beginning of that century, but also by the British in 1705, the city pulled itself together, changed and expanded its economy, and built broad avenues and extravagant houses for its newly prosperous population. This architect-designed extension spreads from the walls of the *Ciutat Antic* as far W as the *Plaça Imperial Tarraco* and fans out S-wards between coast and river. From the visitors' point of view this area is doubly rich, for it contains not only some exciting examples of Modernism, but also some hitherto undiscovered traces of Roman civilisation.

The most important Roman find is the **Paleo-Christian Necropolis** which overlooks the River Francoli. It is accessible by way of the *Avinguda de Roma* (off Plaça Imperial Tarraco) and then left on to *Passeig de la Independencia*, or simply by following the signposts from wherever you happen to be. The Necropolis was discovered in 1923 by a tobacco company when it was starting to build a new factory, and was then persuaded to move the building site a little to one side. Excavations lasted for 10 years and revealed an extensive area of Roman tombs and buildings, the earliest of which were clearly pagan and probably dated from the first years of conquest. Later tombs were equally clearly Christian with some inscriptions which, when pieced together, formed the names of the 3C Tarragona martyrs, *Bishop Fructuoso*, and his two deacons, *Augurio* and *Eulogio*. Over 2,000 tombs were excavated altogether, ranging from the most primitive to the most sumptuous, and over those of the martyrs were remains of a basilica.

Today many of the tombs can be seen *in situ* and the area is protected by a metal roof. The finds, from both tombs and basilica, are displayed in a *Museum* which was constructed in 1930. They include mosaics, statues, superbly carved marble sarcophagi, amphoras and a host of small artefacts. Around the museum are gardens spotted with large chunks of stonework from the many buildings which once stood over and around the tombs.

This claims to be the most important Roman necropolis in Spain, ranging as it does across the whole period of occupation, from early Pagan to late Christian, and revealing such a wealth and variety of artefacts. It is likely to have extended over an even larger area than that which is under conservation today. Do not neglect the displaced Tobacco Factory alongside, a pleasantly eclectic building with imposing neo-classical columns.

Continue along *Passeig de Independencia* to visit the harbour district of *El Serrallo*. Its narrow streets and picturesque waterfront came into being when the railway arrived in the mid-19C, to replace the much older houses which had necessarily been destroyed. El Serrallo (the word means *harem*) is very atmospheric, dominated by the comings and goings of fishing vessels, the buying and selling of the catch, and mending of nets by large ladies seated under coloured umbrellas. Fish restaurants here tend to be rough and ready, but extremely good.

Returning from El Serrallo, turn right off *Passeig de la Independencia* along *Carrer Torres Jordi;* at *Plaça dels Carros* turn left along *C. Apodeca* to *Pl. del General Prim.* Here on the left are the scant remains of a Roman theatre which probably once seated 5,000 people. Continue along *C. Gasometre* to reach the site of a second Roman forum, of which little remains today except traces of a building thought to have been the *Curia*. You are very close now to the *Central Market* on the *Pl. Corsini*, a significant Modernist construction with iron framework and a fine entrance.

Much of the worthwhile building of this period took place along the *Rambla Nova*, a wide tree-lined avenue which forms the backbone of the extension. It is very close to *Pl. Corsini* (along *C. de Canyelles*) and the first thing you will see is the important bronze monument to local heroes of 1811. The Rambla goes up to the seafront, and the statue at the end is that of Admiral *Roger de Lluria*, a 13C hero. Between these two, blending in with a lively array of shops and outdoor cafés, is *Casa Sales*, built in 1907 with a fine gallery and decorated façade, the *Convent de les Teresianes* (1922) in uncovered brick, and also several smaller exuberant creations of the period in a variety of materials.

Environs of Tarragona

Once you have passed through the ugly band of apartment blocks and belching factories, the environs of Tarragona offer a rich scattering of Roman monuments. To the N (off the N240) are the Aqueduct (4km) and the Mausoleum of Centcelles (7km); to the E (along the N340 which was once the Via Augusta) are four sites, already described in the coastal route from Barcelona; these are Tower of the Scipios (6km), the Quarry of Medol, the Villa of Altafulla and the Bara Arch (20km).

The **Aqueduct**, also known as *Devil's Bridge*, is one of the best preserved monuments of its kind in Spain. It soars dramatically across a deep valley and its pure classical line is set off to perfection by the dark pine-clad hills which surround it. There are two ways to see the aqueduct. You can look down on it from a conveniently placed lay-by on the Motorway from Barcelona, which permits full appreciation of its immensity and its glorious isolation. You can also walk right up to it from a lay-by, on the left side of the Valls-Tarragona road (N240), just before the motorway bridge (if driving S-wards). From here there is a path leading through two gateposts to the place where the huge stone columns of the monument emerge from the mass of tangled undergrowth. This short walk is highly recommended for the opportunity it gives of observing at close quarters the superb skill with which the dressed stones have been fitted together. The great height of the central pillars is even better appreciated by walking a short distance beyond and looking back; all is tranquil here; there is neither traffic noise nor modern building to distract the senses.

The exact date of construction is uncertain but it is thought to have been erected at the beginning of 1C AD when Tarraco was experiencing great prosperity, probably during the time of the Emperor Augustus, though it could have been during the time of the Spanish-born Emperor Trajan.

The Romans needed abundant water not only to drink but also for their very important activity of bathing, and for their growing textile and dyeing industry. This elegant and practical monument was built as part of a complex system of canals bringing water from the mountains to the burgeoning city. The Visigoths destroyed the aqueduct but the Moors are believed to have repaired it in the 10C. It then fell gradually into disrepair once more until the 18C when two successive archbishops of Tarragona rebuilt the ruin and even managed to put the water channels back into use. There have been several periods of restoration since then and today the two tiers of arches – eleven below and twenty-five above – look to be in excellent condition, though the water channels have gone.

Approximately 3km farther along the 240 is **Centcelles** in the village of *Constanti*. It started life as a villa but in the 4C AD it was transformed by the Romans into a mausoleum and experts believe that this could have been done in order to house the body of the Emperor Constantine's son, *Constant*, who died in the year 350. Certainly this hypothesis would explain the very ornate character of the main hall with its mosaic-lined cupola.

The mosaics have been allowed to deteriorate quite disgracefully but it is still possible to appreciate the detailed beauty of the hunting scenes in the lowest section. The horses are superbly portrayed, as are the huntsmen, and it is widely thought that the face of the leading huntsman, who appears to be standing apart and gazing up at the sky, could be a portrait of Constant himself. The other three sections of the mosaic represent Old and New Testament stories, scenes of the four Seasons and (barely visible) some unidentified persons right at the top. Below the cupola the walls must once have been covered with paintings. Just recognisable now is the bust of a young woman wearing pearls, some buildings and a herd of antelopes.

The deterioration of what could have been one of the finest Roman mosaics anywhere on the Peninsula is explained by the fact that the whole building has been occupied continuously throughout the years, as chapel and later as country house when it undoubtedly had more than one floor. Recognition of the rare treasures it contained was not made until 1877 by which time irreparable damage had been done, by builders and simply by neglect. Notwithstanding its sorry state, this monument is worth a visit. The mosaic – what is left of it – is now properly cared for, and excavations continue around the building, unearthing significant foundations relating to its early period as villa.

TARRAGONA TO TORTOSA

A. Inland route via Reus. Excursions to Priory of Scala Dei and Tivissa

You have a choice of Motorway or N420 road from Tarragona to Reus (13km).

Reus has been a significant market town for centuries, growing rich on wine from the hinterland of *El Priorato*, and developing its own textile industry. Only the 16C *Church of Sant Pere* survives from the Middle Ages with

TARRAGONA TO TORTOSA

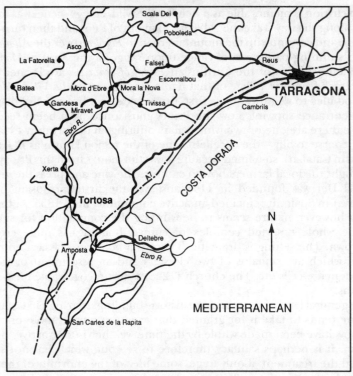

a simple Gothic nave and nice Renaissance door. And the *Casa de la Cuitat* (Town Hall) on *Plaça Mercadal* preserves a Gothic façade.

Reus grew – and grew fast – in the 19C and early 20C and it is the abundant and ebulliant Modernist houses from this period which give the city today a rather special personality. In particular, and also on the Plaça Mercadal, notice *Casa Navas* by *Domenech i Montaner* with an almost Venetian flavour to its windows. There is also the *Banco d'España*, now no longer a bank but a museum (*Museu Salvador Vilaseca*) containing a good prehistoric and archaeological collection which is mainly from the local region. The *Museu Comarcal*, with paintings by the artist *Fortuny* (1838-74) who was born in Reus, is also housed in a Modernist building, known as *Casa Rull*. It is sad, and perhaps inevitable, that so many of these frivolous expressions of a more hopeful age are today dwarfed by huge and uncompromising apartment blocks.

Reus's main *Plaça* is large and traditional and is distinguished by an equestrian statue of the town's noblest son, *General Prim* who, stood up for a constitutional monarchy for Spain at the time of the Revolution in 1868 and was assassinated in Madrid in 1870.

Excursion to Scala Dei

This excursion is memorable as much for the wild, craggy scenery as for the places along the way. Take the N420 for 8km out of Reus and then turn right to *Alforja* and continue up the mountain road to *Poboleda* over the *Alforja Pass* with its stunning panorama of range upon range of the *Serra de Montsant*. The extensive ruins of the Carthusian *Priory of Scala Dei* are located up a rough track from the village of that name (on the way to *La Villela Alta*). It is a good idea to visit the village first, firstly because it has a useful diagram at the entrance showing how the Priory must once have been; secondly because there are one or two wine cellars offering an opportunity to taste – and of course to buy – the excellent wine of the region known as *El Priorato* (*Priorat* in Catalan), so-named because it was the monks from this Priory who first taught the local farmers how to cultivate the vine and press the grape.

Scala Dei was founded in 1163 and was the first Carthusian priory (*Cartoixa*) in Spain. It remained an active community until 1835. At time of writing however, nature seems to be winning the competition for survival and the whole deserted complex of ruined buildings is quite creepily overgrown. The setting is dramatic. There is a bold neo-classical entrance behind which are remains of two cloisters and an assortment of ruined dependencies, cells etc. The church (1228) is just recognisable for what it once was.

The general level of restoration of historic buildings is so high in Catalonia that one tends to take it for granted that even the most remote ones will somehow have been made whole by the time we, the visitors, arrive to look at them. It is perhaps salutary therefore to see one which has not so far received the treatment, if only to get some idea of the enormity of the task.

From Scala Dei it is worth continuing a short way up the road to see the village of *La Morera de Montsant* poised between river and folded rocks in perfect harmony with its surroundings. This is a region of caves and abundant natural springs.

Return to the T702 to visit the two hamlets of *La Villela Alta* and *La Villela Baixa*; the second is particularly lovely looking, from a distance, like some medieval *Sienese* painting. It does not disappoint close up either, with new houses being built in the same distinguished style with high colonnades and evenly spaced windows. There is a charming old bridge over the river.

There are three more worthwhile mountain villages to take in on this trip; all relatively close: *Gratollops*, very steep and cobbled (S from La Villela Baixa on the 710); *Lloa* (712 W of Gratallops) which runs along a mountain ridge and has a rose- covered mirador offering a view which should not be missed, with distant mountain shapes of the *Montsant* beyond slopes of vines and almond trees. Thirdly there is *Torroja de Priorat* (on the road S to *Porrera* and the N420); this is another steep and cobbled village with the by now familar 'Sienese' houses. The remote mountain road belies description, the more wondrous for being so close to the coast and its insensitive urbanisations.

Regain the N420 and turn right for *Falset* (22km), crossing over *La Teixeta* Pass.

Falset, overlooked by ruins of its 12C castle, has a particularly nice arcaded and tree-lined Square (*Plaça de la Quartera*) with a Renaissance palace now containing its town hall. The streets immediately around the Plaça are narrow and worth exploring on foot. Probably the most memorable thing about Falset however is its Modernist Co-operative building – the *Cellar Cooperatiu* – designed by *Cesar Martinell* in 1919 at the W edge of town. You will see several more such buildings in the region, all reflecting the prosperity and power of the wine co-operatives at the turn of the century. This one actually lurks behind a later and more up-to-date version of itself, which cunningly echoes the design of its predecessor whilst conforming to the demands of today's wine industry.

The *Hostal Sport* in Falset is recommended for a hearty and reasonably-priced lunch, with omelette of local snails a speciality (*tortilla de caracolle*).

Excursion to Iberian settlement and Tivissa

Just before reaching *Mora la Nova* and the Ebro river, turn left on to the C230 for *Tivissa*. Before reaching the village take a right-hand turn, (signposted *Poblet Iberico*) which will entail driving for about 6km on track. Probably inhabited since 4C BC, this settlement was destroyed during the war between the Romans and the Carthaginians in 218BC. It is thought to have been of exceptional importance to the Iberians since excavations have revealed rare treasure – ceramics and silver votive offerings in particular, (now in the Archaeological Museum in Barcelona). Still surviving is a very long section of wall, two massive tower bases, which once held the main fortified entrance, and lots of anonymous foundations. It obviously had a view of the Ebro and must have been of considerable value strategically.

Having regained the road, it is worth going on to *Tivissa* itself which pretily crowns a hill. It has a 17C *Church of Sant Jaume* with Baroque W façade, a mirador and an unusual modern fountain with good carving of *Sardana* dancers (*font de la Sardana*). Close by is the tiny *Pla de l'Abadi* with many attractive old houses around. The geranium window boxes and the trill of many canaries make this village almost too good to be true.

Return to the N420 and cross the river to **Mora d'Ebre**, commanded by its castle ruin. At this point there is a choice of two routes towards Tortosa:- the first is to stay on the main road and go through *Gandesa* (with an optional excursion); the second is to take the mountain road via *Miravet* and *Pinell de Brai*, cutting off a corner and leaving out Gandesa.

Route i: From Mora d'Ebre continue on the N420 to *Gandesa* (24km). Capital of the comarca of *Terra Alta*, Gandesa is rather an ugly sprawl but it does have one or two noble buildings and arcaded streets. In particular notice the

Archpriest's Church, which incorporates sections of an earlier church including a magnificent Romanesque door of the Lleida school with five archivolts and some very detailed carving on the capitals of Mozarabic plant and geometrical designs. The old town hall has some good *Ajimez* windows and was once a seigneurial mansion. The much heralded agricultural co-operative building (by *Cesar Martinell*, 1919) stands at the N edge of town; it looks a bit derelict in fact but the design is exciting as always.

The *Terra Alta* landscape is dramatically beautiful and much of it is unbelievably remote. Anyone with a taste for mountain roads, wild flowers (in season) and pinewoods may want to try the following EXCURSION. It includes four striking villages which are still steeped in centuries-old traditions, their people still ready to celebrate the harvest of grape or olive with a folkdance, or mark a religious festival with a procession. Fortunate the visitor who chances upon one of these events.

> From Gandesa drive 7km W-wards and then take the C221 to *Batea*, highly recommended for a stroll especially along its medieval street with nine arches over (*Carrer del Centro*); also recommended is its restaurant *Miravall* whose unattractive exterior should be disregarded in favour of the truly succulent quail with herbs, and other local delicacies within.

> Turn NE to *Vilalba dels Arcs* dominated (like all these villages) by its huge Gothic church. From here take the *Corbera d'Ebre* road and then turn left for *La Fatorella* standing on a high plateau, whose equally huge church has an unexpectedly ornate Baroque front with Corinthian columns. This fascinating village still has its medieval walls (6m thick), gates, arches, and very old houses.

> Lastly, take the T733 to *Asco*; it would be hard to find a wilder or more beautiful stretch of road anywhere in Spain. Asco flows around the base of a hill which has a Moorish castle ruin on top.

After this indulgent excursion, return to Gandesa by way of the N230 and N420 (29km). Continue S-wards along the C221 which passes between the two *Serras* of *Pandols* and *Cavalls* and becomes N230 as it joins the Ebro valley. Just before entering *Xerta* remember to look hard at the river so as to spot the impressive *Zuda*. This is a kind of diagonal dam, designed by the Moors to raise water from the river into a network of canals to right and left. Work continued on it for nearly three centuries after the liberation of Tortosa in 1149 and it is still in use today, restored and adapted to modern requirements. Tortosa is just 12km to the S.

Route ii: Immediately after crossing the Ebro at Mora d'Ebre turn left on to a road signposted *Benissanet*. Miravet village is 7km from Mora and the castle is above it, accessible by rough track and arguably best seen from below anyway. One of the best surviving specimens of Reconquest castles, it is renowned for having been the headquarters of the *Templars* (the Order of Christian knights who helped drive out the Moorish invaders) and also their last stronghold from which they tried unsuccessfully to resist expulsion by the Count of Barcelona in 1308. Thereafter the castle was ceded to the Order of *Hospitallers* who stayed there until 1835.

Most impressive of all, whether from close up or from a distance, are the massively impregnable walls rising sheer out of the rock, reinforced by square towers. One can walk into the castle, part of which is presently under restoration, to see a variety of vaulted rooms as yet difficult to identify. Recognisable however is the shell of a Romanesque church with triumphal arch supported by columns with finely carved capitals.

From Miravet continue to **Pinell de Brai** which has the most striking Modernist Co-operative building of all. You either love it or you hate it. But do take time to come close to see the remarkable comic frieze of painted tiles along the front, telling the story of the grape from its first gathering and pressing through to its eventual consumption as wine by a table of drunken huntsmen. The interior of this hall is an architectural masterpiece of its kind. The village itself is a beauty in soft muted colours on a cliff top. Purists will no doubt question the aesthetic desirability of placing the monstrous co-operative at its feet. Pragmatists will say that this fulfils an essential purpose and is a splendid example of agricultural Modernism to boot.

Shortly after *Pinell de Brai* you join the N230 and turn left for Xerta and Tortosa.

B. Coastal route. Excursions to Escornalbou and Ebro Delta

The quickest way of covering this over-developed stretch of coast is via the Motorway (A7). The alternative is the N340 corniche road, grossly overcrowded in the high season, but worth a try during the rest of the year when tempers and car engines are markedly less heated, and some of the rocky coves (now deserted) are a joy.

The nearest resort (about 10km along the coast) is **Salou** which has extensive beaches, a flower-decked promenade, elegant villas and a host of large hotels. These same beaches, protected as they are by the Cape, were the departure point for James I's armada which successfully won back Majorca from the Moors in 1229, and there is a Monument to commemorate the event.

The most attractive point along the way is undoubtedly **Cambrils**, an old and distinguished fishing town with tourist resort grafted on. The harbour is unspoilt and very atmospheric especially at dusk with sounds of water lapping against hulls and quiet voices of fishermen mending their nets. The place is a fish gourmet's dream and the night air is full of the perfume of scores of fish restaurants. N of the town is the palace and park of *Sama*, built by a 19C marquis and more a curiosity than anything else, with a collection of colonial furniture and 19C paintings.

One of the great attractions of the Catalan coast is of course the ease and speed with which one can reach the comparative wilderness of the sierra behind. From Cambrils there is a worthwhile **Excursion to the medieval castle-monastery of Escornalbou**, high in the *Siurana* mountains, recommended both for its stunning views and for its historic and architectural interest, (approximately 20km there and back).

Take the T312 N-wards to *Riudecanyes*, a small town located below an impressive dam. From here follow the signposts, along a tarmacked road, to Escornalbou. The Romans were the first to discover this pyramid-shaped mountain and its lead mining potential. Later the Moors came and built a castle over the ruins of the Roman fortress. In 1162, after the Reconquest, King Alfonso I ordered a monastery to be erected on the same spot for Augustinian canons under the jurisdiction of the diocese of Tarragona. In 1580 the monastery passed to the Franciscans. It suffered greatly during the wars against Napoleon and in the Carlist wars that followed. In 1836 the Carlists actually tried to blow up the church (but the 2 metre-thick walls withstood the assault). The whole complex of buildings was however looted and fell into general decay, being used as a farmyard and later as a factory for fake coins (using lead from local mines).

The early 20C saw a reversal of fortune when a Catalan philanthropic diplomat called *Eduard Toda i Gell* restored the monastery into a residence for himself. The whole complex of buildings is now in the safe hands of the *Generalitat* who are continuing restoration of the church and have recently put a roof over the simple Romanesque vault to prevent the damp from penetrating further. Today they run a cultural centre on the 2nd floor of the monastery and open the ground floor to the public (every day except Mondays).

A guided tour starts with the *Toda* residence in what were the monastery living quarters. There is an interesting collection of furniture and *objets d'art* collected by this very rich man who had travelled widely, including his library of some 2,000 books, many in English. There are also some splendid 17C and 18C Catalan tiles which were picked out of the ruins by Toda and are now displayed on the walls.

You then pass to the *church* with spacious unadorned single nave, and mainly rounded arches but the beginnings of a Gothic point in some, as one might expect from the late Romanesque/early transitional period of the late 12C when it was built. There is also a *chapter house* with chunks of the ruined cloister stuck on the walls, and a restored *crypt* where further excavations are taking place, revealing Moorish and even Roman work. The one remaining section of the Romanesque cloister was re-erected by Toda as a mirador offering wonderful views of the surrounding countryside, especially the Ebro basin.

There are two more parts to this interesting visit which you will be invited to undertake after the tour of the monastery and church; one is the 10-minute '*Walk of the Friars*' (*Paseo de los frailes*) which takes you along a rocky path around the whole site; secondly, there are the steps up to the *Hermitage of Santa Barbara*, high on the peak and strongly recommended for the view which must be one of the most extensive in Catalonia, said to display 100kms of coastline on a clear day. It also affords an opportunity for a bird's eye view of the restored monastery and church (with its new roof).

Escornalbou is also accessible from *Falset* (on the inland route) via *Duesaigues* but the road is very bad.

Back at Cambrils, continue along the N340 past a succession of towns and developments with camp sites and apartment blocks and fast-food restaurants galore, and every imaginable sort of fun fair and amusement. Amongst all this, the sandy beaches and facilities for water sports are outstanding. Biggest development is *Miami Platje*. *Hospitalet de l'Infant* is named after its now ruined 14C pilgrims' hospice. *L'Ametlla de Mar* still retains its old sea wall and fishermen's houses and has some very good beaches indeed. The port of *Ampolla* marks the beginning of the Ebro Delta. For Tortosa continue 11km to *l'Aldea* and then turn right (13km).

Excursion to Ebro Delta

Take any of the roads going seawards off the N340 between *Ampolla* (N) and *San Carles de la Rapita* (S). This rich, almost tropical region is unique in Spain and should not be missed. Extending over more than 300sq km and still expanding as more and more mud is brought down by the river, it is the second most important wetland in the Western Mediterranean (after the Camargue), with a bird population comprising some 60% of the total number of species found in Europe. Its status as *Natural Park* (since 1983) protects a delicate balance between the outstanding ecological value and its usefulness to man for agriculture (mainly rice) and fishing.

The Moors were the first to discover the Ebro Delta's potential. Then came the Hospitaller Knights who went in for hunting, fishing, salt mining and trading in leeches. Rice was not grown until the 17C when it was introduced by the Cistercians, and canalisation was introduced soon after.

The very humid climate with little variation in temperature makes it ideal for rice and 98% of Catalonia's needs are produced here. Indeed the combination of rice paddy (occupying nearly all the space between the game reserves), the evening cacophony of frogs, the occasional whine of a mosquito and the general humidity over all seem more appropriate to SE Asia than the mountainous Iberian peninsula. In October/November each year, after the rice has been harvested, the still water-logged fields are invaded by thousands of water birds, either passing through or stopping for the winter.

Where there is not rice there are reed beds and lagoons and these make perfect breeding grounds for water fowl and sea birds as well as good stopping places for winter migrants. There are several game reserves, the largest of which are *l'Encanyadissa* and *La Tancada* and a game sanctuary

(*Punta de la Banya*). There are about 300 different species of bird including shoveler duck, teal and shelduck; there are also heron, egret, flamingo, grebe, coot, oyster catcher, avocet and many different types of gull.

The outer edges of the delta are marked by long sandy beaches and dunes, whilst the river and canals are often bordered by poplar and willow. There are said to be over 500 species of wild flower. The deer and wild boar which once roamed the region have disappeared in the face of encroaching human population but there are still some interesting lizards to be found and, of course, countless frogs and toads. Fishing is a traditional activity with many tons of eels and elvers netted every year; there is also pike and bass to be found in the river and abundant red mullet off the coast. Fishing by visitors is controlled but perfectly possible and details can be had from the Infomation Centre. Most hotels and restaurants offer mouth-watering fish menus with assorted shell fish (*mariscera*) and fish stew (*sarsuela*) high on the list.

There is a good network of roads and tracks and at the centre of the peninsula, straddling the Ebro itself, is the sizeable town of **Deltebre** (really a conglomeration of several old settlements). Anyone planning a full and serious visit should call at the *Information Centre* here, which will provide maps, details about the game reserves, and answers to any reasonable questions, (usually in English, French, German, Spanish or Catalan). It is open all day every day (mornings only on Sundays).

For a short visit, simply carry on through the long urban sprawl of *Deltebre* towards *Ruimar*. You will soon come to an area of river restaurants where, besides having lunch you can also hire a fishing boat or take a trip out to the mouth of the Ebro, past the *Isle of Buda*. The latter is particularly recommended: the launches are run by the *Restaurant Nuri* who will time your meal to finish in time for you to catch the boat (just under an hour for the round trip). Or you may simply prefer to walk along the tow path, a refreshing experience after your large plate of shellfish and with who knows what species of bird, reptile, flower or insect to surprise you. You can walk (or drive) right out to the sandy beaches, a few of which are already sprouting holiday villages. Or you can stop in one of the 'protected areas', such as *El Canal Vell*, for some bird watching.

There are two interesting towns in the region – *Amposta*, inland and bypassed by the N340, and *San Carles de la Rapita* on the southern bay formed by the peninsula.

Amposta has a very worthwhile Museum – *Museu de Montsia-Amposta* – which explains the natural formation of the delta and the various periods of human intervention including the early canalisation work; there is also a good flora and fauna collection. Several vestiges of old Amposta remain around its 12C castle ruin (once the headquarters of the Knights of St. John of Catalonia and Aragon). In front, and in total contrast, there soars across the river a magnificent modern bridge: *Puente Colgante*.

The picturesque town of **San Carles de la Rapita** presents a puzzling mixture of old and new, of modest under-statement and grandiose conceit, and herein lies a tale. The Spanish King Charles III, noted for having been the first to allow the ports of Catalonia to trade direct with the New World, intended to turn what had once been the modest fishing village of *Els Alfacs* into a prestigious commercial port, trading in particular with South America. To this end he constructed a right-angled street plan around an enormous square named after him, and a canal joining the town with Amposta. Several neo-classical buildings, such as the vast *Esglesia Nova* (new church) and the mansion known as *La Glorieta* remain in unfinished state as potent reminders of his extravagant but unfulfilled dream; the town was abandoned soon after his death in 1788. Today San Carles is – despite its large and empty plaça – a modest fishing port once more, superbly sited within its huge natural harbour and home to hundreds of fishermen, as it had been since medieval times. The evening market, when the fishermen come in with their catches and all the local hotel and restaurant owners come down to buy, is a dynamic and colourful event.

TORTOSA

Like Tarragona, Tortosa was once a Roman city built over an Iberian settlement. The Romans called it *Dertosa* and constructed a bridge over the Ebro. It became an important commercial centre and port but never received such lavish attention as *Tarraco* and there is very little trace of Roman civilisation left today. Christianity is thought to have taken root about 515 but was cut short by the arrival of the Moors in 715 who stayed more than 400 years and built the defensive Castle of *la Zuda* on the highest point. Probably because of its strategic position as port and river crossing and the fertility of the surrounding land, the Moors established Tortosa as a centre for both trade and learning: it grew in stature and in 1018 became an independent Moorish kingdom, or *taifa*. From that moment on however weakness set in: throughout Spain the *taifas* were beginning to fight with each other and this divided strength was no match for the increasingly confident and powerful Christian forces.

Tortosa was reconquered by Ramon Berenguer IV in 1148 with the help of an armada from Genoa, and the first symbolic act (as in the case of Tarragona after the reconquest) was the building of a cathedral and the re-establishment of the bishopric. There was an initially unsettled period during which the three factions charged with governing the town, one of which was the Republic of Genoa, failed to agree about anything. Fortunately for Tortosa it was then incorporated by James II into the Kingdom of Aragon and in 1279 issued with a Charter – *Els Costums de Tortosa* – which can still be seen today in the city's Museum.

The Middle Ages were a period of great prosperity for Tortosa. Standing astride one of Spain's longest navigable rivers and with all the fertility of Aragon behind, it became a gateway for the export of grain and wool to

Naples and Sicily and an attraction for merchants of many lands. Today's cathedral and the Episcopal palace date from this time, as do the colleges and many of the mansions, and also the conversion of the Moorish castle to a royal residence.

Throughout the centuries, however, Tortosa's advantageous bridgehead position facing the Mediterranean has made it an irresistible military target. It suffered greatly both in the War of Succession and the War of Independence, and during the Civil War it was devastated probably more than any other town in Catalonia as it formed a front between Republican and Nationalist troops. The hard-pressed Republicans were stuck for four months in trenches alongside the river before fighting – and losing – the infamous Battle of the Ebro in January 1939. Today a poignant monument stands on the only pillar remaining after the bridge was blown up, in memory of the thousands who died.

Tortosa now has a rather sad and neglected air. Repeatedly attacked in the past because of its enviable location, it has now lost even that natural benefit since the river is silting up and a great delta now lies between it and the sea. But it does have some atmospheric medieval streets and one or two very important sites and therefore merits a short stay, ideally in the *parador* which has been conveniently and discreetly placed within the Moorish Castle, La Zuda, and consequently commands a splendid view over the surrounding area, and over the cathedral which stands but a few metres away.

The **Cathedral**, replacing an earlier Romanesque building, was started in 1347 and took 200 years to build (if one discounts the W facade which was added in the 18C). Because of its situation at the foot of a hill, it is possible to get an overall impression of this outstanding example of Catalan-Gothic from above – a compact but ungainly building emerging from the medieval scramble at its feet like some huge Goliath. When seen from below, however, the power and the scale are lost to the infinitely harsher outline of the Moorish walls above.

The 18C façade is, to say the least, unfortunate, and it ill prepares the visitor for the pure Gothic style inside. The twisted columns above the central broken pediment, the marble inlays alongside the windows, and the strangely mixed up capitals on the main columns confuse and irritate the eye. Perhaps if the façade had been completed up to its proper height (instead of topped off with a kind of concertina-ed drainpipe structure) the eye of the onlooker would have risen above all this fussy detail, instead of being obliged to dwell on it.

Inside, however, all is harmony and light and this is caused to a large degree by the strikingly lovely double Ambulatory with pierced stone screens and the three tiers of windows which let in a lot of natural daylight. The arches are high and pointed and induce a general feeling of weightlessness and space and this is further enhanced by the fact that the cathedral has no central choir. This is because, during the Civil War a bomb hit the very centre of the nave and the wooden choir stalls, renowned for their delicacy of carving, were virtually completely destroyed. Sections of new stone inserted in some of the central columns of the nave and one or two discernibly new ribs in the vault mark the exact spot today. The choir is unlikely ever to be restored in its rightful place but small sections have been preserved in the somewhat unsuitable setting of a 19C neo-Gothic chapel with pink marble columns at the entrance.

Also worthy of note are the fine memorial stones set in the floor of the central aisle, and two 15C stone pulpits to left and right with finely carved figures of the Evangelists on one side and bishops on the other. On the S wall is a Baroque chapel dedicated to 'Our Lady of the Belt' (*Nuestra Senora de la Cinta*). It is ornately decorated throughout with paintings and inlays of jasper and marble and a picture of Our Lady emerging from a halo of clouds stands over the altar. Always the centre of attention, this chapel is itself the size of a small church and services are nowadays held here rather than in the main body of the cathedral which is left standing as a sad and beautiful museum piece.

In the chapel next door (looking W-wards) is the font of the 'ante-pope', interesting only insofar as it bears the arms of *Cardinal Pedro de Luna* (self-styled *Pope Benedict XIII* in the 15C) who was elevated by French cardinals in *Avignon* but never accepted by Rome.

The 13C **Cloister** on the S side has a peaceful air of austerity and good taste. Slim columns with unadorned capitals, pointed arches and a low wooden vault remain untouched by later 'improvers'. In the walls are one or two very ancient memorial stones (predating the cathedral) inscribed in Hebrew, Latin and Greek.

Also of great beauty is the 14C **Episcopal Palace** standing opposite the cathedral. The courtyard with Gothic arches, delicate windows and incredibly slim columns has a noble staircase up which you should go – to a door marked '*oficinas del obispado*' – to ask permission to view the chapel. It is well worthwhile. From the antechamber you will pass through a highly decorated Gothic arch into the small chapel, noted particularly for its fine vaulted roof in which the ribs are held by splendid bosses with figures of singers and musicians. There is also a carved wooden door showing *Faith, Hope* and *Charity*, and false windows painted on to the chapel walls.

There are two Renaissance buildings in the cathedral area of town which should certainly be seen: these are the *College of Sant Lluis* and the *College and Church of Sant Domenec*. The former was founded in 1544 by the *Emperor Charles V* for the education of young Moorish converts (*conversos*). It is remarkable for its elaborate portal with imperial shield above and for its beautifully proportioned Italian-style inner courtyard with three tiers of arches and interesting carved frieze between the first and second tier; which shows busts of various Catalan monarchs and their wives, ranging from *Ramon Berenguer IV* and *Petronella* to *Philip III* and *Margarita of Austria*.

The *College of Sant Domenec* standing alongside has a typical Renaissance façade of 1578 with Doric and Ionic columns. Its church is now a **Museum** and the home of the city's archives. It contains great treasures, many of which (at time of writing) still await cataloguing and displaying by the overworked and under-funded curator. Roman busts in white marble, and Iberian and Visigothic artefacts in noble disarray compete for attention with priceless documents, many of which are still rolled up in ancient drawers. Most exciting of all is the 1279 Tortosa Charter, *El Costums de Tortosa*, which sets out the rights of the people on being integrated to the Kingdom of Aragon.

Next door to Sant Domenec is the old town hall (*Casa Consistorial*) with Gothic façade. One or two old palaces still remain in nearby streets to evoke memories of a more prosperous age, especially in *Carrer Moncada* and *Carrer de la Rosa* (and notice particularly the extraordinary flight of fancy in the latter street, opposite the entrance to the cathedral cloister). Extensive examination of the town however will most probably not reveal any hidden treasures, apart from those already mentioned. Remembering the various periods of wanton destruction through which Tortosa has lived, perhaps this is not surprising.

ROUTE 3

TARRAGONA TO LLEIDA VIA VALLS AND MONTBLANC

Excursions to Santes Creus and Poblet Monasteries and to cave paintings at El Cogul

Take the N240 N-wards from Tarragona to Valls (21km). Be sure to look at the *Roman Aqueduct* (as you pass under the motorway) if you have not already seen it.

Valls has two small arcaded squares, and if you follow the signs to *Centro Urbano* you will come to *Plaça del Blat*, the larger and more interesting of the two. It has a 19C *Town Hall* (*Casa de Vila*) on one side and, on the other, a *Museum* containing 19C and 20C Catalan paintings. At one corner is the 16C *Gothic Church of St. John the Baptist* (*Sant Joan Bautista*) with rather ugly neo-Gothic bell tower. Inside it is spacious to the point of emptiness, grey and cold, the N and S walls broken only by four single windows on each side and the W wall by a rose window. The E end has a Baroque brown wood retablo with a hint of gilt on the Christ figure. Almost obscuring it are two vertical hangings with black writing on a white ground which read "*ei tu, revoluncionar*" on one side and "*es pais qua*" on the other; in the centre, in front of the retablo, is a modern rendition of the crucifixion, all of this

TARRAGONA TO LLEIDA

probably dating from the year immediately after the Civil War when the church was restored. The lateral chapels merit a look, especially those on the N side which contain a 13C statue of the Virgin, and one or two carved reliefs of historic scenes, including a good one of the Battle of Lepanto. Another redeeming feature is the 18C reclining figure of *Sant Aleix* by *Lluis Bonifac*, at the W end. The second square, *Plaça de l'Oli*, is two minutes walk from the church and has some narrow medieval streets leading off it.

The only other monument of note in this rather disappointing town is the one by the artist *Josep Busquets* to the extraordinary *Xiquets de Valls*, which stands in front of a fountain in the *Plaça del Font* (on the road to Lleida). Valls is renowned for its human pyramids and this monument displays an unbelievable seven layers of humanity, with small children forming the topmost layer. Lucky the visitor who manages to see one of these pyramids in the flesh. They tend to form around midsummer but it is quite remarkably difficult to find out exactly when.

For the *direct route* from Valls to Montblanc take the N240 for a further 17km north-westwards. The road climbs to *Coll d l'Illa* from where there are good views, and the red-roofed village of l'Illa nestles picturesquely in a fold of the hills just beyond.

An alternative and highly recommended route, starting in Valls and ending in Montblanc approximately 60km later, takes in the *Monastery of Santes Creus*, the lovely old town of *Santa Coloma de Queralt* and splendid countryside.

Excursion: Valls – Vila-redona – Santes Creus – Pont d'Armentera – Querol – Santa Coloma de Queralt – Rocafort de Queralt – Montblanc

Take the C246 E-wards out of Valls. After 8km, having passed through the village of Alio, turn left at the crossroads towards *Vila-redona*. This hill-top village is proud of its *Columbarium* – a strange and unexplained chapel-like structure, called Romanesque but looking older and certainly in a very dilapidated state. It is strapped together in several places and is obviously unsafe to enter. It is doubtful whether it is worth following the signposts down a long rough track to see it at all. The same can be said for the castle ruin above the village, which is better admired from a distance.

Santes Creus is about 5km further on and this approach from the S offers by far the best view of the village and monastery in its lush woodland setting. It is one of a trio of great Cistercian monasteries in Catalonia, the other two being *Poblet* and *Vallbona de les Monjes*. The Cistercians arrived in 1150 and, under the protection of the Kings of Aragon and the local nobility, their community prospered and their influence, both cultural and agricultural, spread far and wide. Much of what they created architecturally remains today and has been well restored or preserved for posterity.

Santes Creus is still a living community, though no longer a monastic one for the Cistercians were finally banished in the 19C. The complex of buildings falls into three sections: first comes the outer courtyard which is a

112

pleasant jumble of what must once been storehouses and workshops for the community. Here too stands the modest *Church of Santa Lucia* (1741) and, at right-angles to it, the frivolous Baroque *Door of the Assumption*, which is in fact a complete house and was probably once used by the monks attending to the church next door.

Through the Door is the second section: *Plaça de Sant Bernat* (dedicated to a former abbot of this name), a superb rectangle of houses in soft pinky browns, often decorated with white graffiti in the manner of the Door and some carrying plaques indicating the diverse trades of the monks who once lived there. Some of these now contain craft shops or even small hotels but this concession to modern tourism has been skilfully and discreetly undertaken and does not in any way distract from the overall harmony of the Plaça. The third door on the right is special for it leads to the 16C *Bishop's Palace* which has a tiny inner cloister of just ten arches thought to be part of the Hospital for the Poor which stood here even earlier.

The *Plaça* is dominated by the imposing façade of the monastery Church (started in 1174) with its Romanesque door, single Gothic window and battlements which were added later by order of the king. To gain access to the church and the third, innermost, section of the monastery complex you walk slightly to the right of the church and go through the Royal Gate into the 14C Gothic Cloister. This replaced an even earlier cloister and the hexagonal 'temple' on the S side is all that remains of the first one (probably never completed). It holds a marble basin (filled by a natural spring) and would have served as a wash house for the monks. It is interesting to compare the heavier architectural style of this Transitional building with the much lighter movement of the later Gothic Cloister around it.

The **Cloister** is like a wonderful picture book in stone, its capitals offering a rich sequence of biblical and mythological scenes, starting with Adam and Eve shown on the first great corner column by the entrance. As always one marvels at the exuberance and sometimes sheer inventiveness of these medieval craftsmen (in this case, the Catalan master, *Renardo Fonoll*). There is so much earthy humour here, and why does the theme of pigs eating acorns constantly reappear? Not just the capitals but also the tombs on the walls have been generously endowed with human and bestial figures.

By contrast the **Church** is sublimely simple. It is one of the best preserved examples of the austere Cistercian style anywhere in Catalonia. Its striking beauty depends not on applied decoration at all but on the massive stone pillars, the soaring rhythmic curves of the vault, and the great bare walls with lancet windows shining out of the darkness like jewels. The original Gothic retablo was for some reason taken to the cathedral in Tarragona and replaced by the present one in the 18C. Sadly it is not quite the right size and hides part of the fine rose window in the apse; but its colour has been allowed to fade almost to that of the stone and its role is not a dominant one. The stained glass in the great W window (already seen from the Plaça) is superb and mainly original.

The church is T-shaped and in the crossing are two highly ornate *royal tombs*, a reminder that Santes Creus was also a royal mausoleum. Extraordinary and beautiful in their way, these are not fortunately visible from the E end of the church and so do nothing to distract the eye from the overwhelming Cistercian tranquillity. The tomb on the N side is that of *King Peter the Great* (Pedro III) who died in 1285, and on the S side is that of his son, *James the Just* (Jaime II) with his queen *Blanca de Anjou*. The 14C marble carving of their two recumbent figures clad in Cistercian habit is particularly lovely.

The **Chapter House**, accessible from the Cloister, is a well- preserved architectural joy with a nine-part vault supported by four central columns and the simplest of floral designs carved into the capitals. In the floor are the tombs of the Cistercian abbots. Santes Creus was a very carefully ordered mausoleum: kings in the church, abbots in the chapter house, benefactors in the cloister and monks in the cemetery (E of the church).

Next to the Chapter House are original steps leading up to the *Dormitory*, a surprisingly spacious room – one of the earliest parts of the monastery (1173) and recently painstakingly restored with a new vault built on to the (mainly) original bases. It was not the custom for Cistercian monks to occupy separate cells and this room must have accommodated a very large number of them. A door from the dormitory opens out on to the roof of the cloister (through which the monks would have had direct access to the church at night). From this vantage point today's visitor has a splendid overview and can also appreciate just how fortified the monastery in fact was, with castellations and arrow-slits visible in all directions.

At ground level again a quiet wander amongst the various monastic offices, some ruined, some restored, can be a charming and evocative experience, for it is removed from the modern world and largely unvisited still. There is another simpler cloister which is quietly guarded by noble cypresses. And around can be identified a *refectory*, with decorative band of tiles, a *kitchen* complete with sinks and mill stone, an *infirmary* and a well-preserved *wine cellar* (*bodega*) with vaulting like that of the Chapter House and ancient wine barrels. Also of interest are the ruins of the *royal apartments* built for King Pedro III (buried in the church) and later enlarged by his successors. Small rooms cluster around a two-storey courtyard which has a well in the middle; there is also a polychrome carved wood ceiling and a good scattering of royal coats of arms.

For anyone wishing to stay close to the magic of Santes Creus there is in the village a modest, family-run inn called *Hostal Grau* which, at time of writing, can be warmly recommended. It stands but a few moments' walk from the Monastery and the rooms at the back overlook the wooded banks of the river.

Continue northwards through *Pont d'Armentera* to *Querol*. The road between these two villages runs along the side of a wide valley with pines above and almond trees below. Bordering the road is a spring paradise of wild flowers. They do not display themselves blatantly to catch the eye of passing motorists but hide modestly amongst the aromatic undergrowth so that it really is necessary to stop the car and get out to see the myriads of very tiny, often unidentifiable, shy blooms. There are also wood orchids as well as cistus, broom, and wild honeysuckle. The ear is feasted too in spring when the whole scene is brought to life by waves of muted bird song. Truly a place to quieten the most troubled spirit.

Querol has a jagged castle ruin which is best seen (and photographed) from a distance. There is also a Romanesque church and a lot of houses built in local stone with swimming pools betraying their purpose as holiday homes.

The road continues along the valley of the Gaia river through the villages of *Esblada, Seguer* and *Santa Perpetua.* Seguer has hilltop ruins, but Santa Perpetuas's 10C castle, set on a rocky crag over dramatic gorges is more dramatic.

Go through *Pontils* to **Santa Coloma de Queralt**. This small medieval town is still walled and retains much of interest in a compact area. From its 12C castle, of which only the round tower (*torre de homenaje*) survives, the Counts of Queralt played an important role in expelling the Moors from Southern Catalonia. The town has an exceptionally charming triangular central plaça (*de la Esglesia*) with colonnades supported by slightly leaning pillars. The *Plaça Mayor* is similarly arcaded and many houses have wrought iron balconies. A dominant feature is the 14C *Church of Santa Coloma* which contains a remarkable alabaster retablo carved by a local artist, *Jordi Joan* in 1387, and also has a fine Romanesque door. Three of the town's original monumental gates remain in good condition: *Portal de Cervera, Portal del Castell,* and *Portal dels Jueus* which leads to a picturesque Jewish quarter (*Barri Judio*).

Outside the town walls in a direct line from the parish church and about one third of a kilometre from it, is a second church – *Santa Maria de Bel-loc,* once part of a monastery and built a century earlier than the church of Santa Coloma. It has a glorious Romanesque door of the Lerida school with five archivolts, fine capitals and a carving of the *Adoration of the Magi* in the typanum, and inside the church are the alabaster tombs of the Counts of Queralt. Today it is known as the *Sanctuario* and is used during religious festivals when processions go between it and the parish church. It is obviously much treasured and a discreet garden has been planted in front with seats from which to admire the door. Nearby is a 17C fountain – *Font des Canelles* – next to which stands a copy of the Gothic boundary cross, the original being inside the church.

Turn S-wards now and take the C241 to **Rocafort de Queralt** which has a massive fortified church with a badly cracked 18C façade. Like Santa Coloma, Rocafort retains the original tower of its castle, once the residence of the Counts of Queralt. Modern houses have now been built inside the old walls, using the local stone. What makes Rocafort different however is the possession of a splendid Modernist wine cellar. The clear sweeping lines of its internal framework are reminiscent in design of the vault of Gaudi's church (*La Sagrada Familia*) in Barcelona. This is not surprising since the wine cellar was designed in the early 20C by *Cesar Martinell,* a pupil of Gaudi. Several similar wine cellars exist in the region, notably in the villages of *Serral* and *Barbera de la Conca* to the S, all built at about the same time when the wine industry was recovering from a deadly outbreak of phylloxera and was changing from the old system of land tenure to a new one of co-operatives; hence the need for very spacious cellars.

A slight detour from the route to the hilltop village of *Fores* (about 3km west of Rocafort) is wholly justified by the magnificient views – *of* Fores as you approach, and *from* Fores over the wide expanse of surrounding countryside. A closer look at Fores reveals a rather derelict village but with a restored church with good door. The road passes through the villages of *Serral* and *Pira* and rejoins the N240. Turn left here and almost immediately you are in *Montblanc.*

Montblanc is a charming and unspoilt medieval town which has managed to retain a rare tranquillity because the only gaps in its 14C crenellated walls are too narrow to allow main roads to penetrate. It is a very compact town and its narrow atmospheric streets can easily be explored on foot.

Founded in 1162 by King Alfonso I on the hilltop site of an Iberian settlement, Montblanc prospered from the beginning: a castle was built on the highest point (of which sadly there is now no trace) and in 1366 the impressive perimeter ramparts were erected with twenty-eight watch towers and two fine tower gates: that of St. George (*San Jordi*) on the W wall and *Bove* on the E wall, both still bearing traces of portcullis and battlements. In 1392 the town received a royal seal of approval with the creation of the first Duke of Montblanc.

Undoubtedly the best view of the walls, said to be one of the most important medieval constructions in Catalonia, is to be had from the Lleida road to the N of the town, and the section just to the right of the approach road is in particularly good condition. The 12C bridge over the river *Francoli* leads straight into the main street (*Carrer Mayor*) and makes an excellent starting point for a tour of the town. Today's road leads over a modern bridge but the old one (*Pont Vell*) alongside deserves a closer look. It goes back to the beginnings of Montblanc, and has been many times restored but still retains sections of primitive carving in its walls, some of which look as if they have come from an even older structure. (Certainly the gross female figure on the wall furthest from the modern bridge has a counterpart on the façade of the parish church).

After the bridge, on the left-hand side of the road approaching the town walls, is the 14C church and hospital of *Santa Magdalena.* Here, tucked away behind an unpromising façade, is a delightfully harmonious and peaceful little cloister, recently restored and with an ancient well in the middle. It has three tiers, hexagonal columns and Gothic arches below, twisted columns and flatter arches above, and short, stubby columns with completely flat arches on top. Such an unexpected joy as this encapsulates much of Catalonia's irresistible charm.

The *Carrer Mayor*, with helpful map of the town on the wall just inside the gate, cuts through the centre of town. On the left, down *Carrer Sant Josep*, is the 14C *Alenyas House (Casal dels Alenya)*, once the most important civil building in Montblanc. Its elegant windows bespeak former glory and its creators, the *Alenyas*, were a greatly respected philanthropic family. Behind the house is the Street of the Jews (*Carrer dels Jueus*) with its original gate in the wall and picturesque houses. Continue down Carrer Mayor towards *Plaça San Miguel*, named after its Romanesque church with typical high tower and beautifully proportioned door. The church had its moment of glory in the early 14C when the central government of Catalonia (*Corts*) assembled here on several occasions. It was the parish church until the larger *Santa Maria* was finished at the end of the century.

On the opposite side of Carrer Mayor, five minutes' walk in a westerly direction, is the *Plaça Mayor*, a delightfully spacious, tree-filled square with colonnades on two sides. There are four interesting features here: the first (on the left as you enter) is *Casa Desclergues*, 14C residence of the King's representative and acquired 200 years later by the family Desclergues who added the splendid porticos and coats-of-arms; on the other side of the Square is the town hall (*Casa de Vila*) with a fine Gothic window preserved from its 13C origins and the rest dating from 17C and 18C; the whole façade has recently been restored; next door are the Arches (*Porxos*) where the official grain measures of the town were kept; the stone measuring vats are still in place, probably last used in 18C; next to the arches is a 19C fountain with moulded front and large Spanish shield. Behind the *Plaça* (W-wards from the back of Casa Desclergues) is the old residence of Catalan kings (*Palau Reial*). It bears very few traces of its former grandeur now, having been insensitively modernised with two vertical drainpipes running up the centre of the main façade.

A short distance N of the Square is the most important sight inside Montblanc: the **Parish Church of Santa Maria**, begun in 1352 by the architect *Reynard des Fonoll* (said to be English) on the site of a much earlier church. It is believed that the original design was never completed. The distinctive 'Baroque' façade in warm yellow stone is liberally covered with statues and columns in a quite bewildering variety of styles. At the top are some very primitive figures indeed and it seems that relics from the earlier church may well have been inserted in places, alongside later carvings. It is even possible to spot different styles in the same statue – with finely carved heads on primitive bodies and vice versa, and the very coarsely carved naked man at the very top seems not to belong at all (though he could be the partner of the lady on the *Pont Vell*). The overall effect of the façade is pleasing, if a little confusing.

The interior of the church is dark and well proportioned with buttresses and side chapels in typical Catalan Gothic style. The tall stained glass windows are particularly lovely, though they let in very little light, and the 16C polychrome wood carving of the Virgin is a joy. Also remarkable is the 17C organ believed to be the oldest in Spain, and restored in 1977. Visitors are obviously welcome in this church for there is abundant information in four European languages (besides Catalan), which is more than can be said for the majority of churches in the region. A walk around the outside of the church is a rewarding experience and it is quite easy to detect the various periods of building, including at the back a pure Romanesque arch, obviously remaining from the earlier structure. The streets in the immediate vicinity have retained their medieval character: narrow, sometimes arched, sometimes stepped, always atmospheric.

Next door to the church is the Regional Museum (*Museu Comarçal*), originally the residence of the Josa family who enlarged it in the 18C. In 1958 it was converted into a museum and traces of the original 13C structure were discovered, believed to have been part of the Notary's office. Today it houses a collection of ceramics, paintings and documents relating to the beginnings of Montblanc.

Behind the W end of the church is the *Pla de Santa Barbara* – the small hill or 'white mountain' where 12C Montblanc was born, over the remains of an Iberian village. This was the site of the original castle (which was later taken down) and today has been turned into a pleasantly inoffensive mirador. It is well worth the short steep walk up to the top for a rewarding view of the city's red-tiled roofscape and, most particularly, of the perimeter walls. It is possible to identify at least nineteen surviving watch towers, many with houses built in to them or up against them, and to appreciate the compactness of this charming town so naturally protected from ugly modern intrusions.

Also clearly visible from this high point are two more historic sights which merit a closer look if time permits. In a westerly direction and standing just outside the walls is the 13C Convent of the Mountain (*Convent de la Serra*). This outwardly austere building which is now used as a school should be entered for a sight of the appealing and beautiful alabaster figure of the *Virgin of the Mountain* (patron saint of Montblanc), set in a chapel on the S wall against a retablo displaying four medieval paintings. The fourth one, depicting the martyrdom of the Virgin whilst God sits in a cloud above and awaits her soul, is particularly charming. The chapel is lit by natural light filtering through the stained glass window above and glows like a gem in its otherwise fairly unremarkable setting.

In the same direction, within the angle of the town walls, is the 14C *church of St. Marçal*. It was originally intended as a hospital for the poor and now houses a collection of paintings and sculpture (open only from 11 to 14 hours).

L'Espluga (6 km) is a pleasant but unremarkable town on the bank of the Francoli river. It has one or two points of interest, notably the *Church of St. Michael* in Transitional (Romanesque-Gothic) style which overlooks the *Plaça Mayor*, a 14C Hospital opposite the church with fine interior patio and staircase, and the rather unusual *Casal de l'Espluga*, built in 1963 in traditional style as a recreational and cultural centre. L'Espluga also has a Modernist wine cellar, in the manner of Serral and Rocafort. This one boasts three naves and looks rather like some great contemporary cathedral; in fact it is another sign of the prime importance of co-operative wine growing in the early 20C. It was designed by *Lluis Domenec* and opened in 1913.

Excursion: From L'Espluga take the T700 road 4½km to the **Monastery of Poblet**, which was founded by the Cistercians in 1151. It was paid for by *Ramon Berenguer IV* in gratitude for his victory over the Moors. By the end of the 12C, church, hospital and library were all in place. Building continued and the Order prospered and achieved power over a wide area. The high point was reached in 1367 when *King Peter IV* (the *Ceremonious*) decided to turn the church into a royal mausoleum for himself and his descendants, and to move the tomb of *James I* there from Santes Creus. At this time there were over 100 monks in residence and the Monastery's influence over vast tracts of countryside and countless towns and villages was unassailable.

Fortunes changed however and by the 16C decline had set in. The Cistercians were finally expelled in 19C, leaving the Monastery vulnerable to thieves and vandals (though it was never at any time sacked or burned). Many treasures disappeared and the despoliation was only halted at the beginning of this century when the Government stepped in and began restoration work. In 1940 a small community of Cistercians returned and today there are some 30 in residence. Since this is once more a working monastery, visitors are required to take a guided tour, rather than wander freely. This takes about an hour; opening times are between 10 and 12.30 and between 15 and 18 hours each day.

The monastery complex is encircled by three walls. The outer one, 5 metres high and 1½km long, encloses storehouses, workshops and utilitarian buildings, once used by peasants attending the monks. Here too, on the right, is the *Chapel of St. George* (*Sant Jordi*) built by *King Alfonso V* in gratitude to God for his conquest of Naples in 1442.

You pass through the second wall by way of the *Golden Gate* (*Puerta Dorada*), started in the mid 15C but only completed after *King Ferdinand of Aragon* (husband of *Isabella of Castile*) visited the monastery to give thanks for the discovery of the New World by Columbus and the final removal of the Moors from Granada in 1492. It became the 'golden' gate when *Philip II* ordered the plates covering the door to be gilded in 1564. (These are no longer gold, but copper).

Inside this wall is the *Plaça Mayor* with the pure Romanesque (12C) *Chapel of St. Catherine* (*Santa Caterina*) on the left and the ruined 16C *Abbots' Palace* on the right. Straight ahead, the third (inner) wall is pierced by two contrasting doors: on the left is the 14C **Royal Door** (**Puerta Real**) held tight between two massive hexagonal watch towers like the entrance to some fortress. On the right is the joyous Baroque façade of the Church. This was not added until the 17C, the Cistercians having originally built a completely plain W façade, as was their wont. Opinions differ as to whether this one is entirely suitable, and purists question particularly the need for the two ornate side windows flanked by twisted columns which were added fifty years after the entrance itself.

You enter by way of *Puerta Real* which leads through a passageway into the very fine **Cloister** which, unusually, lies at the N side of the church. The wing alongside the church wall is the oldest (1178) and has round arches in pure Romanesque style, whereas the other three wings have typical Gothic traceried windows. All four wings have a ribbed quadrapartite vault which is supported at intervals by bundles of slender columns with capitals which are simply adorned with plant or geometric motifs. This conforms with early Cistercian austerity and contrasts markedly with the rich panoply of life displayed by the cloister at Santes Creus (built two centuries later to replace an older one). The tombs of noble benefactors in the walls of this cloister are mostly in poor condition, having been repeatedly damaged by robbers over the centuries.

The hexagonal fountain or 'lavabo', looking like a little temple and sometimes referred to as '*la Glorieta*', is contemporary with the S wing of the cloister and echoes its open Romanesque style. Here the monks would have had their daily wash in natural spring water before entering the refectory, whose entrance stands opposite it.

There are three rooms leading off the N wing of the Cloister. The first door leads into a kitchen of monumental proportions with a hole in the wall through which food was passed to the refectory next door. The refectory itself, still in use by today's monks, is a simple and noble rectangular hall lit by twelve undecorated windows. There is a plain octagonal fountain at one end where, it seems the monks were again required to wash their hands, and a lectern from where the daily scriptural reading was (and still is) given during the otherwise silent meal. Fortunately for today's monks, a modern kitchen has been built behind the medieval one.

Next door is a small utilitarian room known as the '*Calefactorio*' where old and frail monks could come and warm themselves in front of the small open fireplace. All of these three rooms were completed by the early 13C.

The *Library*, off the NE corner of the Cloister, is rarely open to visitors, presumably because its priceless volumes and manuscripts are in daily use by the Cistercians.

At the E end of the Cloister, next to the Library, is the beautifully proportioned **Chapter House** with its 9-part vault supported on four delicate columns. Former abbots lie buried under the floor, and for the living there are wooden steps around the walls which serve as seats.

The **Church**, begun in 1170, is a masterpiece of the pure and unadorned architectural line so characteristic of the early Cistercians who believed that decorations, statues and paintings served only to distract the senses. The noble uncluttered interior of creamy golden stone, with plain cradle vault over the nave, is quite simply breathtaking.

The main altar is backed by a magnificent alabaster retablo by the 16C sculptor, *Damian Forment.* Divided horizontally into four sections, numbers 1 and 3 show scenes in the life of Christ, no. 2 shows the Virgin Mary and saints, and no. 4 shows the twelve Apostles flanking the central Christ figure.

A notable feature is the apse which is ringed by an ambulatory and has seven radiating chapels. This was probably not part of the original architectural design but was incorporated soon after construction began to accommodate the needs of the growing community for several altars to be in use simultaneously. Another afterthought was the atrium (known as the *Galilea*), built on to the W end in 1275. From here, guests (sometimes royal ones) were able to participate in services held inside the church which was originally reserved for the monks). Inside the Galilea is a striking Renaissance altar depicting the burial of Christ.

Most remarkable of all of are the **Tombs of the Kings and Queens of Aragon** which span the N and S transepts in the form of low arches. They were raised on columns thus so as to enable the monks to pass underneath, for they had complained bitterly about the disruption to their daily offices. The carving of the horizontal figures is very fine and guides enjoy recounting details of every single one. Notice particularly the recumbent figure of King James I who was a monk and had no wife, and so is shown twice, dressed as king and as monk. Others have their wives alongside, including Peter the Ceremonious who had three. Many of these tombs were desecrated in the 19C but have now been restored and in some cases redecorated by the contemporary sculptor, *Frederico Mares.* This church has great spirituality and equilibrium and it is sometimes possible to slip back in through the W door after the guided tour has ended, to appreciate these qualities in comparative silence.

From the *Choir* of the church you will be taken upstairs to the *Monks' Dormitory.* This is a spacious hall, 87m long and built over the Chapter House and Library, its massive arches specially designed to distribute the weight and not put undue pressure on the earlier rooms below. From here you can step out on to the roof of the Cloister for a rewarding overview of this wonderfully harmonious section of the building, the four dark cypresses standing in stark contrast against the mellow stonework. From here, too, you can see the hexagonal Cimborium which was built in 14C over the Crossing by the *Abbot Copons* (responsible with King Peter IV for the royal mausoleum). The Cimborium was later sealed off and is no longer visible from inside the church.

Also accessible from the upper cloister walk is the **Museum** which contains fragments of tombs which were desecrated and not restored, pieces of sculpture and other interesting relics, all well displayed and labelled. But the main significance is the hall itself with massive Gothic vault supported on four columns. It is apparent that there was once a floor at the base of the columns and that this was once two rooms. This was indeed so: the upper one was a dormitory for lay brothers, and the lower one was first their refectory and later a wine cellar. Restoration work is currently taking place here.

Returning from Poblet to the main route (N240), the next point of interest is the village of **Vimbodi**, which has a 12C parish church and a rather magnificent castle of *Riudabella* which was once a farm belonging to the Monastery at Poblet.

Vinaixa comes next with a 13C *Church of Sant Joan*. This has a good Romanesque door which it is difficult to stand back from and fully appreciate because later buildings are hard up against it. Perhaps this is just as well as the single round window over the doorway is irritatingly off centre. *Carrer Forn*, close by, is a street which exudes former elegance with some lovely monumental doorways and *Ajimez* windows still in place.

Excursion to Cave Paintings at El Cogul: Just beyond Vinaixa is a turning off left to *l'Albi*, worth a diversion in its own right. It has a tranquillity all its own with a lovely arcaded square (*Plaça de la Vellesa*) where old men sit around the ancient tree discussing better times, a picturesque *Carrer Mayor* leading off the *Plaça*, and a castle ruin on a hilltop.

From l'Albi you can take a direct route to *El Cogul*, through *Cervia de les Garrigues* and *Albages* (approximately 25km) or a more leisurely semi-circular drive through *El Vilosell, Bellaguarda, La Granadella* and then N-wards to *Albages* (about 62km). The dry stony land of *Les Garrigues* (meaning 'the thickets') is not without charm and produces the best olive oil in the Region as well as notable carved objects from its stone.

The cave is called *La Cova de Moro* and is located up a short track from the village of *El Cogul*. The paintings are known to be at least 12,000 years old and were discovered only in 1908. There are typical hunting scenes involving men, bison, deer and a giraffe, and there is an unforgettable one of women wearing what look like skirts dancing before a single naked man. The very devoted guide, who seems to sit outside every day except Sundays, will point out what he believes to be two different periods of painting, the one appearing spikier and older than the other. He will also explain that the paintings have been badly damaged by misguided attempts in the past to make them more visible by rubbing (even scrubbing) them with water; this to the point where some of the figures are barely discernible. Nevertheless this is a remarkable sight and it is a pleasure to be able to visit it with so little fuss. The wall is simply railing-ed off from the road, the rest of the cave presumably having long since disappeared.

From El Cogul you can go direct to Lleida on minor roads by way of *Aspa* and *Artesa de Lleida*, or simply return the way you have come, which will enable you to take in **Les Borgs Blanques** on the main Route (N240) to Lleida. This ancient, once walled, town has been an important oil producer for centuries and has what is probably the only oil museum in Catalonia (*Museu del Aceite*) full of old olive presses. The town retains an arcaded *Plaça Mayor* with an old palace as its town hall and some nice Renaissance façades. The parish church is neo-classical (late 18C) and one or two arches still standing in the Municipal Park are all that remain of a Baroque cloister of a Carmelite monastery. There is a weekly market every Tuesday which dates back to the 14C.

Lleida is 24km away.

ROUTE 4

LLEIDA

The provincial capital of Lleida is an intrinsically ugly town redeemed only by its superb medieval cathedral (*Seu Vella*) which dominates it from on high, and by a few isolated and (at time of writing) poorly preserved churches and civil buildings.

Lleida's origins go back a very long way indeed: to a warlike tribe of Iberians known as the *Ilergetes* who had a sizeable settlement on the hilltop (where the *Seu Vella* now stands) which was known as *Ilterda*. They successfully defended their hilltop and a large part of the surrounding plain against wave after wave of first Carthaginian and then Roman invaders until finally the superior might of the latter wore them down in 205BC. Even so they continued for some years with frequent and damaging rebellions under their legendary leaders, *Indibil* and *Mandonio* (whose statues stand outside the old town gate by the river).

When lasting peace was finally achieved the Romans expanded the town from the hilltop down on to the plain and called it *Ilerda*. They built an encircling wall and a bridge across the river Segre (of which the foundations still remain today under the 'old bridge' or *Pont vell*). They also built a *Via Augusta* parallel with the river (where today's *Carrer Mayor* runs). Around 417AD the town became a Christian diocese but was then sacked several times by successive Gothic invaders. Finally, in the mid-eighth century, the Moors arrived; they changed the name to *Lareda*, built a mosque on the hilltop and a castle (*la Zuda*) of which vestiges still remain around the *Seu*). The town expanded again and retained both a Christian and a Jewish sector (*el Romeu* and *la Cuirassa*). It was later regarded as a strategically important point on the northern limit of Moorish Spain and in 1023 became a small, independent kingdom or *taifa*, until it was 'liberated' in 1149 by the Christian Count of Barcelona, *Ramon Berenguer IV*. Thereafter it achieved steady growth and prosperity which led to the construction of the cathedral and of the first ever Catalan-Aragonese university.

Like many Catalan cities, Lleida suffered greatly in the various wars which followed, most notably in 1464 when the city walls and over 400 buildings were destroyed, in the War of Succession (1707) when virtually the whole of the upper part of the city around the *Seu* was destroyed, and in the Napoleonic War in 1810 when the French general, Suchet, blew up the Moorish castle and the area known as *La Magdalena* on the east side of the hill. Most of what we see today therefore is an untidy 19C and early 20C sprawl and what is left of the old city (*Casc Antic*) is concentrated in a small area next to the river to the south and west of the *Seu*.

The Seu is an unmitigated architectural joy as it stands lonely and indomitable, and witness to so much destruction around its walls over the years. After 241 years of damaging occupation by the military (when it was used as a barracks and ammunition depot until 1948) it is now being lovingly restored and is well set up for visitors, with plenty of information available, including photographs of 'then' and 'now'. It is possible to drive right up to it through the untidy waste land of half finished buildings, attempted gardens and ongoing excavations. Or to take a lift.

Construction of the *Seu* started in 1203 on the foundations of an earlier primitive church which in turn had been sited over the remains of the mosque immediately after its destruction in 1150. (There are traces of the first church in the N wing of the cloister). The main body of the *Seu* was completed in 75 years, and it is a splendid example of the transitional Romanesque-Gothic style with characteristic features from both periods. The cloister and octagonal tower were added a little later.

The interior consists of a nave and two aisles and five apses, four of which contain chapels; the third one along has particularly good vaulting and glorious bosses, and there are vestiges of paintings on the walls of the main apse, behind the high altar. The dome over the crossing is a Romanesque feature and its alabaster windows create a suffusion of golden light. Both transepts and the W end have rose windows which are of a later date and add to the general impression of space and lightness.

However it is the primitive and lively carving on the capitals throughout (and nowhere more so than in the cloister) which deserve particular attention. Another remarkable feature is the number of exceptionally fine monumental doors, best of these being the Door of the Annunciation (*Porta de l'Anunciata*) on the S side: Romanesque style, its archivolts and capitals are richly decorated with plant and animal designs, many of which have a definite Moorish flavour. The empty niches on either side once held statues of the Virgin Mary and the Angel Gabriel, which account for the name.

A similar Moorish influence can also be detected in the fine carvings on the Door of the Children (*Porta dels Fillols*), leading off the S aisle. The term 'Romanesque School of Lleida' is largely based on the distinctive features and fine proportions of these two doors, and is used to describe the same characteristics in churches throughout the Region.

A third remarkable door is that of the Apostles (*Porta dels Apostols*). Late 14C and Gothic in style, it stands at the W end, leading into the cloister, and there is a large empty platform outside from which to view it. Only the tympanum has remained intact and represents the *Last Judgement*. It is sad that all the apostle statues have been lost, though the presence of some fragments inside suggest they may be going to be restored or replaced at some time. There is no doubt that the lack of proper surround for this door is aesthetically unsatisfactory, especially when it is seen from a distance, and one can only imagine how it must originally have looked with a properly proportioned section of masonry above it instead of its cruelly truncated crown. To the right of the door is the 70m high octagonal tower, which probably served originally as a watch tower.

Inside the Apostles' Door (though now only accessible from inside the church), is the **Cloister**. Its unique siting at the W end is thought to relate to the position of the original mosque which would probably have had a forecourt there. The Cloister was completed in the late 14C and is predominantly Gothic in style with huge traceried windows (all different), those on the S side affording a panoramic view of the town below. They are interspersed with gargoyles some of which are highly amusing and some having floodlights attached to their foreheads. This is no closed inner cloister made for quiet contemplation, but rather a bold statement uniting the church with what was once the populace at its feet. The wing nearest the body of the church is the oldest and has some of the finest carved capitals of all – with human and bestial figures in extraordinary contorted shapes. There are three good doors from here giving access to the church, corresponding with the nave and two side aisles.

The Zuda: On the way up to the *Seu* you will have noticed a somewhat confusing miscellany of walls and fortifications and even a tower or two. These are the remains of the Moorish *Zuda* (Arabic: *el sudda* – castle) which in the 14C was converted into a royal castle for the Kings of Catalonia and was in fact the location for the momentous marriage of the Catalan *Ramon Berenguer IV* with Petronella of Aragon. It was blown up in 1812, and again in 1936, and of the central building itself but one wing remains today, with three towers, one of which has been restored recently.

There remains the old city (**Casc Antic**) below: compact, interesting in parts, but not worth a great deal of time. The best place to start your walking tour is at the end of the old bridge across the river (*Pont Vell*) where stands, appropriately enough, the statue of the two Iberian heroes, *Indibil and Mandonio*. Go through the neo-classical portal (*Arc del Pont*) and notice the tourist office actually inside the 15C arch on the right hand side, behind a glass front saying "Knock the door": it is particularly well supplied with helpful leaflets. Through the portal you come to a very lively and picturesque arcaded area known as *Els Porxos de Dalt y Els Porxos de Baix* which was an important shopping street in medieval times. To the left is the *Plaça de la Paeria* where stands the 13C town hall (*Paeria*) with its splendid Romanesque façade. The south front facing the river was added in 1868 and the whole building was restored in 1927. Inside is an archeological museum containing a 14C Code of the Constitution of Catalonia.

The *Carrer Mayor* leads out of *Plaça de la Paeria* (following the line of the Roman *Via Augusta*) and presents a stimulating mix of Modernist, neo-Gothic and Gothic buildings. On the left is *Plaça de San Francisco* which is dominated by the unlovely Baroque façade of the church of that name. A little way further down, on the right hand side, is the 15C *Chapel of St. James* (*Santiago*), also known as *Peu del Romeu*. Legend has it that St. James passed through Lleida on his journeys across northern Spain and, at this very point, got a thorn in his foot which angels came down from on high and removed. Carvings inside the church illustrate the legend.

At the end of Carrer Mayor, on the right, is the 'new' cathedral (*Seu Nova*), built during the 18C when the old one was taken over by the military. The Neo-classical façade has a clean and symmetrical look; the interior is undistinguished and much of the original decoration, including the carved wooden choir stalls, was destroyed during the Civil War. It does however contain an interesting collection of Flemish tapestries. Opposite the cathedral is the 15C *Hospital of Santa Maria* with forbidding exterior and charming Gothic-Renaissance style interior courtyard with staircase and galleries. Today the Hospital houses the Institute of Lleidan Studies and also the town's main archeological museum containing an abundance of Iberian, Roman and Paleo-Christian pieces found in the region.

The Church of St. Laurence (*Sant Llorenc*) stands in a maze of narrow streets behind the new cathedral and is sadly hemmed in by modern buildings but is worth seeking out. Its date – c.1230 – suggests it was built immediately after the final departure of the Moors and its style is basically Romanesque (central nave) with Gothic additions (two side aisles, doors and bell tower). This apparently neglected little church possesses some singular treasures including four magnificent Gothic retablos: the main one shows scenes in the life of St. Laurence; the others are dedicated to St. Ursula, St. Lucia and St. Peter (the last is gloriously simple by contrast and has the horizontal figure of the 'donor' above). The exterior of the church is dominated by an imposing octagonal tower which has a fine Gothic door next to it, protected by a portico.

The Romanesque Church of St. Martin (*Sant Marti*) stands at the end of the street of that name and presents a much purer, simpler line with single nave and a fine west door with archivolts and typical wall belfry. Like the *Seu Vella*, it was used by the army during the 18C and has now been replaced for purposes of worship by a modern church. It now houses the medieval sculpture section of the Diocesan Museum.

Finally – on a hilltop to the W of the city and accessible by way of the 'ring road' or *Passeig de Ronda* – is the unmistakable outline of the ruined *Castle of Gardeny*. The land was ceded to the Knights Templar by Ramon Berenguer IV in 1149 in recognition of their part in driving out the Moors, and the castle became one of their principal stations in Catalonia. They also built the austerely beautiful Church of *Santa Maria* alongside. Later both castle and church were handed over to the order of *Hospitallers* who remained in occupation until 1772. Incidentally this hilltop affords a magnificent view of the surrounding countryside.

LLEIDA TO LA SEU D'URGELL

A. Via Artesa de Segre. Excursion to Solsona

Balaguer lies 26km NE of Lleida and can be reached by either of the two roads running beside the River Segre. It sits astride the river, new town on one side, medieval quarter on the other. The latter is dominated by the huge buttressed *Colegiata de Santa Maria* (14C-16C) which was once used as a prison. It is worth driving up there if only for a splendid view over the jumble of roofs below, also a sight of the ruined 9C Moorish castle (*Castell Formos*) and of sections of the old town walls. (You may wish to avert your eyes from the high-rise blocks across the river).

A short wander through the old town can be very pleasant. The focal point is the huge arcaded square of the *Mercadal*, full of vegetable stalls and cafés. The Town Hall stands here and contains a small museum. A smaller prettier square (or rather triangle) is the *Plaça del Pou* and between the two is many a colourful street hung with window boxes and flower baskets and packed with every kind of shop.

Down by the river, at the end of the old bridge, is the 14C *Cloister of Sant Domenec* – a lonely survivor from the War of Succession which all but destroyed its church and monastery (much of which has now been rebuilt). Its still unblemished slender columns have a poignant beauty all their own. *Gaspar de Portola*, whose statue also stands at the end of the bridge, was a *conquistador* who discovered San Francisco Bay and was made Governor of California. He was born in Balaguer and the people of California donated the monument.

From Balaguer you can either proceed along the 1313 to *Artesa de Segre* (25km) via *Cubells*, or divert to *Agramunt*, then join the 240 to Artesa, adding an extra 15km to your route. The second option is recommended, and for this you need to turn right 3km out of Balaguer.

Agramunt was liberated from the Moors in 1070 and rapidly became a prosperous market town which at one time had its own coinage. Today the town walls are gone but many of the old streets remain. The most distinguished monument by far is the Romanesque *Church of Santa Maria* in

LLEIDA TO LA SEU D'URGELL

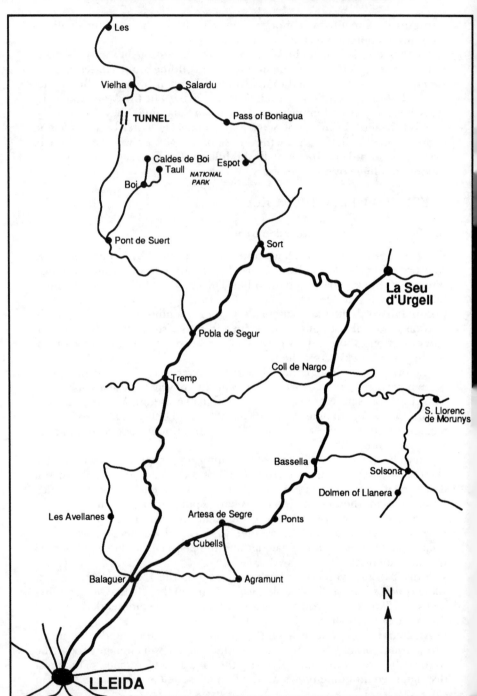

the centre of town, commenced soon after the liberation and completed in 1280. Its most striking feature is the magnificent door at the W end facing the square: typical of the Lleidan school with plant, animal and geometrical motifs all intertwined, it has eighteen archivolts supported by eighteen slender columns on each side. To anyone who had not already seen the door at Ripoll, it is quite simply breathtaking. The figures in the centre – the Virgin and Child, flanked by the Three Kings on the left and the Annunciation on the right – were donated by the Weavers' Guild in 1283. There is another door on the N side, of similar design but much smaller, and with two simple figures in the tympanum.

The church's three apses have typical blind arcading on the outside and columned windows with carved capitals; the bell tower is Gothic and was added in the 15C. The interior of the church is calm and very simple, with plain stone barrel roof and austere understated shapes throughout.

The 18C Town Hall stands alongside the church overlooking the square and presents a disciplined Baroque façade with important town shield above the main balcony. The square itself is the scene of a particularly lively market every Wednesday.

Cubells, (for those who took the direct route to Artesa or who are minded to turn back (6km) and have a look), is an ancient, once-walled town retaining still its 12C *Church of Santa Maria* which now serves as the front section of a larger neo-classical building. It is distinguished by another splendid door in the Lleidan style with six archivolts and typical carvings.

Artesa de Segre has one distinction only and that is its very fine arcaded square dominated by the mansion known as *La Granja* with Renaissance façade.

Continue along 1313 to **Ponts** (14km). This rather ugly town is now filling up so fast with industry and new buildings that it is no longer dominated by its famous hilltop, known as Les Forques, with scant remains of *Reconquest castle* and 11C *Church of St. Pere* on top. However, it is worth following the signpost to *La Collegiate* and driving for 10 minutes up a roughish track (past a cement works) to see the church. St. Pere has three circular apses, with fine Lombard decoration and paired windows, built in the form of a cross; also an octagonal central tower. Inside it is quite startlingly simple, with plain barrel roof which seems surprisingly high, tiny windows and a dome under the tower. Construction probably started c.1000, immediately after the Reconquest, and it would have stood at the foot of the castle. In the 16C it became part of a small Augustinian convent and the nuns added one or two connecting doors and also the Choir (which accounts for the Gothic touches here). In 1838 all the buildings were virtually completely destroyed during the Carlist wars. The church has recently been well restored.

As you pass the turning to Gaulter (2km after Ponts), notice the ruined 12C monastery church. This was blown up in the Civil War and only one or two arches, one apse and one wing of the cloister remain.

At *Bassella* (16km) a road turns off right to *Solsona*. Adventurous spirits with a day to spare will wish to take in Solsona and then do the highly recommended mountain road (tarmacked) from Solsona to *Sant Llorenc de Morunys* which offers unforgettable alpine views and has plenty of stopping places for admiring them. The road between Sant Llorenc and *Coll de Nargo* is also extremely picturesque. The diversion adds approximately 110km to the route. Scenically and culturally it is well worth it.

Solsona, Iberian *Setebona*, Roman *Setelix*, has a cathedral, one of the best museums in Catalonia, and an evocative old quarter. Old Solsona stands on the right bank of the river *Negre* beneath the ruins of its castle; it preserves sections of its 14C walls, three town gates, of which the neo-classical *Portal del Pont* is the most impressive, and a good scattering of noble mansions, including the Renaissance *Town Hall* on the *Plaça Mayor*. The town was recaptured from the Moors by Wilfred the Hairy in 886. It was made into a bishopric in the late 16C by Philip II as part of his stand against the rising tide of Protestantism.

The great bulky *Cathedral* lacks harmony and needs to be understood before it can be appreciated. It started life as a 12C Augustinian canonry; it was then almost completely rebuilt in the 15C and added to in the 18C. Surviving from the Romanesque period are the three round apses with typical Lombard arches (and some nice columns and capitals inside), the door to the cloister (of the 13C Lleida school), the bell tower, and a statue called *La Mare de Deu del Claustre*, carved in black stone and standing in its own chapel. A dominant feature of the exterior is the seven-sided Gothic apse with butresses which stands where the old transept would have been. The W facade of the cathedral is 18C with important Baroque doorway.

Closeby is the **Diocesan Museum** housed in the 18C Episcopal Palace. It is open from 10 to 13 and from 16 to 18 hours (16.30 to 19 in the summer) every day except Monday. A visit is highly recommended. After useful prehistoric and archaeological sections (including samples of Iberian 'writing' on stone), you pass into the Romanesque rooms. Here you are confronted by a screen showing slides of some 86 local churches of that period, each slide lighting up at the press of a button. This makes a good appetizer for what comes next: some outstanding frescoes which have been transferred here from their mother churches by the process known as *Strappo* (described on page 19). One of the most remarkable is the 12C painting of God with arms outstretched to touch the circle of Heaven, and with a phoenix above, symbolising immortality; this was taken from the apse of *Sant Quirze de Pedret* (near Berga). There is also a wealth of 12C altar frontals and some movingly simple madonnas of that time; also some notable fragments of stone work (capitals etc) saved from the original Solsona church.

The Gothic section contains some fine paintings and retablos and a single crucifix (14C) standing in the middle of a room, well lit and with its shadow reflected on the wall: possibly the loveliest exhibit of all.

The Museum, created only five years ago, is at time of writing labelled only in Catalan. The Director complains he has no money but intends one day to translate into Spanish, French and English. Such a notable collection of treasures deserves wider understanding.

An added curiosity – in the same building – is the Salt Museum, which is devoted to household objects such as chairs and tables, carved out of nearby Cardona's rock salt deposits.

Keen archaeologists will wish to extend the excursion further to take in the **Dolmen of Llanera**, one of the best preserved and most accessible megalithic burial chambers in Catalonia. Leave Solsona by *Portal del Pont* on the *Tora* (*Llobera de Solsones*) road. Go as far as *Hostal Nou*, take a left turn for 1km and then a track for 2.7km to *Vila*, which is a farm. The Dolmen is 5 minutes' walk from the farm along a line of telegraph poles (and there are some not very visible signposts to it). Prehistoric remains are said to abound in this part of the Region. Here at least is one which is relatively easy to track down, probably dating from around 2000BC. It has a single chamber with four huge stones on each side, one at the end and three on the top. Unlike other dolmens (*Cova d'en Daina* in particular, described in Route 7) these stones do not stand up from the ground but are still covered by a hump of soil with a passageway leading in. It is, incidentally the highest point around and well worth the time spent in finding it.

The lovely old town of **Sant Llorenc de Morunys** in a spectacular setting, still retains parts of the original walls, four of its gates, and enough narrow winding streets to make a short wander thoroughly enjoyable. Its 11C church with three apses decorated in Lombard style is somewhat hemmed in by later buildings. Inside, two highly ornate retablos stand in striking contrast with the severely simple Romanesque structure. Most remarkable of all is the S chapel with painted vault and walls and a richly coloured wood retablo which is the work of the 18C artist, *Josep Pujol.*

Walk up *Carrer de Esglesia* (Church Street) for a good view of the apse decoration and to reach an enchanting cloister: once part of the Benedictine monastery to which the church belonged. Only one or two of the original arches remain and bigger, rougher ones have been introduced later. There are hopes that the cloister will be restored. The town also has a small museum: *Museu de la Vall de Lora*, with an archeological section, Baroque sculpture and local crafts.

The 50km of mountain road from Sant Llorenc to *Coll de Nargo* is a delight, passing scattered farmhouses and, here and there, a ruined church or castle. The direct road from Bassella runs along the left bank of the *Oliana* reservoir, passing first through the small agricultural town of Oliana made prosperous by the fertile irrigated land surrounding it.

Coll de Nargo, at the northern end of the reservoir, is blessed by one of the most enchanting small churches in Catalonia: *San Clemente*, which stands alongside the Tremp road, on the edge of the village. The distinctive pre-Romanesque bell tower is wider at the base than it is at the top which adds greatly to its primitive charm; it has a horseshoe arch on each side, which betokens Moorish influence. The top storey with triple windows and blind arcading was added later, when the main body of the church was built, probably around 1000. There is similar arcading on the W end, on the apse and on the N wall, but the S wall is plain. Inside, the tower is open to the rest of the church and looks like a N transept. There appears at some time to have been a S aisle and the foundations of this are still visible.

If you continue up the Tremp road as far as *Les Masies* (3km) and then turn left along a rough track through pines and oaks which leads right down to the valley floor, you come to what must be the most remote church of all – that of *Santa Roma de Valldarques* with unusual round windows in its bell tower (about 10km in all). It is not so much the church as the whole sylvan setting which makes this short excursion magical: the sound of mountain streams, the smell of pines, the almost overwhelming forest, all so far removed from 20C bustle. There are derelict cottages beyond the church and even – just showing in the distance – the round tower of what could have been a castle. The forest has taken over what must once have been a complete village. (The road continues by way of *Isona* to Tremp, 58kms, and is beautiful all the way.

Back in Coll de Nargo, continue on up the 1313 to *Organya* (5km) which is best known for its unmistakeable (and rather ugly) round monument by the roadside which commemorates the discovery nearby of the earliest known document written in Catalan – 'the Sermons of Organya' (*Les Homilies d'Organya*). There is also a Romanesque church (*Santa Maria*) with a lovely original door of four archivolts and Lombard arches above. There are trefoils on the stones beneath the arches.

The road then passes through the Organya Gorge (*La Garganta de Organya*) with dramatic cliffs on either side and continues (24km from Organya village) to *La Seu d'Urgell.*

B. Via Sort. Excursions to Boi Valley and Aran Valley

For Lleida to Balageur, see page 127.

From Balaguer there are two alternative routes northwards which converge some 20km south of Tremp. The main N147 road follows the long, narrow *Camerassa* reservoir, at the N end of which are the hilltop ruins of *Sant Oisme* castle with its distinctive round tower. A short distance away is the 11C *Church of Sant Bartholomeu* with typical Romanesque apses in clover-leaf formation and a charming square bell tower. It is said, incidentally, that the mountains above Camerassa contain the largest concentration of birds of prey anywhere in Catalonia.

The second of the alternative routes, also very scenic but somewhat longer leaves the N end of Balaguer in a westerly direction towards *Les Avellanes* and *Ager*. It passes several ruined monasteries, notably that of *Santa Maria de Bellpuig de les Avellanes* with lovely 12C cloister and tombs of the *Counts of Urgell*. The small town of *Ager* (10km before the two roads converge) contains the sizeable ruins of the 11C church of *Sant Pere* and, in its parish church of Sant Vicenc, a very distinguished 3C Roman sarcophagus in marble with pagan scenes of nymphs and nerieads.

The N147 now crosses the wild and wonderful *Sierra De Montsec* and follows the *Terradets* reservoir to **Tremp**, a town preserving three towers of its ancient walls, one of which stands at the E end of the huge Gothic, buttressed parish church of *Santa Maria de Valldeflors*. The church was rebuilt in 17C after a fire two centuries earlier. Its greatest treasure is the gilded wooden statue of the Virgin which presides above the main altar and which, according to legend, was once discovered in a nearby valley covered in flowers; this was deemed a miracle since it happened in midwinter and so the church acquired its attactive name. Other interesting sights in the town include the 16C *Hospital de Pobres* (poor house) and the 17C *Casa de Cuitat* (town hall). Tremp stands at an important cross-roads and has a lively market on Mondays.

Salas de Pallars (10km N of Tremp and off the main road to the right) retains its medieval, now somewhat derelict, character with walls and three fortified gates. The parish church of *la Mare de Deu* stands on the highest point – where the castle once was, but the most attractive feature of the town is the charming arcaded square – *Plaça del Mercat* – with lovely views of narrow streets through its many arches. It was once the site of a renowned cattle fair first documented in the 14C.

Pobla de Segur (8 km) has always been an important centre of communications because of its situation at the confluence of the two rivers *Flamicell* and *Noguera*. It was made prosperous by its wood trade and became famous for its raftsmen (*raiers*) who skilfully navigated the timber along fast flowing rivers. A surge of building in the early 20C has given the town some rather striking Modernist houses, particularly the *Can Mauri* with its castellated tower and decorative tiles.

(From *Pobla de Segur* a road crosses the mountains northestwards to *Pont de Suert* and the *Boi valley* (see Excursion on page 127)).

The N 147 follows the *Noguera* river to Sort. The mountain scenery is spectacular and the river is much used for canoeing. On the way look out for the *Benedictine* monastery of *Santa Maria* at *Gerri de la Sal*. It was founded in 807 and was in use until 1835. Its imposing church dates from the mid-12C and still retains its nave and two aisles with massive columns, three apses with Lombard arches and a distinctive 3-tiered belfry. Notice also the salt flats at Gerri, evidence of a once thriving salt industry which brought prosperity to the town in medieval times. The once abundant springs of natural salt water finally disappeared under flood water in 1982 when the river was dammed higher up.

Sort has become something of a holiday centre, surrounded as it is by mountains offering ski-ing, fishing, hunting, canoeing and considerable opportunities for walking. There are good hotels both in town and in neighbouring villages which turn in to lively ski resorts in winter. Sort itself flows gently downhill from its 11C castle ruins towards the fast-flowing

Noguera river below, which has itself changed course. The castle, which retains three towers and a Gothic wall, was once a residence of the *Counts of Pallars Sobira*. Below it was the medieval town, of which only a few decrepit houses now remain immediately below the Gothic wall. Below that is the original *Carrer Mayor*, still a lively and important street with good shops and picturesque arches.

A walk along the *Carrer Mayor* is recommended: park the car in the main Plaça near the church. From the church steps there is a path up to the castle (or it is possible to scramble up one of the narrow alleys leading off the *Carrer Mayor* and come out immediately below the Gothic wall). The point of the castle visit is the view (which is even better if you climb to the top of one of the towers). Lift the eyes over the medieval roofs of the modern town far below, in which the old river bed shows as a grassy sward dotted now with trees and shrubs. When you regain the main road, notice the one or two Modernist houses along it, including the bank (*Caixa*).

The Route now requires a right hand turn from Sort towards *Adrall* (unless you are doing the Excursion to the Aran Valley in which case do not turn right). The mountain road (42km) is currently being upgraded. The few villages along it are on the whole sad and uncared for, but this may change with the upgrading of the road. At Adrall turn left for La Seu (7km).

At Castellciutat notice the impressive castle ruins which are now part of the grounds of a very expensive hotel (Hotel el Castell).

Excursion up the Boi Valley (Val de Boi)

From Pobla de Segur take the N260 (formerly C144) to Pont de Suert (22km). This is a picturesque mountain drive with high peaks appearing after Sarroca (6km). You cross the Perves Pass at 1530m, from which there is a nice view on to the village below.

Pont de Suert is a pleasant resort town with an unusual modern church. The separate bell tower and the W façade are arresting and brave but the rest is a disappointment.

Just after Pont de Suert turn right in to the **Val de Boi**. A visit to this blissful valley is a total experience. Not only does it offer what are generally considered to be the most important Pyrenean Romanesque churches in Catalonia (*Coll, Barruera, Durro, Erill la Vall, Boi* and *Taull*), but also a wealth of charming villages which are quite genuinely unspoilt and uncommercialised. This is probably because there are no large hotels along the valley's length and only one or two small guesthouses (*hostales*) and discreetly hidden away campsites.

The scenery and the churches get better and better as you move up the valley – some 20km from start to finish. The churches – all 12C – have fine bell towers with Lombard arching, which is often repeated around the nave and apses, and good doorways with archivolts and original iron work. A few, like Erill la Vall and Durro, have later additions such as porches. Most have had their frescoes taken to museums (which is good or bad depending on

Erill la Vall. Romanesque church of Sta. Eulalia, Boi Valley, Pallars Jussa.

where you happen to be at the time, but ultimately necessary for their conservation); the famous 'Stoning of St. Stephen' at Boi, for example, can be seen at the Museum of Catalan Art (*Museu d'Art de Catalunya*) at Montjuich, Barcelona.

Some villages are better than others. *Coll* (the first one as you enter the Valley) is reached by a narrow lane bordered with wild iris, broom and euphorbia and has superb mountain views. *Barruera* deserves special mention: it is on the valley bottom and right by the river which offers excellent fishing, good walking along an enticing tow path into the distance, a small camp site, and delicious homemade bread and cakes from the nearby *Forn de pa* (bakery). The church here however is not one of the best, having suffered from later additions. It is redeemed only by the mouldings on the W door and the arching on the central (original) apse.

Boi, after which the Valley is named, is one of the access points to the *National Park of Aigues Tortes* and has an information centre and Land Rovers available to take parties in. It also has one or two simple but very adequate *hostales* and a lovely church, still very much at the centre of village life, with one original apse and a fine belltower.

Far and away the most entrancing village is **Taull** with its steep slate roofs in perfect harmony with the dramatic mountain backdrop. This village has not one church but two, built by the same powerful family and both consecrated in the year 1123. The lower church is *San Clemente* and it is necessary to walk to the main Plaça in the upper part of the village (3 minutes) to find the key-holder. For this is a church which should be entered. The interior – nave and two aisles – is movingly simple with wooden roof and great cylindrical columns, without capitals, leaning quite severely outwards. In the chevet is a reproduction of the original painting which has been taken to the Museum of Catalan Art in Barcelona. But the exterior of the church is even more memorable, with its perfect proportions, its slender 6-storey bell tower, and the colour of the stone blending most beautifully into the setting, with no tell- tale variations to betoken later restoration. This is an aristocrat among churches.

The village runs in orderly disorder between its churches. There seems not to be one house which is out of step. The upper church is similar in structure with an equally fine bell tower and similar reproduction wall paintings inside, the originals also having gone to the Museum. It has a different key holder, also with a house on the Plaça, and which any passer-by will willingly identify. There are no hotels of any sort in this village but several small bars and restaurants and even a camp site below, kept well out of sight. It is fortunate that Taull is the furthest point along the Boi Valley. It really should be kept till last for anything coming afterwards is bound to seem dull by comparison. The road does not continue anyway except as far as *Caldes de Boi*, a modern spa with a bottling plant, an accommodation block and little charm.

Back in Pont de Suert, you have the choice of continuing northwards by way of the Vielha tunnel to the *Aran Valley* or returning to Pobla de Segur and rejoining the main Route.

Excursion from Sort to Les, through the Aran Valley

The **Aran Valley** is an exceptionally beautiful area of some 600km2, located between two arms of the Pyrenees. It is the only Pyrenean valley to have an Atlantic climate and it is surrounded by some of the highest peaks of all, giving rise to several great rivers such as the *Garonne*, the *Noguera Pallaresa* and the *Noguera Ribegorçana*. The people of the Aran Valley live mainly along the banks of the Garonne and still retain their Aranese language which is part of the linguistic family of the *Langue d'Oc*. It is not unlike Catalan, into which they will switch very easily; they also speak Castilian and sometimes French. Their cuisine is regarded by many as the best in Catalonia with strong French influences and many delicious slow- cooked stews designed to keep out the winter cold; their churches and the treasures within them are outstanding. In short, this uniquely rich and hidden corner of Catalonia should not be missed.

There are two possible approaches from the south. The first is via the Vielha tunnel from Pont de Suert and the N230 – a straightforward and all-season route which follows the boundary between Aragon and Catalonia. The second, which is described here, starts at Sort. It is a high and fairly demanding mountain road with breathtaking views, which follows the Garonne all the way to the French border and beyond. The highest point, and the start of the Aran Valley proper, is the *Pass of Boniagua* (2072m). From then on it is downhill all the way as far as Les, the last village before reaching France.

From Sort you pass through *Rialb de Noguera* with several modern hotels which serve the nearby ski resort of *Llesui*. The road follows the Pallaresa river over this point which is much valued along its length for fishing, particularly by the French who tend to pop over the border and stay at one of the many excellent *hostales* down by the river.

Shortly after *Escalo* you reach the left-hand turning to *Espot* (7km from main road). This pleasant village, full of hotels and restaurants for the ski stations (Super Espot) above it, is also one of only two access points to the **Aigues Tortes National Park**. This is one of nine National Parks in Spain (the only one in Catalonia) and a visit is highly recommended. The tarmacked road from Espot takes you 8 km to *Lake St. Maurici* which is ringed by jagged peaks and where immediately you feel as if you are in a different world. A number of tracks and paths start here and, for serious walkers, there are over-night shelters and a few camp sites.

This exceptionally beautiful Pyrenean region is by definition very wild and walkers are advised to discuss their proposed routes with wardens at Espot (or at Boi on the other side), especially if attempting to cross from one side to the other. Pines, silverbirches and beech trees cover the lower slopes and there are some fifty lakes and countless streams and waterfalls. The temptation to introduce hydro-electric projects must have been enormous and all credit is due first to the national government, and later to the autonomous government of Catalonia, for resisting it and protecting this remarkably accessible wilderness from anything which might damage it environmentally.

From *Esterri d'Aneu* (a little further along the main route) there is a tarmacked road to *Islil* – a recommended mini-excursion of some 11km alongside the very young Noguera Pallaresa. The point of this drive besides the beauty and the peace of it is the 10C *Monastery of St. Joan d'Islil* at *Gil* (about 8km along), with its wonderful door with archivolts and stylized capitals right by the road/river-side. In the upper frieze over the door are primitive low reliefs of Adam and Eve before and after the Fall (though 'after the Fall' is on the left and so appears to come first). There are also some remarkable carved human and animal heads. 3km further on is the *Church of Sant Lliser* in the village of *Alos d'Islil* which is similar in design, even to having Adam and Eve carvings either side of the door (the right way round this time). The door itself, however, is less fine.

Back at Esterri the road now begins to climb in earnest, its bends becoming ever tighter and the scale of the landscape ever grander up to the *Pass of Boniagua.* You are now in the comarca of *Aran Valley* and from here on the road goes downhill. It is narrow in places and not as well maintained as it might be, presumably because a far greater volume of traffic (including the lorries) uses the simpler Vielha Tunnel route.

The first point of interest, having passed through the ski resort of *Vaqueira* with its hotels and abundance of ski-lifts, is *Tredos.* This tiny village has a 12C church with free standing bell tower, arcaded apses and a S door with *Chrismon* (a monogram representing the first 2 letters of Christ's name in Greek); also a modest but excellent bar-restaurant called *Saburedu,* serving Aranese food and hiding so successfully in the centre of the village that it takes several sets of directions to get there. One of the most delicious dishes of this region is *Olla Aranese,* an aromatic bean stew containing chunks of black sausage and bacon and reminiscent of cassoulet. For some reason it is not usually regarded as the main course but comes between the salad and the charcoal-grilled meat. A very satisfying 4-course meal with wine and coffee to follow costs (at time of writing) the equivalent of £6 a head.

A few kilometres further on is the small hillside town of **Salardu**: its 17C houses around the *Plaça Mayor* and its transitional Romanesque-Gothic church are good but, compared with what is still to come, not outstanding. The church has a very heavy fortified Gothic bell tower, a pure Gothic window at the W end, and three Romanesque apses at the E end. The S door has four archivolts and is typical of the Lleida school. Inside is a fine 13C wooden figure of Christ nailed on a cross which has panels at its four extremities.

Gessa, which is 1.6km off the main road, is worth a quick look for its picturesque cobbled streets and its charming *Plaça Mayor* with medieval houses, one of which incorporates a cylindrical tower from the original walls. The 12C church has suffered some rather unfortunate 18C and 19C alterations.

The small town of **Arties** is one of the jewels of the region and, unlike Vielha, has retained its quintessential character and seems content to stay the size it is. It is not however unwelcoming to visitors and displays a helpful plan of available facilities and walks to historic sites outside its prestigious parador, dedicated to the conquistador, Gaspar de Portola who was born in Balaguer. The house, now tastefully enlarged, has a pyramid-topped tower and a tiny 17C chapel.

One can park near the parador, and walk across the bridge over the Garonne to the delightful *Plaça Ortau*. Then take the *Carrer Mayor* up to the church. On the way notice the 16C *House of Paulet* with grotesque faces either side of the window. The 12C parish Church of Santa Maria has a good N door with six archivolts and some artistic treasures inside including a fine baptismal font and some good retablos. In front of the church stands a circular tower which is all that remains of the medieval castle. On the opposite side of the main road from the parador is the *Chapel of Sant Joan*, transformed from Romanesque to Gothic in 1385 and recently restored. It is now a miniscule museum, open only from 17 to 20 hours on weekdays and from 11 to 14 hours at weekends.

Escunhau is a tiny stone village off the main road, 1km E of Vielha and worth a look for its quiet unspoilt charm. Its 12C church retains a particularly good door with a simple image of Christ in the tympanum. The two columns have small faces carved into the capitals, all of which, without exception, look very miserable. The rest of the church has been much altered through the centuries (which could be a reason for their misery).

Several of the old houses around the church double up as restaurants serving both Aranese and Catalan food. They are listed by the Tourist Office in Vielha and are beginning to become popular (deservedly); they tend either to be completely deserted or full to capacity, depending on the season, so it is best to book in advance.

Vielha, capital of the Aran Valley, stands at an altitude of 980m at the confluence of the rivers Garonne and Nere. Its strategic position at the meeting point of valleys, and therefore of roads, has given it an embattled history as wave after wave of invaders have seen it as a crucial prize to be won before continuing southwards. It is first mentioned in the history books as the meeting place of French and Catalan diplomats at the end of the 13 C when Philip (le Bel) of France occupied the area.

Today the only invaders are friendly tourists. In its glorious setting and with so much to offer, Vielha is a rewarding place either to pause a while or to be energetic, with fishing, canoeing, walking (along marked trails), mountaineering and ski- ing in season being just some of the many attractions on offer (full details from the Tourist Information Office near the church). It has many good hotels of all categories and a splendid modern parador, built in the local style, which stands on a hill on the edge of town and has one of the most magnificent mountain views anywhere in Catalonia, with valleys cutting their ways through dramatic massifs in every direction. There is a huge amount of building going on in and around the town, most of it in suitable local materials. Can all these new apartments and hotels really ever be filled? Given the attractions mentioned above and the remarkable accessibility of Vielha – from France, from Spain by way of the Vielha Tunnel and by this Route – the answer of course is *yes*.

Despite all this activity the old quarter, up the hill behind the Tourist Office, retains a quiet dignity and has some good 16C and 17C mansions, one of which contains the *Ethnology Museum* for the whole Aran Valley. It is recognisable by its polygonal tower and distinctive slate spire and is well worth a visit (open 11-13 and 17-20 hours each day).

Vielha's most distinguished historic site is the parish *Church of Saint Michael* (Sant Miqueu) which dates from the transitional Romanesque-Gothic (12C-13C) period. Notice particularly the doorway with typical Romanesque carved archivolts but pointed Gothic arches; the tympanum seems to predate the door and depicts St. Michael and the Flagellation of Christ. The bell tower, square at the base, octagonal above and crowned with a slender spire, was added in the 15C.

Treasures inside the church include a 12C baptismal font with floral decoration, a 15C retablo dedicated to St. Michael with 13C paintings, the central one of which shows him slaying the dragon. Then there is the famous *Christ of Mijaran* – an unforgettable wooden bust, very large and very moving, known to be part of a set of figures representing the Descent from the Cross (probably 12C). On the wall behind the figure is a helpful drawing which shows the complete group of figures as they would have been, with the hand (lower right on the torso) quite clearly belonging to someone helping to take the body down from the cross. The bust comes from the Augustinian *convent of Santa Maria de Mijaran* which is 1km to the N of Vielha, right by the road. The church has been many times destroyed, the last occasion being the Civil War, and is now being rebuilt again. It is thought to be the place where the Governer of the Valley once swore to respect its privileges, in the presence of all the local dignitaries.

There are several more villages to go before reaching the French border, some straddling the river, some perched on the hillside. The biggest is *Bossost* with a lively riverside high street and a notable 12C church which is well worth entering. Its two side aisles are separated from the nave by simple arches resting on massive round columns, and there are vestiges of some original painting on the walls of the main apse. Outside there is a good W door with tympanum of Christ in Majesty, a chessband design above, and primitive carved capitals. Despite its 4-storey bell tower, this church has a rather squat appearance.

Les has plenty of shops, hotels and restaurants to catch the cross-border trade and a 12C *Chapel of St. Blas* where the last Baron of Les is buried.

Really to get away from it all, continue a short way down to the road from Les towards France and take a right hand turn to *Canejan* (5km). This is an isolated village perched on (or rather clinging to) the mountain side so precariously that it seems from below that the weight of just one more car might well push it over. The main square has been thoughtfully provided with a mirador and there is even an Aranese restaurant opposite it (open only in high summer). The drive itself is memorable with spectacular views. It is not for the faint-hearted however.

This excursion ends at Les. You have a choice of returning the way you have come and rejoining the main Route at Sort, or leaving Vielha by the southern road through the tunnel, which leads to Pont de Suert. Or crossing into France.

ROUTE 5

LA SEU D'URGELL

La Seu d'Urgell, capital of the mountainous comarca of *Alt Urgell* (High Urgell) is best known for its cathedral, a surperb example of Italian-style Romanesque. The town itself, standing at the confluence of the rivers Segre and Valira, has been the seat of the bishops of Urgell since its liberation from the Moors in 820. But there are documents in existence which mention the diocese of *Orgel-lie* as early as 516 (in the time of the Visigoths).

The Middle Ages were a period of great prosperity for the town and under a treaty signed in 1278 the bishops of Urgell became joint rulers of Andorra, together with the Counts of Foix. (The bishops are still co-rulers of the Principality, but the President of France has taken over from the House of Foix). Over subsequent years the town's proximity to France and Andorra have brought it continuing affluence in times of peace but also devastating involvement in the countless wars which raged throughout history, particularly in the 19C.

Today a small and very charming medieval quarter survives with arcaded streets and a few elegant mansions, and on the end of this stands the **Cathedral of Santa Maria** which replaced two earlier churches. The rebuilding was in the hands of the Italian master architect, *Raimondo Lombardo* (whose name is still used to describe a style of decorative arcading to be found on late Romanesque churches throughout Catalonia). It was completed in 1175 and has been several times restored since then, notably in the 18C when Baroque touches were added, and again at the beginning of this century when it reverted to pure Romanesque.

The W façade is flanked by two octagonal towers and has three doors corresponding to the nave and two side aisles. It is also divided into three sections horizontally with the lowest one quite plain except for two noble lions over the main door. A narrow frieze of animals and humans divides this from the middle section which is also very simple. Above however, all is joyful, even frivolous, decoration with typical Lombard arches of almost lace-like delicacy rising to a pediment which in turn is lightly topped by a square belfry of red and white stone. A walk around the outside of the cathedral is recommended. The N front is quite severe by comparison with the W – almost like a fortress and with minimal ornamentation. The main apse (E), with an upper gallery of double-columned arches and three windows below, is an architectural gem – a Lombardian masterpiece. It can be admired in comfort from a seat in the garden below.

The interior is majestic with a nave and two aisles, a very long transept (with remains of wall paintings on the S end), and a dome over the crossing. The vault is supported on engaged columns scattered with tiny faces or rosettes (stone masons' marks) which give a feeling of lightness amongst so much awesome solemnity. Many of the interior arches are similarly decorated. There are five apses and four of them are interior. The effect of golden light playing through arches and windows of the central one on the main altar and the central 13C figure of the Virgin is near sublime.

The cloister is reached by way of the **Diocesan Museum** on the S side. This museum is a treasure house, containing a wonderful range of illuminated manuscripts, richly coloured retablos and other ecclesiastical objects. The most rare and valued exhibit is the 10C *Beatus de Liebana* manuscript of St. John's Commentary on the Apocalypse with seventy-nine miniatures. There is also a Papal bull in papyrus dating from 1001 given by the Pope Sylvestre II to the Bishop of Urgell, a charming shield-shaped fragment of a 16C wooden retablo depicting the Annunciation, three recognisably Arab vessels, and so on. It is all well worth the 200 peseta entrance fee.

On the other side of the Museum is the Cloister with three Romanesque galleries and one (E) rebuilt in the early 17C. The carved capitals are of the Roussillon school and one can only marvel at the imagination and humour of the medieval masons who have created such grotesque entwinements of plants, animals, musical instruments and human figures, many of the last in process of being devoured by monsters.

A door leads off the SE corner of the Cloister into the small *Church of St. Michael*, built in the early 11C by St. Ermangol (whose cape can be seen in the Museum) and therefore predating the present cathedral. It has the three apses and plain stone barrel vault typical of its period and the remains of a fresco on the W wall. The church gives on to a square overlooked by the elegant neo-classical Bishops' Palace which contains the cathedral's archives (in Latin and Catalan). Around the square are the delightfully colonnaded streets of the period: of particular charm is the herb and spice shop faced with picture tiles, and notice the grain measures at the top of *Carrer Mayor*, one dated 1379 and the other 1840 and looking almost exactly the same despite the passing of nearly five centuries. There is a splendid view to be had from the E end of the cathedral away down the valley towards the mountains.

Environs of La Seu d'Urgell

The Pyrenean scenery around La Seu d'Urgell is outstanding and the area is well provided with tracks and paths from which to admire it. There is excellent fishing, especially in the more remote streams, and canoeing has been developed on the rapids of the two major rivers – Segre and Valira. Cross country ski- ing is well organised in season and there are facilities for mountaineering on several challenging peaks such as the *Salonia* (2,789m). In Spring and Summer the valleys and lower slopes come alive with butterflies, lizards and grasshoppers and the wild flowers belie description. Above are the dark forests and tumbling streams and above that the bare craggy peaks. For those wishing to explore further afield there are several rough but driveable tracks for excursions and picnics, often with the added interest of a ruined church or two along the way. But it is the setting itself which counts.

One such is the drive to *Bescaran* by way of *Estaramiu* (30km there and back). Take the 1313 from La Seu in the direction of Puigcerda and, after roughly 5km, turn left for 10km of piste driving. Estarmariu has an 11C ruined apse, nave and one aisle, sadly almost completely taken over by brambles. Bescaran does have a handsome 6-storey bell tower and a village fitting neatly in to the head of the valley.

Another somewhat longer excursion leaves the 1313 just S of La Seu at *Castellcuitat*, passes through *Aravell* and on to *Castellbo* where there is a 13C Romanesque-Gothic *Church of Santa Maria* with some good iron work on the door. This large church was once a canonical college and was restored in 1955. The track continues through the tiny villages of *Carmeniu* and *Turbiasto* to the *Sanctuary of Sant Joan de l'Erm Nou* and nearby is the cross-country ski refuge of *La Basseta*. This is a wonderful place for walking (with or without skis), with paths in all directions through forests and across open fields with glorious views on all sides.

It remains only to say that the Pyrenean state of *Andorra* lies 9km N of La Seu d'Urgell. The main road follows the Valira valley and is exceptionally picturesque.

LA SEU D'URGELL TO RIPOLL

A. Via el Cadi tunnel and Pobla de Lillet

Take the 1313 road out of La Seu which follows the river Segre through dramatic mountain scenery. The excursion to *Estaramiu* (a left-hand turning about 5km out of La Seu) has already been described. Roughly 8km after the village of *Martinet* take a right-hand turn to *Bellver de Cerdanya*, a fortified hilltop village founded in 1225 and still retaining sections of its original walls. There is a charming arcaded *plaça* and an early Gothic (but much modified) *Church of Santa Maria*. (A more worthwhile and earlier church can be found at the village of *Tallo*, just S of *Bellver*, it is pure unspoilt 12C, a one-time Augustinian canonry, and its lovely 13C image of the Virgin has not been taken off to a museum but remains where it belongs).

Do not return to the 1313 but continue a few km along this road until it joins the N1411, at which point turn right and proceed through the 5km long *Tunel del Cadi* to **Baga**. Baga was founded in 1233 and retains many of its old buildings and portals. There is a particularly charming *Plaça Mayor* and significant sections of the original town walls still stand. Just outside the walls is the Gothic church (early 14C) of *Sant Esteve*, with some important pieces inside including a 10C Byzantine cross. Just below the old town, a medieval bridge (*Pont de la Vila*) crosses the *Bastareny* river.

Guardiola de Bergueda is the next town and 1km NE of it is the Benedictine *Monastery of Sant Llorence prop Baga*. Much of the monastery building has been modernised but the 11C church remains, albeit in poor condition. The most interesting feature is the enormous crypt under the church which is thought to have been an earlier church (the monastery was founded in 898). The crypt-church has a particularly good early Romanesque door with archivolts and the foundations of two apses have recently been discovered at the W end.

At Guardiola de Bergueda take the B402 road eastwards to **Pobla de Lillet** (9km). The road follows the *Llobregat* river and offers splendid scenery. Just before getting to Pobla, and up a very rough track, is the tiny circular *Church of San Miquel.* You come first to the ruins of an Augustinian monastery (on to which a rather scruffy farm has been built) and it is worth taking a moment to peer over the wall at the neglected remnants of what must once have been a fine cloister. The church stands opposite the farm on a hillock and, as there is no marked path, you just scramble for a few minutes up a hillside. The setting is glorious; the silence is broken only by distant cow bells and the occasional cock crow.

The church was built in the 12C and a close look reveals the skilled grading of the horizontal rows of stones needed to achieve the perfect spherical shape. There is an embedded apse and a south-facing door with classic Roman arch. The whole has been extremely well restored. It is probable that it was once the chapel serving the *Castle of Lillet*, the remains of which can just be discerned on the neighbouring hill.

LA SEU D'URGELL TO RIPOLL

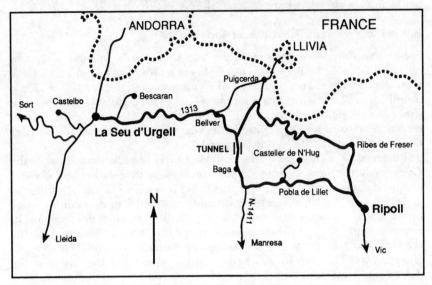

The village of Pobla de Lillet has an arcaded plaça and no less than four bridges across the river, including a Romanesque one (*Pont Vell*). The modern parish church proudly displays a Baroque door which was taken from the old *Church of Santa Maria* on the edge of the village.

From Pobla a short excursion up to the mountain village of **Castellar de N'Hug** (alt. 1,750m) is recommended (18km there and back), both for the scenery and for the enchanting 20 minute walk from the village up to the Source (*Fonts*) of the *Llobregat* river. It is hard to believe that the thin translucent springs gushing out of the rock face eventually become the sluggish and polluted mega-river S of Barcelona. Castellar is well provided with a variety of modest chalet-type hotels and restaurants and has something of the air of a holiday village about it.

As you return, notice – just below the village on the left- hand side of the descending road – the *Church of Sant Vincenc de Rus*. It is a perfect example of Romanesque simplicity. Built around 1105 it has a single nave, single apse with Lombard band, and small belfry. The buttresses on both sides were probably added later to prevent the walls from leaning any further outwards because of the weight of the vault.

The road now winds its way over the *Merolla Pass* (1,090m) 15km to the village of *Gombren*, founded in 1278 and retaining one or two medieval streets. Of interest is the dramatically sited *Sanctuary of Santa Maria de Mogrony* with the tiny Romanesque *Church of Sant Pere* on an outcrop of rock above it and connected by a rough stairway. The church stands on the site of a one-time castle which was first documented in 885.

145

A further 9km brings you past the little *Church of Sant Llorenç* with 11C belfry to *Campdevanol* where you join the N152. Ripoll is 4km to the S.

B. Via Puigcerda and Ribes (Excursion to Llivia)

Follow the previous route as far as the turn to *Bellver de Cerdanya*. Then stay on the 1313 which follows the upper Segre valley through some glorious mountain scenery. This is an area of forest and glacial lakes and is ideally suited for walking and cross country ski-ing. There are several mountain shelters (*refugios*) and the local tourist offices will provide maps and recommend routes. The river itself offers excellent trout fishing and licences can be had either at Bellver or Puigcerda.

Puigcerda was chosen by King Alfonso I in 1177 to be the capital of the *Cerdanya*. Since then, its strategic position close to the frontier and close to a natural corridor across the Pyrenees into France has caused it to suffer in countless wars. Today it is a rather sad and unattractive town retaining some of its walls and only the bell tower and fine marble doorway of its Romanesque – Gothic *Church of Santa Maria*; the rest was destroyed during the Civil War and has not been rebuilt. The monastery *Church of St. Dominic* (now the parish church) has been heavily rebuilt but has inside it the deteriorated remains of three original frescoes (on the N wall) and a striking modern stained glass window on the S side. Puigcerda is only 2km from the town of *Bourg Madame* in the French *Cerdagne*.

A visit to **Llivia**, 3km N of Puigcerda (but still in Spain) is recommended. Originally the Roman settlement of *Julia Lybica* and later capital of the Cerdanya until the foundation of Puigcerda, Lliva now forms a unique Spanish enclave in France and is reached by way of a 'neutral' road which runs within sight of the Customs post on the main road. The anomaly arose out of the fact that the *Treaty of the Pyrenees* in 1659 ceded thirty-three villages to France but not *Llivia* which had the title of *Villa* or town, and was therefore not included.

Llivia is now an important tourist centre with hotels and apartments serving ski resorts in the Spanish and French Pyrenees and Andorra. In its historic sector to the N there is a unique attraction in the form of the oldest **pharmacy** open to the public in the whole of Europe. This is the key exhibit of the little Municipal Museum opposite the church and probably dates from the 15C. There is a fascinating collection of 17C and 18C apothecary jars and painted wooden boxes, laboratory instruments, drugs, glass receptacles, weights and measures, and a book of recipes lying open on a desk. Other exhibits in the Museum include capitals from the 9C church which stood originally on the site of the present one, and Roman coins.

Between the Museum and the parish church stands the defensive tower of *Bernat de So*, named after the nobleman who bought the rights of the town in 1319. It now houses a permanent exhibition of dioramas of the flora of the region. Beyond the tower stands the transitional Gothic church which was fortified with three cylindrical corner towers in the 16C after the King of France had destroyed Llivia's castle in 1479. Llivia has an important music festival every August when choirs and orchestras from all over Europe come to perform in the parish church, said to have excellent acoustics.

The mountain road from Puigcerda to *Ribes* is wide and well graded as it climbs up and over the *Toses* Pass at 1800m, passing the ski resort of *Super Molina* on the way. What a pity about the single ugly building on the top, which is *hostal* and petrol station combined and makes no attempt to blend in with the wonderful mountain scenery around.

Ribes de Freser is an unremarkable town with a parish church which was rebuilt in the 1940s and now incorporates three Romanesque apses from the earlier church as side chapels. Of interest however are one or two Modernist buildings visible from the road between Ribes and Ripoll. Notice particularly the Hydroelectric *Centre-Montagut* in neo-Gothic style, and (better still) the *Balneario-Montagut* with colourful glazed balconies.

ROUTE 6

RIPOLL

The small Pyrenean town of **Ripoll** stands at a height of 2,400m in a valley created by two major rivers, the *Ter* and the *Freser*. Its mountainous location made it a natural refuge for Christianity during the Reconquest and the Benedictine *Monastery of Santa Maria*, around which the town originally grew, played a very important role in revitalising and sustaining the Christian spirit throughout northern Catalonia.

The monastery was founded in 879 by the Catalan Count, Wilfred the Hairy (*Guifre el Velloso*), but the inspirational force behind its greatness belonged to *Abbot Oliva* who built the church in 1032 and turned the monastery into a centre of learning and creativity which generated hope and energy throughout a huge and hitherto under-populated area. Oliva was one of Catalonia's great men: the son of a *Count of Besalu*, he was both *Abbot of Ripoll* and *Bishop of Vic* (38km to the south in the same valley). Deeply religious, intellectual and essentially a pragmatic man, he set about energetically organising the entire life of the surrounding region which had been backward and impoverished for so long. This he did by setting up markets and small industries and showing people how they could make use of the God-given resources around them. Under his guidance the monastery became a great centre of learning and its library was renowned throughout Europe. Above all he made it a centre of spirituality and truth and encouraged the creation of churches and smaller monasteries throughout the region. He was the personification of Romanesque – in the purest sense of the word.

Today little is left of the original 5-naved basilica Church of Santa Maria except the truly magnificent **W door**, the lower sections of both towers and part of the Cloister. Inestimable damage was done by an earthquake in 1428 and a fire in 1835 destroyed a great deal more. Major rebuilding according to old drawings was carried out between 1886 and 1893 and the main body of the cruciform church, the seven apses, the cimborium and the tops of both towers, date from this period. At the same time a wise decision was taken to build a glazed 'porch' in front of the W door to protect the already decaying stone work from further weathering. The door – in the form of a triumphal arch with horizontal bands of biblical and allegorical figures – is considered by many to be the finest example of Romanesque sculpture anywhere in Catalonia. Considering that it dates from the mid-12C (completed by Oliva's successors) it is in remarkably good condition and this is partly due to the narrow, stone overhang at the top of the door, added in the late 13C. Best preserved of all are the figures in the archivolts which are doubly protected.

It adds greatly to one's enjoyment of these superbly executed biblical scenes to be able to identify them:-

The central figure in the top row is God the Father, with angels on either side; on the left is a winged man (symbol of St. Matthew) and on the right an eagle (symbol of St. John). The other two evangelical symbols appear below: a lion (St. Mark) and a bull (St. Luke) and beside them are the twenty-four elders of the Apocalypse. Left of the door are scenes from the Book of Kings: moving downwards, these are (first row) Elijah ascending to Heaven and four scenes involving David and Solomon; (second row) David with musicians, the Ark of the Covenant, the plague of Zion and God speaking to David. Below that is another representation of David with musicians and, finally, a lively scene of monsters fighting.

Scenes on the right of the door represent stories from the Book of Exodus. These are (from below the symbol of St. Luke): Moses striking the rock and bringing forth water; God's people guided by a flight of quail; manna falling from Heaven and (round the corner) the crossing of the Red Sea. In the row below is Moses standing with his arms raised in victory, and cavalry in battle. The five sadly deteriorated figures below are believed to be David with four of his people. At the bottom (as on the left) are huge figures of monsters fighting.

Badly damaged statues of St. Peter and St. Paul stand on either side of the doorway. The decorations in the archivolts themselves are however in excellent condition still: on the outer one are roundels containing animal and plant motifs, next are scenes from the lives of St. Peter and St. Paul, still astonishingly sharp in outline. Inside again are scenes from the lives of Jonah and Daniel; the innermost arch has the Christ figure at the centre and scenes in the lives of Cain and Abel to right and left. On the two columns supporting the innermost archivolt are the twelve months of the year.

The interior of the church is pleasantly harmonious but rather dark. The stone is a cold grey colour, unlike the soft creamy gold of the W portal, and the lower windows are of alabaster. The only decorations in the main body of the church are the carved capitals on the massive columns separating the double aisles, and the vault is quite magnificently simple. In the N transept is the tomb of Wilfred the Hairy marked by a 19C monument; but the real treasure is to be found in the S transept – the original carved sepulchre of *Ramon Berenguer III* set on eight splendid columns, with wonderfully detailed capitals.

The *Cloister* retains one original wing (dated c.1170) which is the one nearest the church. The rest followed in the 15C and the upper storey was added a century later. Predictably, the carved capitals are a joy and worth examining closely for the imaginative and sometimes gruesome carvings of the medieval sculptors; and displayed around the gallery walls are miscellaneous pieces surviving from the original church such as bosses and stone retablos.

Next door to the church is a rewarding and unusual **Museum** in the heart of which stands an authentic 17C forge. During the 16C, 17C and 18C the Ripoll area was renowned throughout much of Europe, London included, for the superb qualilty of its firearms and also its metal nails. It was only when modern technology arrived in the 19C that the local industry died and was replaced in Ripoll by textiles. The museum is a lot more extensive than would at first appear: there are countless rooms containing diverse collections of local artefacts and a fascinating array of sheep-rearing paraphernalia including massive collars worn by sheepdogs to keep off the wolves.

Apart from the monastery church and the museum, there is not much else to see in Ripoll except for an ancient plaça and some old mansions. There are also a few modernist and neo-classical buildings scattered around, symbols of the prosperity created by the textile industry.

RIPOLL TO FIGUERES VIA BESALU

RIPOLL TO FIGUERES - RIPOLL TO GIRONA

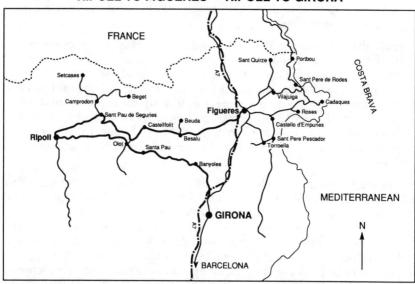

Take the 151 road 10km north-eastwards to **Sant Joan de les Abadesses**. This small town grew around a Benedictine nunnery founded, like Santa Maria at Ripoll, by Wilfred the Hairy who installed his daughter Emma there as the first Abbess. History relates that scandalous behaviour occurred during the time of one of Emma's successors, the *Abbess Ingilberga*; this was duly reported to the Pope by the neighbouring *Count of Besalu* and in 1017 the nuns were sent away in disgrace. Their place was taken by a religious community led by the son of the said Count who was, conveniently enough, the *Bishop of Besalu*.

150

The **Church** was founded in 1150. It takes the form of a Greek cross and has five apses, three at the E end and one in each transept. The apses are decorated both inside and out with arches and columns of great delicacy. Originally there was an ambulatory but this was destroyed by an earthquake and local masons replaced it with a series of columns which form a deeply satisfying and harmonious pattern of shapes around the crossing.

The church is celebrated for the unusual group of seven polychrome wood figures, dated about 1250, in the central apse. This striking rendition of the Descent from the Cross is remarkable for its simplicity, for its realistic action (it appears that Christ's right arm has just been removed from the cross), for the expressive faces (especially that of the Virgin) and for the portrayal in detail of two additional figures – the crucified thieves on either side of Christ. The monument is also known as the '*the Holy Mistery*' (*el Santissim Misteri*) because in the 15C an unbroken host (wafer used in celebrating Mass) was found in the carved head of Christ.

There is a small Gothic cloister with slender columns and the remains of an earlier Romanesque one have been uncovered in one of the galleries. Next door to the church, the 15C *Abbot's palace* has recently been restored. It has a tiny double cloister of just two arches on each side which is quite delightful. Two minutes' walk from the church, downhill on the right, is the ruined *Sant Joanipol* (once the parish church); so ruined in fact that the centre section has disappeared and only the Romanesque W door and the trefoil apse at the E end remain. If nothing else, it offers the visitor a glimpse of a medieval stone wall in cross section.

From *Sant Pau de Seguries* (8km along the Route from *Sant Joan*) an EXCURSION of some 45 km is recommended; it takes in three (or even four) Romanesque churches with villages, and some gloriously remote mountain scenery. In winter this is a region beloved by skiers; in summer it is virtually deserted. From Sant Pau take the C151 to *Camprodon* (6km): a rather plain town at the confluence of the rivers *Ter* and *Ritort*, which grew at the feet of the 10C *Monastery of Sant Pere*. Of some distinction is the 'new' bridge (*Pont Nou*) which was built across the Ter in the 14C and stands next to a defensive tower which is all that remains of the town walls. Camprodon, incidentally, is the birthplace of the composer, *Albeniz* (1861-1909).

Then take the road (which follows the Ter) north-westwards 3km to the tiny unspoilt village of *Llanars*. In the middle is the simple 12C *Church of St. Stephen* with minimal decoration outside (no Lombard bands) and a good doorway with columns and carved capitals. The real treasure inside is the polychrome wood altarfront with central painting of Christ and four scenes in the life of St. Stephen. How refreshing to find it in place and not removed to a museum.

The road actually continues as far as the ski station of *Vallter*, very near the French border; the scenery is wonderful; the traditional wooden houses, particularly in *Setcases*, have been replaced by modern apartment blocks, which probably look less ugly in the snow. The recommended route for this excursion however is to go back to Camprodon, then northwards on the C151; very shortly after joining the 151 turn right for *Rocabruna* and *Beget*. This road has some idyllic picnic spots with mountain streams and flower-filled meadows in abundance. Rocabruna village is more memorable for its setting than for its 12C church, which nevertheless does have some fine ironwork on the door. The drive from Rocabruna to Beget is only about 6km but seems longer because the road is single track and very lonely. Beget and its 12C church are however worth the effort. The church has a charming 4-storey bell tower and an exterior in complete harmony with its natural setting. Inside, harmony is less apparent and one is immediately struck by the later addition of several rather heavy and dominating Gothic and Baroque retablos and paintings which unfortunately distract the eye from the lovely 12C Christ in Majesty carved in wood over the altar. It is rare to see the crucified Christ portrayed wearing a robe, and the treatment of the beard and tendrils of hair falling over the shoulders is also unusual. The village itself is rewarding to explore and has two restaurants and a *hostal*.

The best way back to Sant Pau is to go back the way you have come, perhaps taking in the village of *Mollo* (with another gem of a church) 3km to the N of the turning on to the C151.

At *Sant Pau de Seguries* take the 153 for approximately 21km to la *Canya de Dalt* where there is a turning left for *Sant Joan les Fonts* and *Castellfollit de la Roca* (4km). Sant Joan is named after its 12C Monastery whose church has good apse decoration, and relief sculptures on the font; also of interest here is the fortified mansion of about the same date, called *Casa Juvinya*, which is said to be one of the best preserved civil monuments from the Romanesque period in Spain. Castellfollit stands dramatically on a spur of black basalt overlooking the confluence of the rivers *Fluvia* and *Turonell*. The extraordinary rock formation is the result of volcanic upheavals in prehistoric times which gave rise to *La Garrotxa* region (described on page 161) which also includes *La Canya* and *Saint Joan*. Most of the village of Castellfollit has been rebuilt since it was almost totally destroyed by earthquakes in the 15C. Here you join the 150 and continue approximately 13km for Besalu.

BESALU is an unusually harmonious and well preserved small town with a number of outstanding Romanesque and Gothic monuments set in medieval streets and picturesque squares. Founded by the Romans at an intersection of two of their roads, Besalu was later occupied by both Visigoths and Arabs. Reconquered by the Christians in the 9C it quickly became very prosperous and was until 1111 the capital of an independent county extending from the Ter valley as far E as *Figueres*. During this time it acquired fortified walls and a castle, of which there are scant remains on *Tallaferro Street* which runs off the fine porticoed principal square – *Plaça de la Llibertad*.

Arguably the loveliest monument of all is the 12C **Church of Sant Pere**, the only surviving part of a Benedictine monastery which was destroyed in the early 19C. It is immediately recognisable by the sculpted lions which flank the small and perfect window above the W door. Very few churches strike you as purely beautiful the moment you enter, but this could be one of those few. It is imperative to go inside. The interior is simple – a nave with two aisles marked by massive stone piers. Then there are four pairs of columns around the apse with fine capitals and arches above, the whole showing a distinct Italian influence. There is no other decoration.

Outside the church, off one corner of its huge square (*El Prat de Sant Pere*), is the *Cornella House*: a medieval noble residence with a nice 3-storey courtyard inside. This is one of several fine mansions to have survived, albeit with later additions. The square, incidentally, used to be a cemetery and this accounts for its size since nothing can be built on top of it. Next door to the church is the original façade of the hospital *Church of Sant Julia* with an exceptional door whose capitals show beasts consuming humans. The rest of the church has been much restored and is disappointing.

There are two other churches of some interest: one is *San Vincente*, in transitional Romanesque-Gothic style (probably imposed upon an earlier 10C structure) with a side door reminiscent of the one at Ripoll's monastery, and a Gothic rose window; the other church is *Santa Maria*, which once formed part of Besalu's castle and was the See of a bishopric created here in 1017. It is now a sad ruin with only three apses, part of the transept and some columns surviving.

Besalu is justly proud of its exceptionally fine angled **bridge** over the river Fluvia. It has seven arches and a battlemented tower with portcullis in the middle and probably dates from the early 12C, but has been many times restored. A very good overall view of it is had from the modern bridge alongside; a feel of it, and the fortified town it protected, can be had by walking across to the other side. In the same street as the bridge, there is a *Mikwah*, or Jewish ritual bath, which probably dates from 13C and would have formed part of a synagogue in the Jewish quarter by the river. It is being excavated at time of writing and is said to be unique in all Spain.

Besalu clearly deserves a half day of your time. Should you wish to stay longer, there is the very acceptable *Fonda* and Restaurant *Siques – Cal Parent* within easy walking distance of all the sites described.

From Besalu you may wish to visit nearby *Palera* and *Beuda*: take a left turn off the Figueres road immediately outside Besalu. *Sant Sepulcre de Palera* is down a roughish track 1km off the road, set in pinewoods and thickets of wild rosemary. It is an 11C Benedictine priory with a squat, heavy church. The austere priory was once a meeting place for a local chapter of knights of the *Holy Sepulchre*. Now it is occupied by a caretaker who is happy to show you round it and the farm alongside. There is even a little bar with dust-covered leaflets written for the occasional visitor who ventures this far off the beaten track. *Beuda* (5km in all from Besalu) is just big enough to have a *Plaça Mayor* wherein stands its 12C church with three apses, a good doorway with scrolled ironwork, a carved font in the SW corner and some very ancient marble tombstones in the floor of the nave. For peace and perfect mountain setting, these two hamlets would be hard to beat.

Back on the 260 road, **FIGUERES** lies 27km, to the NE, by way of *Navata* whose 12C church has a good door with archivolts, ironwork and tympanum intact. The name Figueres derives from the Visigothic word *Ficaris*. Before that, the Romans called it *Juncaria* and built the *Via Augusta* through it. Were it not for the fact that the surrealist painter, *Salvador Dali*, was born in Figueres in 1904, it is doubtful whether today's visitor would wish to stay there very long, or even at all. The medieval town (*Villa Vella*), once under the jurisdiction of the Counts of Besalu, and later made an independent city for the purpose of resisting those same counts, is now all but swamped by industry and tasteless residential development. Only the large 14C *Parish Church of Sant Pere* remains from the past, sustaining its Gothic style throughout despite major rebuilding after the civil war. One section of the original city wall also remains nearby, known as the *Torre Gorgot*.

However ... all is forgiven because the splendid **Dali Museum** is here. And should not on any account be missed. Whatever your preconceptions about Dali, his life-style and his work, it is impossible not to find some evidence within that the man was a genius. On arrival, most people stare at the outside of the building in sheer incredulity, for on the roof, on the very edge as if waiting to be tipped off, are what can only be described as giant eggs; there are also loaves of bread; it is all great fun. This building was once the municipal theatre and was converted to a museum in 1974 – with design inside and out by Dali himself.

Inside, one is struck by the number of different media that Dali tried – from pink plaster to driftwood, from dressmakers' dummies to chunks of rock; indeed, some of his most satisfying creations are huge primeval human figures made out of lichen-covered rocks and pieces of wood. The decor is sometimes outrageous: the ceiling of the main hall is painted with two huge pairs of feet – his own and his wife, Gala's – as if both were dropping in from above; the Mae West room is a joke in the worst possible taste; one's tolerance level is being manipulated throughout. And yet, despite all this, it is impossible to deny that his draughtmanship is often sublime, his paintings are powerful and sometimes deeply moving. The world would have been a poorer place without him.

Not far from the Dali Museum is the pleasant, tree-lined *Rambla* which displays a monument to the 19C inventor of the submarine, *Narcis Monturiol*, who was born here. Also on the Rambla is a more traditional museum – *Museu del Emporda* – with local paintings and archaeology.

Just outside town, on the NW corner, is the hilltop fortress of *Castell Sant Ferran*, built in 18C. It has walls in the form of a star (known as the *Vauban* style) which give maximum visibility from inside. It has to be said that the fortress is hardly worth visiting today; it is used as an army barracks and visitors are not welcome inside; moreover the view of greater Figueres from the perimeter walls merely confirms one's initial impression that it is essentially ugly.

Two EXCURSIONS follow, which can obviously be combined, extended or shortened depending on the time available. The first takes in the *Monastery of Sant Pere de Rodes* and the seaside resorts of *Cadaques* and *Roses*; the second explores part of the *Emporda Natural Park* and adds on two Romanesque churches for good measure.

1. Figueres – Vilabertran – Peralada – (Sant Quirze de Colera), – Sant Pere de Rodes – Cadaques – Roses – Castello d'Empurias – Figueres

Vilabertran is only 3km out of Figueres on the *Portbou* road (N252). Its late 11C *Church of Santa Maria* was part of an Augustinian canonry and has an exceptionally fine 3-storey bell tower with typical Lombard arcading and paired windows. The simple interior of the church (where King James II married Blanca d'Anjou in 13C) has been much restored though the floor appears to be original. Its proudest possession is a magnificent 14C processional cross in gold with precious stones and enamelled medallions, which stands in the N chapel. The small restored cloister on the S side has delicate paired columns and carved capitals and offers the best view of the bell tower). Nearby, on the *Plaça del Monestir*, is a 15C abbey built in rough golden stone. Its façade is quietly memorable with pairs and triplets of windows separated by slender columns and arranged in no particular order. Inside is a ruined courtyard with castellated fortress walls.

From Vilabertran continue to *Perelada* distinguished only by its 17C palace (once a Gothic castle) with two ornate round towers. It is now a casino and is not accessible to the casual visitor. Go on to *Garriguella* (6km) where you may be tempted by a diversion off the main route. If so, turn left to *Vilamaniscle* (4km) and then continue over rough track to *Sant Quirze de Colera*, which is close to the French border. It takes time (at least half an hour), determination and a strong vehicle to get there, but the reward is the sudden appearance (just as you are about to give up) of the most remote church and monastery ruin ever, set in wild and wonderful Pyrenean scenery. Built by the Benedictines at the head of the valley (for defensive purposes), the monastery is known to have existed in 927. The church, extended and reconsecrated in 1123, must have been extensive and one can see traces of Lombard arching on two out of three apses, as well as vestiges of a simple cloister. Alas, the church is now used as a barn and the gnarled ruins of the monastery dependencies are clearly abandoned and will probably remain so. The effect, on a stormy day, is quite eerie.

Back at Garriguella, make now for *Vilajuiga* where you will turn left for *Sant Pere de Rodes*. Before doing this, you may be tempted (again!) to continue 5km to *Palau Saverdera* which has an 11C church of striking Romanesque simplicity with huge primitive arches supported on squat round pillars. It has recently been restored and is once more in use as a parish church.

The 8km mountain drive from Vilajuiga to the deservedly popular monument of **Sant Pere de Rodes** is quite simply spectacular. At the end stand the substantial remains of what must be one of the most dramatically sited monasteries of all time. Perched on a high cliff, Sant Pere de Rodes overlooks the *Cape of the Cross* (*Cap de Creus*) on the one hand and the Mediterranean coastline sweeping up towards France on the other. It is dear to the heart of all Catalans because it represents one of the earliest Christian communities in the Region and because, architecturally speaking, it is perceived as the cradle of the Catalan Romanesque style. It is much visited, especially at weekends. Flat shoes are a must since there is a 10-minute walk uphill from the car park and the floor of the building itself is very uneven.

The first document to mention Sant Pere de Rodes is dated 879, but even then the monastery was described as 'ancient'. There is much speculation as to its origins; some historians firmly believe it was built on the site of a Greek temple dedicated to *Aphrodite*. This is based on actual accounts and maps made by travellers of the 3C and 4C AD referring to such a temple standing on a rugged cliff 'jutting out more than any other'. The theory is strengthened by two significant facts: firstly the discovery of foundations extending beyond the perimeter of the present building and suggesting a much larger edifice at some time; and secondly the excavation of several obviously pagan carvings, some of which have since been integrated in the Christian walls.

Much more dubious is the legend, said to originate from the transcription of old parchments by a 17C Catalan scholar, that parts of the bodies of St. Peter the Exorcist (son of St. Peter the Apostle) and of three contemporary martyrs lie under the crypt. The story tells that in the early 9C some priests were told by Pope Boniface IV to take these holy relics to a safe place, away from the threat of desecration by invaders. They sailed westwards and landed on the beach of *Cap de Creus*, hid the sacred objects in a cave on the cliff top, sealed the cave and returned to Rome. Months later, the danger having passed, they returned and could not find their hiding place. Deeply troubled, they remained and built a simple church over the most likely place; the relics were eventually discovered and properly buried in the crypt underneath the altar. This legend certainly explains the dedication of the monastery.

What is certain is that by the early 10C the building had already suffered considerable damage from Moors and Franks and that the monks had come under the control of various powerful and disputing abbots and were leading an unsettled and unhappy existence. Fortunately, in 934, the monastery was declared independent and directly answerable to Rome and – by command of *King Louis IV* of France – it was rebuilt for the Benedictines and greatly enriched under the direction of a wealthy nobleman – *Count Tassi*. (One of the Count's sons was subsequently made the new resident abbot).

At the same time as the monastery was being regenerated, a local community was forming around it, many of whose members would have been in the service of the monks. The most notable evidence of this today is the tiny ruined *Church of Santa Elena,* which is visible in silhouette from afar and stands above the monastery, accessible by a steepish path. In the simplest possible pre- Romanesque tradition it consists of a single nave and transept and very typical primitive belfry (atop a fortified tower). It faces on to what was undoubtedly the main square of the village of *Santes Creus de Rodes* and two gateways remain of its fortifications; there are also foundations of several cottages (which probably numbered around thirty). Further protection was given by the *Castle of San Salvador,* sections of whose substantial walls still remain today in remarkably good condition. This was built on the highest point of all (above the monastery and village) from which it was possible to spot any potential enemy approaching, by sea or by land, pirate or Moor, and protect not just the community below but the whole of the vulnerable hinterland of the *Emporda* Plain.

The fortunes of the monastery continued outwardly to improve. Much of the surrounding region came under its domination and its fame spread far and wide, to the extent that – in the 13C – the nobility lavished it with gifts and the Pope advised the faithful that they could gain indulgence by making pilgrimages to Sant Pere. All was not well within the monastery however. Too much attention and renown was beginning to turn the heads of the monks, many of whom had been living outside the monastery for some time with their own servants and indulging in practices which were certainly not permitted under the *Rule of St. Benedict.* By the beginning of the 14C local feudal lords, long jealous of the monastery's domination, were taking advantage of the growing demoralisation and helping themselves to land and possessions with the greatest of ease. Even worse, the French began to step up their raids across the Pyrenees and discovered they could plunder Sant Pere's legendary treasures virtually without opposition. These included a very beautiful 11C illuminated bible almost certainly produced by the monks in their scriptorium; its presence today in the National Library of Paris is a poignant reminder to the Catalans of this period of monastic decadence.

The end of Sant Pere took a surprisingly long time in coming, as a few monks stoically hung on. By 1730 eight still remained (though the village above had long since been abandoned). In 1798 those who were still alive moved out to *Vila-Sacra* nearby. All remaining objects of value were removed by local people and the building remained, a stark and ruined shell, until in 1935 the *Generalitat* of Catalonia undertook the very first efforts at restoration. The work was interrupted by the Civil War and was recommenced in 1973.

So what is there to see today? There is the very fine church with a nave and two side aisles, transept, three apses, crypt and cloister; there are three towers and sundry domestic and monastic quarters, all in varying stages of arrested ruin and restoration. You enter the W end of the church by way of an atrium and notice, as you descend the steps, the carved woman's head set into the wall above the door which is believed to have come from an earlier, pagan, building. The main portico, now bare, was once lavishly covered with carvings; some of these have appeared in other parts of Catalonia, including a famous one of St. Peter in a boat (now in the *Federico Mares Museum* in Barcelona).

The nave is immensely tall with two storeys of columns, four on either side, standing on high bases. The lower capitals are in Corinthian style with wolves' and dogs' heads, whilst the upper ones are cubic and decorated with loops. Both betray Byzantine and Mozarabic influences (rather than Lombardic which is more common in Catalonia). One of the loveliest features of the church is the ambulatory in the central apse and beneath this is the crypt which can be entered down a ramp. It is here that the remains of St. Peter are said to rest. There are two doors in the N transept: one leading up to St. Michael's chapel and tower (the smallest of the three towers); the other leading to various outbuildings.

The way to the 12C *cloister* is through the S transept. The well- restored carved capitals and delicate paired columns look ill at ease against the jagged ruins of the monastery's massive defensive walls. On the S and E sides are various kitchens, a refectory and a well preserved wine cellar, also a chapter house and library. On the W side is the door leading to the base of the magnificent bell tower and it is possible to stand inside and look up into it. But by far the best view of this tower can be had from a walkway which has been constructed above the cloister; the lower half is contemporary with the church, whilst the upper part, with twin windows and Lombard arching, is obviously some 150-200 years later (like the cloister). The other tower, similar in size, is a much grimmer affair and was built solely for the purpose of defence.

From the monastery a road winds down to *Porta de la Selva* – a tiny community clustered around its natural harbour from which the local people have fished for centuries. The corniche road continues northwards through the resorts of *Llanca* and *Portbou* to the frontier with France. For the purposes of this Route, it also goes southwards 21km to the glistening white village of *Cadaques* with its diminutive beaches and plethora of tiny bars and cafés.

Depending on the season, **Cadaques** may appear as an unspoilt fishing community of some 2,000 inhabitants, or as a bustling resort of many times that number. The permanent occupants (besides the fishermen) are mainly artists who are following in the footsteps of the notorious *Dali* who lived here with his wife *Gala*. They are joined in the summer months by owners of prestigious city galleries, promoters of festivals, writers, musicians and art collectors of sometimes international renown, all wanting to see and be seen and to share in the cycle of intense creativity which is still dominated by surrealism. Then, of course, there are the summer visitors who are needed to enjoy, and to pay for, the huge variety of exhibitions of contemporary painting and sculpture on offer. Cadaques has an exciting and non-exclusive cultural tradition. The balance between its creators and those who come to appreciate it is a precarious one which, for the moment at least, is well observed.

Long before it was discovered by artists (and Dali was not the first) Cadaques was a fortified seaport, very exposed to attacks from Moors and pirates. It still preserves a small medieval sector with one or two segments of original fortifications dotted about, and a 16C church with a sumptuous Baroque retablo said to be one of the best of its kind in Spain. Cadaques also has a healthy sprinkling of Modernist houses dating from the turn of the century and coinciding with the first wave of creative energy which arrived about that time. From Cadaques there is a road, of sorts, which goes out to the lighthouse on the point of *Cap de Creus* (the most easterly tip of Spain).

The coast road from Cadaques to *Roses* is predictably picturesque: one can become pleasantly addicted to the sparkling sea and cliff scapes, the freshness of colours, the glint of sun on wave-tops, the clarity. It is also possible (and quicker) to take the inland route which is mountainous and also beautiful. It is approximately 17km to the crossroads where you turn left for Roses.

Roses, superbly dominating the Gulf of the same name, has become a popular resort with over 4km of sandy beaches, its present-day popularity understandably boosted by the proximity of an airport serving the tourist complex of *Empuria-brava* to the S. Besides stunning views and sheltered swimming, Roses offers every conceivable facility for water sports and an endless assortment of hotels and restaurants.

From the beginning of history, Roses' position at the head of a natural bay has attracted visitors, not all of them friendly. Indeed Roses, like so many strategically placed Catalan towns, has suffered severely in all the wars, especially from the French. The first invaders were the Greeks and substantial archaeological evidence of their occupation has been discovered in the area known as *la Ciudadela* (the citadel) which can be seen on the left as you enter the town from Figueres. Most of this evidence has now been taken to the Archaeological Museum in Girona, as indeed have later Roman and Visigothic pieces from here. Recently the remains of a Paleochristian church have been excavated beneath the 11C *Church of Santa Maria de Roses* which was itself severely damaged by the French in 1792. An apse of this church with typical Lombard arcading has recently been reconstructed. Nearby are traces of a pre-Romanesque apse and cloister. All of this rich but somewhat confusing site has been enclosed since the 16C by massive defensive walls, for it was here that the Emperor Charles V chose to build his citadel. Easily visible from the road is the well-preserved Renaissance style *Porta de Mar* which was the seaward gate to the citadel. This was matched by a *Porta de Terra* on the opposite side which is now in poor condition, as are all the walls on that side (a fact which has the advantage of allowing some modest exploration by the keen visitor).

The other monument of interest is the ruined castle (*Castello de la Trinitat*) which overlooks the bay from a rocky outcrop at the other end of town (towards *Falconera* point) and was built shortly after the Citadel. Between the two historic sites, and indeed beyond them, there now sprawls a homogenous mass of white apartment blocks, hotels and villas which continue to spread unabated up the hillside and along the coast.

Castello D'Empuries is 9km W of Roses and half way along is a left turn to *Empuria-brava* – a large holiday complex by the beach. Castello was capital of the independent county of Empuries until it was made part of the Catalan-Aragonese kingdom in 1402. Before the Moorish invasion Empuries had been a diocese and the counts had several times tried to restore it, building the great *Church of Santa Maria* in 11C. The church was rebuilt to serve as a cathedral in the 13C and 14C but the fine battlemented tower dates from the earlier period. The Gothic door (15C) with six arches rising from six apostles on each side is probably the finest feature of the church but is much decayed and some of the figures are crumbling. Inside is an exceptional retablo with six scenes in the life of Christ and a Virgin and Child looking like the finest stone carving; but it is all, in fact, alabaster. The figure of Christ underneath the Virgin is particularly sensitive. Apart from the church, one or two sections of city walls surviving from the time of the counts, and a good Gothic bridge over the river Muga (visible from the modern road bridge) there is not much of interest in this town.

You can either return to Figueres at this point or take a further (much shorter) excursion before doing so.

2. Castello D'Empurias – Sant Pere Pescador – Sant Tomas de Fluvia – Sant Miquel de Fluvia

From Castello turn S-wards towards *Sant Pere Pescador*. You are now in the S section of the **Emporda Natural Park** which was set up in 1983 to protect vast areas of marshland and former lakes from total destruction by encroaching tourism (like Empuria-brava which already forms a wedge between N and S sections of the Park). Further areas were undoubtedly in danger of disappearing under housing developments and marinas and were only saved by a successful campaign leading to government action.

Today the Emporda wetlands are second only to those in the *Ebro Delta* as refuge, feeding ground and nesting ground for thousands of migratory birds. In Spring, when the Pyrenees are made impassable by a cold wind from the N known as the *Tramontana*, flocks of birds alight on the lagoons, rivers and marshes of the Natural Park and bird watchers have claimed to have seen over a hundred species in a single day. Permanent residents include coot, duck, geese, heron and snipe; also kingfisher, bee-eater and the great spotted cuckoo. White storks have been known to nest in the Park and there is now a project underway to encourage and protect them. As well as birds there is also a wealth of small mammals, amphibians and reptiles, and a predictably varied display of marshland plants. The whole alluvial plain is criss-crossed with drainage channels which produce reed beds and an abundance of iris and purple loose-strife in the Spring. Along the banks of the waterways are strips of woodland of poplar, elm and ash.

There is a particularly rich and accessible area of Park E of the road between Castello and Sant Pere, which is dotted with eight lagoons close to the sea, surrounded by a large steppe of salt marsh. At *Mas Cortalet* (turning left off the road) there is an Information Centre where they will explain where you may wander and what you can expect to see. Another exceptional area, lying to the E of Sant Pere Pescador is the *Island of Caramany* in the river Fluvia and formed when the course of the river was being corrected. The fact that it is an island greatly enhances its value as a bird refuge and usually the visitor must be content with standing on the river bank and watching from afar, preferably with binoculars.

From Sant Pere take a minor road W-wards to *Sant Miquel de Fluvia* (via *Torroella de Fluvia*). The 11C **Church of Sant Miquel** is mainly Romanesque but has some Gothic and later rebuilding at the W end. Apart from carved capitals, very much in the early style of Sant Pere de Rodes, and a fine bell tower with twin windows and blind arcading, this church is disappointing and parts of it are in poor condition. Notice the battlemented fortress wall complete with arrow slits which has been added to the main apse and elsewhere.

Less impressive at first sight but well worth seeing inside is the neighbouring **Church of Sant Tomas de Fluvia**. This much smaller, simpler village church contains some fine frescoes, recently discovered and well restored. The Catalans have decided (and rightly in our opinion) never to re-paint sections which are actually missing at time of discovery, leaving (in this particular case) large expanses of blank wall where the early work has disappeared without trace. The farmer next door holds the key to this church and, in true entrepreneurial style, requests 100 pesetas before turning on the light to enable you to see the paintings. They are worth it, especially one of the Last Supper.

Return to Torroella and take the 252 road to Figueres.

RIPOLL TO GIRONA VIA OLOT

From Ripoll take the N260 eastwards over the *Canes* pass (1120ms) to *Olot* (31km). The road takes you through the **Garrotxa Volcanic Zone Natural Park** which starts about 6km W of Olot and covers altogether 119 square kilometres. The Garrotxa is an area of exceptional geological interest with cones, craters and lava flows dating from a period of intense volcanic activity in prehistoric times. Most of these are now covered in dense vegetation; the area is extremely fertile with superb oak and beech woods and a rich selection of both flora and fauna. About 25% of the land is under cultivation – and has been for centuries – so the woodland is pleasantly broken up by farms, fields and villages, as well as the occasional stark volcanic cliff and even the occasional marshy spot creating its own misty atmosphere. In 1985 the region was created a Natural Park which assures its environmental protection and prevents further incursions by farmers. An Information Office has been set up in Olot with a good range of publications and audio visual materials and the possibility of a guide for anyone wanting a serious tour.

The earth was to move again and the original walled town of **Olot**, documented since 9C, was almost completely destroyed by an earthquake in 1428. It was energetically rebuilt and by the early 17C was one of the region's most prosperous textile-producing centres. The huge parish church of *Sant Esteban* was built in neo-classical style in the 18C and is approached by a broad tree-lined avenue called *Paseo del Firal;* it really deserves to be called '*Ramblas*' because of all its lively open-air cafes, its casino and theatre and shops. Moreover it has two good Modernist houses: one (at No.40) is the outstanding *Casa Soler Morales* by *Domenech y Montaner* (1926) with balconies, sculptures and floral oramentation; the second, built in 1905, stands just below the church and is worth a close look for its wealth of detail.

Olot has three museums, all different and all worthwhile. There is the *Parochial Museum* in the *Chapter House* of the church itself (and not open on Sundays) with the wonderful picture of Christ carrying the cross by *El Greco* as its proudest possession. Then there is *Museu Comercal de Garrotxa* housed on the third floor of a large empty-looking building, known as the *Hospici* which is to be found in a side street just S of the church. The Museum is dominated by the paintings of the well-known *Olot School of Landscape Painters*, a collection of 18C and 19C artists who were inspired by the splendid scenery around them. There is also a good deal of Modernist sculpture and a worthwhile section dealing with local traditional crafts such as charcoal burning and various textile processes. The third museum is that of *Natural Sciences* housed in the *Casal dels Volcans* in the Botanical Gardens on the outskirts of town (off the *Vic road*). It sets out to explain the geological formation of the Garrotxa and includes the Information Centre mentioned above. The gardens surrounding it are pleasant and include areas of natural wood and meadow land as well as a trout farm and a meteorological section.

From Olot the road continues to **Santa Pau**, a delightful fortified village (still in the Natural Park) with houses built in to its original protecting wall, a glorious triangular arcaded square known a *El Firal dels bous* (fair of the bullocks) and some outstanding mountain views. Facing on to the square are a 15C parish church and the substantial remains of a medieval castle. 2km away is the 9C Sanctuary, *la Mare de Deu dels Arcs*, severely damaged by the 1428 earthquake. The surviving sections have now been integrated into farm buildings and the end result is not really worth the drive along a very rough track.

20km further on and nicely situated on the shore of the *Banyoles lake* is the village of *Porqueres*, equipped with hotels, restaurants, facilities for water sports and a lake steamer. Porqueres has an 11C church with an unusually tall belfry and a fine portal of three very wide, almost horseshoe-shaped, arches resting on slender columns with plant motifs carved on the capitals and with medallions around the doorway. Inside there is a powerful triumphal arch between nave and apse displaying intricate carvings of humans and monsters.

The road goes right round the lake (6km) to reach the charming town of **Banyoles** which has an old sector (*Vila Vella*) centred around the monastery of Sant Esteban, all but destroyed by the 15C earthquake and finished off by the French in 1655. It was later rebuilt in neo-classical style but conserves a door and fine retablo from the earlier Gothic period. Close by is the 14C church of *Santa Maria dels Turers* which has been much rebuilt. Banyoles also has a new sector (*Vila Nova*), 'new' in this case being a purely relative term. The main feature is a charming porticoed market square (*el Mercadal*). Here too is the house of *Pia Almoina*, once the town hall and now containing an archaeological museum which includes in its collection a replica of the famous *Neanderthal* jaw found by the lake and thought to be the oldest human bone in Catalonia. The road continues 21km to Girona.

ROUTE 7

GIRONA

History *Girona* was a settlement of the Iberian tribe of *Ausetani* until the Romans came and turned it into a fortified town (*oppidum*), one of many along the *Via Augusta*. Roman Girona, or *Gerunda*, was built in the shape of a triangle along the E bank of the Onyar river, with its three angles marked by the *Portal San Cristofol, Portal Sobreportales* and the end of *Carrer Force.*

Not for nothing has Girona been called *the City of Sieges.* Its strategic position just S of the Pyrenees had laid it open to repeated devastations by Franks, Moors, French and countless warring factions of Catalans. It has been built and rebuilt over and over again, each time managing to preserve a vestige of architecture as evidence of its tormented and colourful history. As if this were not enough, its unique location astride four rivers has rendered it subject to constant flooding which in times past has proved disastrous. The first invaders to disrupt the Roman idyll were the Franks and Alemanes who poured over the Pyrenees in the 3C, and laid waste all before them before passing on. Christianity crept in to Girona at the beginning of the 4C but the Romans were not ready for it yet and burned the believers. The 4C sarcophagi discovered in a martyrium and now displayed in the church of *St. Felix* (*San Feliu*) bear witness to this. In the 5C, with the conversion of the *Roman Emperor Constantine* and the arrival of the Visigoths, Girona became a Christian diocese.

The Moors took Girona in 718 and it was liberated again by the combined Frankish-Catalan army in 785. It was now the turn of the Catalan counts to quarrel amongst themselves and this they did, with Count Wilfred the Hairy emerging as the most powerful and annexing all the liberated counties to existing possessions of Barcelona, Girona and Osona in 9C. There followed a period of peace and prosperity and great architectural creativity which extended well into the 14C. The Cathedral, many of the great churches, the Arab Baths and the Jewish sector all date from this time and the town expanded across the Onyar river to form the area known as *El Mercadal.* Trade and culture flourished and Girona was the second city of Catalonia (after Barcelona).

Catalonia's Golden Age was cut short in the second half of the 14C by a combination of pestilence and the first of the many wars of succession which were to plague it through the centuries and devastate the economy. Girona suffered more than most particularly from the French who besieged the city over and over again. Undoubtedly the worst of all were the horrific sieges by Napoleon's troops in 1808 and 1809, the last of which the townspeople resisted for seven months before starvation and disease and lack of arms forced surrender on them. By 1814 Napoleon had withdrawn definitively and the economy slowly began to recover throughout Catalonia particularly in the field of textiles. Girona was no exception and her new-found confidence was greatly helped by the extension of the railway from Barcelona to the town in 1862. The town grew and grew and developed an industrial belt on the periphery, and latterly an airport to serve the tourists bound for the nearby *Costa Brava.*

Girona has emerged from the troubled first half of this century a proud and prosperous town which takes good care of its exceptional architectural heritage. The floods still occasionally occur; the sieges, fortunately, do not.

Sight-seeing Arriving from the N, you come in on the N11 road which crosses the northern tip of the *Devesa Park* and brings you to the left bank of the Onyar river. The old city of Girona lies compactly along the right bank and you will see the distinctive shapes of the *Cathedral* and *St. Felix church* reflected in the river as you enter the town. Cross the river and follow signs to *Centro Ciutat.* The delightful confusion of steep streets and ancient walls and buildings is quite small and is best explored on foot. There are signposts to all the major monuments. Parking may be a problem but there are car parks in the area around the Cathedral.

The logical starting point for any visit is the Cathedral Square (*Plaça de la Catedral*) from which ninety-six steps lead magnificently up to the imposing mass of the **Cathedral of Santa Maria**. The W front with its fussy 18C Baroque decoration of assorted statues and columns topped by a single ornately framed occulus is greatly flattered by the regal approach. From immediately below it is possible to avoid seeing the single bell tower (completed in 1764) which from any other angle gives the façade a decidely lop-sided look in uncomfortable contrast with the absolute symmetry of the Baroque section.

Apart from the W front, the church is pure Catalan Gothic with plain, fortress-like unadorned walls, few windows and massive internal buttresses. Examples of this confident no-nonsense style abound in Catalonia reflecting the growing prosperity and energy of the 14C fostered by cultural and trading links with France and Italy.

Two earlier churches are known to have stood on the same spot and the first was undoubtedly destroyed by the Moors. The second, Romanesque in style, was built in the 11C. Surviving from this period are the cloister and the lovely '*Charlemagne's tower*' with typical paired windows and Lombard arching which now forms part of the Gothic N wall and is best seen from the cloister. The main body of today's church was begun in 1312 and continued through various stages until well into the 15C. Notice the Apostles' Door on the S side which was begun in 1394 and has recently been restored, so only two of the terracotta figures are original.

The **interior** is serenely and soberly beautiful with a gallery of nine arches surrounding the High Altar, a triforium of 105 delicate niches and some magnificent stained glass, much of it original, which provides just the right amount of colour to the stark grey walls. The nave is the widest of any European Gothic cathedral. Originally it was intended that there should be two side aisles, as can be seen from the positioning of the chancel arches. However in 1417 the progressive architect, *Guillermo Bofill*, persuaded his sceptical colleagues that a single nave would create a more spacious effect and could safely be spanned by a 22m wide vault, albeit supported by internal buttresses which are 6m thick. The elegant fluted columns which are the only other visible signs of support have tiny capitals which in no way interrupt the soaring line to the vault. The main retablo is a remarkable piece in silver gilt highlighted with enamel and surmounted by a canopy which is also covered in silver.

The side chapels – thirty in all – are well lit and well labelled and mainly heavy Baroque. Two deserve special mention: the first chapel on the N wall which contains the 15C tomb of *Bernard de Pau*, and the fourth chapel on the same wall with the very lovely horizontal figure of *Cardinal Berenguer de Anglesola* carved in marble by the 15C sculptor *Pere Oller*. The apsidal chapel immediately behind the High Altar contains a powerful carving of the dead Christ. This is in fact a modern work (1958) and its strength lies in the remarkably wasted and cavernous quality of the body which is deeply moving.

The irregular-shaped **Cloister** is an important relic of the Romanesque cathedral with simple rounded arches supported by seventy-four paired columns, and eleven square pillars at the corners and at the centre of each gallery. The pillars are decorated with carved friezes depicting scenes mainly from *Genesis* which must be some of the finest in Catalonia, particularly those in the S gallery which is the oldest. The paired columns have somewhat coarser carvings, mainly of birds, monsters, plants and even some

GIRONA, OLD CITY

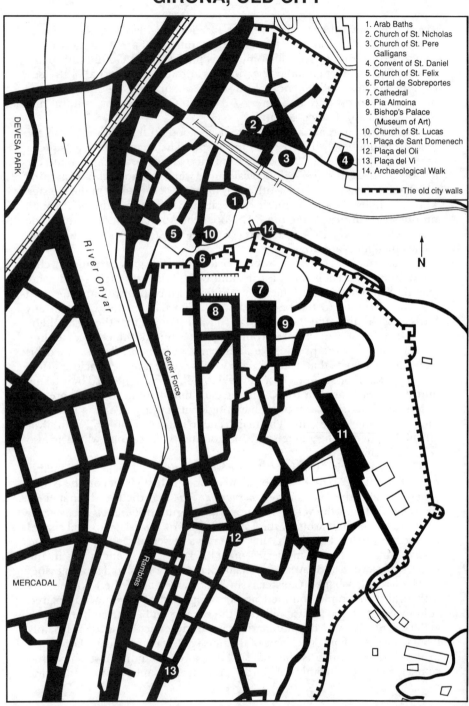

1. Arab Baths
2. Church of St. Nicholas
3. Church of St. Pere Galligans
4. Convent of St. Daniel
5. Church of St. Felix
6. Portal de Sobreportes
7. Cathedral
8. Pia Almoina
9. Bishop's Palace (Museum of Art)
10. Church of St. Lucas
11. Plaça de Sant Domenech
12. Plaça del Oli
13. Plaça del Vi
14. Archaeological Walk

▪▪▪▪▪▪ The old city walls

N

DEVESA PARK

River Onyar

Carrer Force

Ramblas

MERCADAL

geometrical designs looking distinctly Islamic. The Cloister affords the best view of *Charlemagne's Tower*, described earlier, and looking quite dwarfed by the massive Gothic walls around it.

In the *Chapter House* is a well-organised **Museum** of cathedral treasure with comprehensive guides written in all the major languages which you can take round with you and hand back at the end. There are some quite exceptional pieces in the four salons, including an 11C wooden figure of Virgin and Child, a 10C Book of the Apocalypse, and a 14C alabaster statue of King Peter IV, also known traditionally as the 'statue of Charlemagne', possibly because the people of Girona revered Charlemagne as a saint for having driven out the Moors. Most remarkable of all however is the 11C **Tapestry of the Creation** in the fourth salon where there is also an unobtrusive electronic machine which talks you through the piece. The picture of birds and fish being created in the bottom segment of the circle is especially charming, but everyone who is lucky enough to see this tapestry will have his or her own favourite sections. It is embroidered in wool on silk and is in good condition except for the right-hand and bottom borders which are badly deteriorated. This Museum should not be missed.

S of the Cathedral is the former Bishop's Palace, of little charm in its own right but housing since 1979 a Museum of Art including paintings of all periods up to the present day and a huge collection of Gothic retablos. The most notable exhibit however is the painted beam from the 11C church at *Cruilles* showing a procession of monks (it is worth coming to the Museum for this alone); also, from the same church, a magnificent Christ in Majesty.

On the right side of the Cathedral Square is the distinguished *Pia Almoina* building with Gothic façade and exceptionally good windows, which is now occupied (appropriately) by the *College of Architects*. On the left side is the *Portal de Sobreportes* between massive cylindrical towers. It was built on the site of the original Roman gate which stood here guarding the *Via Augusta* and some of the original Roman stones are visible within the medieval gate. The street leading off it is called *Carrer Force* and follows the line of the old Via Augusta. A walk up here is highly recommended for it is picturesque and full of interesting shops. On the left hand side is the old Jewish sector (11-15C) which is characterised by incredibly narrow streets, often stepped, many containing collectors of rare books or antiques. On the right hand side of Carrer Force is the *City History Museum*, housed in a former convent.

On the left of the Portal is the **Church of St. Felix** (**San Feliu**) instantly recognisable for its truncated steeple which was struck by lightning in 1581. This is one of the most historically interesting monuments in Girona, built on the site of an earlier church which stood over a 6C Martyrium containing the tombs of Christians who had been put to death by the Roman Emperor *Diocletian* in the early 4C. It would therefore have been outside the city walls as was the custom for cemeteries in Roman times.

Today's church has a 14C Gothic vault over a 12-13C nave. The huge clumsy pillars and poor lighting overall give the interior a somewhat grim

Girona. Cathedral of Santa Maria. W front. 18C.

aspect with the only redeeming feature, architecturally speaking, being the delicate triforium. However, there is treasure to be found in this forbidding setting, in the form of eight magnificent pre-Constantine **sarcophagi** which were found on the site of the martyrium. These have been embedded in the walls either side of the main altar. The scenes are as follows:-

N side	(left)	Saint Susanna (also martyred by Diocletian) A lion hunt with Roman soldiers
	(right)	The sacrifice of Isaac A new testament scene
S side	(left)	A new testament scene The Good Shepherd
	(right)	Roman figures The Rape of Proserpine

The last two date from the second century; the rest from the fourth.

Also of interest is the Baroque chapel to *St. Narcissus* (on the N wall) which stands in place of the original cloister destroyed shortly after it was built in 1374. It contains a silver sepulchre with recumbent figure of the saint above, who is believed to have been martyred when he was saying mass in the catacombs possibly on this very spot. St. Narcissus was bishop of Girona. He was put to death three years after St. Felix and the church appears to contain far more in memory of him than it does of the humble missionary, Felix, to whom it was dedicated. Contrary to popular belief, the tomb of St. Felix is not here and it is doubtful whether his mortal remains were ever found. At the W end of the church is a recumbent Christ figure dating from 1350 and carved in alabaster; a truly timeless and powerful piece.

On the right side of the Portal de Sobreportas, past the austere neo-classical *Church of San Lucas*, are the lovely **'Arab' Baths** dating in fact from the 13C, but built over earlier *Mudejar* baths. Inside is a domed room containing an octagonal pool with slender columns. The top of the dome is open, so daylight pours in to enhance the contrast between elegant columns and rough stone surround. There are niches in one wall where people would have left their clothes, and the four windows would undoubtedly have looked out on a garden. There is also a *tepidarium* (warm room), a steam bath room with double floor and hypocaust, and a *caldarium* (hot room) which at time of writing is being restored. These baths, believed to be one of the finest specimens of their kind anywhere, are open for public view only between 10 and 13 hours each day.

Beyond is the *Archaeological Walk* offering good close-up views of the ancient town walls on the right, including the tower of the 12C church of *St. Pere Galligans* which undoubtedly served originally as a watch tower. It leads up to the second Roman gateway, that of *Sant Cristofol,* from which there is a splendid view of the surrounding countryside and of the ruined *Gironella*

Tower. Across the valley on the left are the ruined walls of the *Montjuich Fortress,* destroyed by the French in 1809 and almost completely hidden now by modern houses.

The **Church of St. Pere Galligans**, fortified by fine apses as well as its distinguished tower (octagonal above and square below) is worth a visit. The interior is unadorned except for a fine rose window and high carved capitals and now houses part of the *Provincial Archaeological Museum,* the main body of which is the Cloister. The original Cloister was destroyed by the French in 1809 and again by floods in 1843 after which it was splendidly restored to its present state with paired columns, carved capitals and blind arcading above with animal heads. The second storey was added at this time. The exhibits include some interesting Iberian and Jewish tombstones and various Greek and Roman sarcophagi from Empurias. Opposite is the immaculately restored 12C *Church of St. Nicholas (San Nicolau)* with cloverleaf apse and fine Lombard arching all round.

A road leads up the valley eastwards from here to the *Convent of St. Daniel,* founded in 1025 by the *Countess Ermesenda of Barcelona.* You can drive, or walk for about 10 minutes. The church, which has been embedded in a later building, has a small and appealing Romanesque cloister with paired columns and Corinthian capitals and a Gothic gallery added above. Because the Convent is still occupied by nuns, the Cloister can only be viewed from the church through a grille. The church is a simple structure with single nave, three apses arranged in clover-leaf formation, and fine arcading around the crossing. In the N apse is the sepulchre of St. Daniel showing six scenes in his life. To visit the church simply knock on the main door of the Convent and a nun will come and show you around.

A walk in the upper part of town in the general area S of the Cathedral is an evocative experience and leads you through a maze of steep streets, many of them stepped, past ancient walls, and buildings of many periods. Notice particularly the sweeping stairway of *Escola Pia* street with its medieval walls and defensive tower; also the *Plaça de Sant Domenech* which displays remains of a pre-Roman, *Cyclopean* wall of huge stones, the façade of the 16C university destroyed by *King Philip V* in 1718 and currently being rebuilt, and also the 14C monastery itself with its huge Gothic church.

If at the end of *Carrer Force* you bear left, you come to *Plaça del Oli* and then *Carrer de Ciutadans* which is lined with noble mansions with impressive portals and often a glimpse of a patio beyond. The most memorable is the *Fontana d'Or* at no.19 with fine Romanesque façade. The house has been restored both inside and out, and is now used as a cultural centre. At the end of this street is the charming arcaded *Plaça del Vi* overlooked by the Town Hall and the Municipal Theatre. There is such a concentration of old churches and fascinating buildings in the old town that it is not possible to describe more than the principal ones; the alert and patient wanderer will discover even more.

A walk along the *Ramblas* which, together with the River *Onyar* effectively divides the old from the new, is recommended. It is reached by turning right at the end of *Carrer Force* and then almost immediately left. Like all Ramblas it is broad and tree-lined and colourful and for pedestrians only. It is arcaded on the left-hand, 'old' side and connects with the new town by way of footbridges across the river. There are several Modernist houses along its length.

Immediately across the river is the sector known as *El Mercadal* which marks the first expansion of the medieval town in the 14C. It started as an area of monasteries and simple housing for the growing population. Today the elegant *Gran Via de Jaume I* follows the line of the ancient walls, and the monasteries have given way to office blocks and shops. There is a good sprinkling of Modernist and eclectic houses, especially along the Gran Via itself, and just a few vestiges of old buildings particularly in the region of *Carrer Santa Clara*, parallel with the river, and *Carrer Nou* leading off the *Pont de Pedra* bridge which preserves arches of a Gothic cloister.

Not to be missed is the *Devesa* Park which lies to the N of the Mercadal sector in the angle formed by the joining of the two rivers, *Ter* and *Onyar* and extending westwards as far as the river *Guell*. With broad avenues between tall plane trees, canals and gardens, it is a delightful place to catch your breath and rest a while after your energetic walk around this fascinating city.

Excursion to Empurias and Ullastret

This excursion is based on the two most important archaeological sites in Catalonia: **Empurias** (Greco-Roman) and **Ullastret** (Iberian). The *Lower Emporda* is an agricultural region rich in hill-top villages, ruined castles and Romanesque churches and we have suggested a route which takes in the best of these. Inevitably there are some which are not included and still await discovery, and the reader will shorten or lengthen the excursion as time permits.

Take the N11 or the motorway N out of *Girona* and at approximately 16km turn right for *Vildamat* and *L'Escala*. L'Escala itself has grown from fishing village to major tourist resort with the usual plethora of hotels and campsites and fine sheltered beaches. **Empurias** lies 2km to the N and comprises three sections, two of which have been excavated and can be visited. There is also a good museum.

History: Paliapolis, ('old city') was the first trading post to be established by Greeks from Asia Minor in 6C BC and was, at that time an island. Today the site is occupied by the village of *Sant Marti d'Empurias* and the island has become part of the mainland. By 550BC the island had become too small and the Greeks moved down the coast a little way to establish a second enclave. This much larger settlement which archaeologists called *Neapolis* (new city), played a leading role in the expansion of Mediterranean trade in the 3C and 4C BC; it prospered greatly even to the point of minting its own coins. The arrival of the *Carthaginians* in 3C BC upset the equilibrium

171

somewhat and *Emporion*, as the enclave was called by the Greeks, stood firmly on the side of the Romans in the Punic War.

In 218BC the Romans invaded. Their primary objective was to root out the Carthaginians and prevent them from recruiting Iberians for their armies. They came first to Emporion and within a short time had established a permanent military camp on the hillside behind *Emporion-Neapolis*. This settlement forms the third section of Empurias. Initially the Roman arrival meant even greater prosperity for Emporion because it became the point of entry for vast quantities of merchandise from Rome intended for the soldiers. Relations were good between the two peoples since each benefitted from the presence of the other. When in 150BC the greatly enlarged military camp was declared a city it was intended by the Romans that it should exist on equal terms with the Greek town of Neapolis – a fair enough consideration in view of the Greeks' unswerving loyalty since the arrival of the first soldiers. Inevitably however the one grew faster than the other. Roman culture dominated and, during the reign of *Augustus*, the Greeks were granted Roman citizenship which *de facto* united the two settlements into one city – *Municipium Emporiae*.

With the emergence of Tarragona as capital of the province of *Tarraconensis*, and later of Barcelona as the second Roman city of the province, *Municipium Emporiae* began to fall into decline and during 1C AD many Romans abandoned their homes and went to live in one of the more fashionable centres. The remaining population stayed on until 3C AD when Emporias was devastated by Frankish invaders from the N (along with the rest of Catalonia). Those who survived returned to live in *Paliapolis* whose size was more commensurate with their reduced numbers. But the excavation of a 4C *Paleochristian Basilica* in Neapolis indicates that a fair number of people must have stayed on there too.

Documentation has revealed that *Empurias* was capital of a Visigothic diocese between 516 and 623 and it is thought that a cathedral might well have been sited on Paliapolis (now Sant Marti). When the region was reconquered from the Moors in the late 8C, Empurias became capital of a *Carolingian* county, but it was only the Santa Marti-Paliapolis section which was repopulated because it offered the best possibilities of defence and had an excellent natural harbour. The ruins of Empurias-Neapolis were left alone until 1907 when the first excavations began. These were interrupted by the Civil War but restarted in 1939. Since 1982 the whole process has been greatly stepped up. The whole of Neapolis, as it was during the Roman period has been uncovered; though much of what predates the Roman arrival in 218BC has still to be unearthed. Sant Marti-Paliapolis however presents serious problems to archaeologists because it has been continuously and, at times, densely inhabited for 1700 years.

A walk around the ruins of Neapolis and the Roman city can be a confusing experience. This is because many of the earliest structures have been partially or completely dismantled by later builders who have then used the materials for similar, or perhaps quite different, purposes, either alongside or directly above. The following **itinerary** is designed to help the visitor around the site in a clear and logical way. The numbers correspond with those displayed on posts *in situ*, and also with those in the official Guidebook, an erudite document with a wealth of detail which is probably better read before or after your tour, rather than during it.

The tour begins in Neapolis with the 2C BC Greek wall **(1)** marking the southern boundary. You can see the remains of two square towers at the entrance and of a massive tower on the SW corner. This was later attached to the wall built by the Romans to enclose the whole of *Municipium Emporiae*. The huge limestone blocks come from an earlier Greek wall (4C BC) which ran parallel to the later wall. This was almost completely dismantled and any remains were purposely buried under tons of earth to raise the level of the city.

At **(2)** can be seen the foundations of a 4C tower with a later wall built over it. Also at (2) in front of the 4C Greek wall is the *Proteichisma* or defensive parapet built by the Greeks in 3C BC to protect their earlier wall from enemy attack.

The religious therapeutic centre marked **(3)** would have consisted of various temples and archaeologists have named it the *Asklepion* after *Asklepios*, the god of medicine, whose broken statue was discovered amidst the ruins. This is now in the *Museum of Archaeology* at *Barcelona* and the site of the discovery is marked by a reproduction. A marble head of *Aphrodite* was also found here and is in the same museum.

Above the Asklepion – at **(7)** – is a watch tower which formed part of the defensive system before the 4C wall was built. Beside the watch tower is a large cistern intended to provide water to soldiers defending this highest point of Neapolis. Of great interest is the 3C water filter made from cylindrical amphorae which would have contained sand or gravel to purify the water and is believed to be of Carthaginian origin. W of the watch tower is a huge oven thought to had been made in the 17C by the builders of the monastery (which now houses the Museum) where they burned the limestone of any monuments – statues, walls etc – they could lay their hands on to obtain lime necessary to produce mortar. No wonder so little remains of this part of Neapolis.

Below the Asklepion is a square **(4)**, and to the N of this there were three shops or *tabernae*. **(5)**, the *Serapion*, is a square to the SE of (4) which was probably created in the 2C when the new wall was being built using the material from the older one and fitted neatly between the two. The square was porticoed and stood on ground which had been artificially raised by taking earth from in front of the *Proteichisma* (where there is now a ditch). Later it seems that a temple was built on the W side of the Serapion dedicated to the Alexandrian god *Zeus Serapis*. The evidence for this was a broken stone plaque found here which tells of a man born in *Alexandria* called *Numas* who was charged with the building of a temple to Serapis.

(6), **(9)** and **(10)** were *tabernae* or shops, facing on to the wide main street which led from the sea up to the public square. **(8)** marks a fish salting factory. **(11)**, set back off the main road, is a house of the Augustan period when the Greek and Romans towns were first united as one city (Municipium Emporae). It has a full complement of domestic and public rooms around a central courtyard with well and peristyle. There is another house **(17)** of the same period over the other side of the street, behind the tabernae, which had a more compact, 4-columned atrium.

At the end of the main street is the Agora **(13)**, a large rectangular square porticoed and bound to the N by a *Stoa* **(14)**, a kind of shopping arcade. Together these formed the general meeting place and commercial nucleus of the town. Archaeologists have noted that this whole area was built over the ruins of earlier houses.

N of the Stoa are the scant remains of a *Paleochristian Basilica* **(15)** of the 4C which experts believe made use of the walls of a building previously housing public baths (the niches in the wall are supposed to be places for clothes). The rounded apse at the E end is clearly visible, as are fragments of a white marble floor. All around was a cemetery and some sarcophagi remain from the early Visigothic period.

Turn up now towards the *Museum.* Just before reaching it, at **(16)**, you see the remains of a Hellenic house famed for its mosaic with Greek inscription. The significant point here is that the Greek language should still be in use as late as 1C BC, at a time when Roman culture was thought to be swamping everything. The Museum is housed in the 17C Monastery of *Santa Maria de Gracia.* It contains many of the finds excavated from the Greek and Roman sites including a lovely mosaic of the *Sacrifice of Iphigenia.*

From the Museum pass to the Roman town built above and behind Neapolis and overlooking the Bay. It occupied some 20ha and had an important forum in the centre of a regular network of N-S and W-E streets. Not all of the perimeter walls have been excavated as yet. You enter on the E side where three significant houses have been discovered. The first **(18)** was built in two periods – early and late 1C BC; the earlier part had rooms arranged around a hexagonal atrium; then new rooms were added on the N side, plus peristyle and gardens and more rooms on the S and E sides. The black and white mosaics in some later rooms are still in place. It is interesting to note that the new rooms extend beyond the city walls in some places, indicating that they were built after the uniting of Greek and Roman towns (at which point the walls had become obsolete). **(19)** is a much smaller house with atrium, and **(20)** is another palatial one covering a vast area, with innumerable peristyles, pools, mosaics and columns. One wall has been reconstructed showing the Roman method of rough-casting adobe with painted lime.

Walk now towards the *Forum*. You come first to a section of blocks of stone (**22**) remaining from the original fortification built when the Romans first arrived. Beside it are public cisterns (**21**) of roughly the same period. The *Forum* (**23**) – (**28**) is of course the heart of the Roman city. In the early Roman period it probably had a pagan temple in the centre surrounded on three sides by porticoed buildings. Later, when Municipium Emporiae was created, it would have been greatly enlarged with civic buildings and shops. A *Curia* (meeting place of the municipal council) was added at the S side and a civic *Basilica* for judicial assemblies was built on the E side.

From the S end of the Forum the *Cardus Maximus* (main N-S street (**30**)) leads to the S gate of the Roman city. It would have been porticoed and lined with shops. The S city wall is the best preserved part of the perimeter. It dates from late 2C and the main gate (**31**) is clearly identifiable with original lintel intact and supported on modern blocks. There was another gate at the SW corner of the city and between these two, outside the walls, was the *Amphitheatre* (**33**) designed for gladiatorial contests. The elliptical foundations are visible and there has been some reconstruction but it is far less impressive than the only other Roman amphitheatre in Catalonia – in Tarragona. This is a good place incidentally from which to appreciate the huge stones of the city walls. Also outside the walls, just E of the S gate, is a rectangular area thought to have been a *Gymnasium* (**34**).

This completes the Roman city. Plenty of imagination, and a measure of knowledge as to how it ought to look, can make the visit a memorable and educational experience. It remains to mention the excavations currently taking place in the Car Park S of Neapolis (**35**) where foundations are believed to be those of an early 1C BC factory for working lead and silver. Beneath it are earlier buildings and possibly a Greek *necropolis* from 4C BC.

The village of *Sant Marti d'Empurias*, where it all began, is clearly visible from the Roman city, high on a rocky crag dominating the bay and looking impregnable still. Many layers of history must still be there awaiting excavation and this has never been possible because the site has been continuously inhabited for seventeen centuries at least. The 16C church is thought to stand over a 13C one and a 10C one and probably a 7C Visigothic cathedral which, in turn, possibly replaced a Greek pagan temple. Some of these are documented on tablets found in or near the church and now embedded in the main façade. Finds from the Greek temple, such as a frieze showing sphinxes back to back (discovered upside down because they had been re-used as building material at a later date) have been taken to the main museums in Barcelona and Girona. Sections of defensive wall can still be seen near the church, mainly medieval and making use of stones from earlier walls whose traces they probably followed. There are also remains of the 12-14C castle dating from the time when this was the capital of the County of Empurias, before the honour was granted to *Castello d'Empurias*.

Between Sant Marti and the Greek city of Neapolis, a little way out to sea, are the stark remains of a jetty dating from the Greco-Roman period (1 BC) and still withstanding the onslaught of the waves, probably because the builders used lime as mortar.

The whole region is full of necropolises, indigenous Iberian, Greek and Roman, and not always easy to identify because some are on farmland. Probably the easiest to find is a Roman cenotaph on the top of *Les Corts* hill at *El Castellet*. It is surrounded by small funeral monuments in which were placed the urns containing ashes of the dead. This is thought to be the earliest Roman necropolis in Empurias. Enthusiasts will wish to arm themselves with the official guide book and take time to discover many more. The main site is open every day except Mondays (10-14, 15-19 hours in summer; 10-13, 15-17 hours in winter).

Return to Vildamat and turn left 9km for *Verges*. Verges has preserved much of its medieval rampart, but is primarily renowned for its unique and ancient Dance of Death which is performed every Maundy Thursday by villagers wearing gruesome skeletal costumes. Continue S to *Parlava* (4km). Turn left and shortly right for *Ullastret*.

The ruins of the Iberian settlement of **Ullastret** are located 2km NE of the present village. Anyone who has travelled extensively in Spain can be forgiven for regarding signposts to Iberian settlements with a degree of sceptism. All too often there is simply nothing to be seen, the land having long since been ploughed up. Ullastret is the big exception. There really are substantial remains here and a visit is worthwhile if only to put the rest of history into perspective.

The settlement was built on a hill called *Puig San Andreu* which was surrounded by a lake. The lake dried up during the last century but has several times been refilled after floods, notably in 1965 and 1977. Finds of flint tools and stone axes suggest that the site was inhabited in the Upper Paleolithic period. The first settlers however probably dated from the transitional Bronze-Iron Age towards the end of 7C BC. The Greeks arrived from *Asia Minor* a century later and founded Emporion. They also came to Ullastret and the fortified town excavated here combined indigenous Iberian and Greek culture. It is thought to have flourished for three centuries until the beginning of 2C BC when the hill was abandoned. No-one quite knows what brought about the end of Ullastret since there are no signs of destruction or violence. It was presumably eclipsed by Emporion and people simply moved away.

The ruins of Ullastret were not discovered until 1931 and excavations did not begin in earnest till 1947. There is much still to do, not just on Puig San Andreu but on other smaller hilltops nearby where some artefacts have been found. The visitor will find that Ullastret comprises three sections: outer ramparts, acropolis on the crown of the hill, and the town itself built in between the two. There is a small museum in the acropolis area.

The **outer rampart** is very impressive indeed and would at one time have enclosed the whole settlement. The western section is where excavations began and is the most solid part, consisting of seven massive circular towers joined by sections of cyclopean wall. If you go through the gate marked *no. 1* you will come to the main street leading uphill to the acropolis. Crossing this are a number of side streets following the contours and along which the houses were ranged. The lowest horizontal street leads to a public square, or *agora* which was colonnaded though the bases of only two columns survive today. The square is punctured with small holes which were silos used for storing cereals or sometimes bits of household equipment such as pots. There are some 230 of those across the settlement and many of them have yielded significant pieces to the Museum.

Houses in the town were single-storey and made of stone, possibly lined with mud and with mud floors. Each house had a fireplace made of small stones or pottery shards, and at least one stone bench against a wall. Three large cisterns have also been discovered, the largest of which is on the acropolis, a second near the second horizontal street leading to the right off the main uphill street. Cisterns were for collecting rainwater and were cut out of the bedrock. They were lined with slabs of sandstone faced with lime mortar and covered by more large slabs.

The **acropolis** is also known as 'the sacred quarter' because the remains of a pagan temple were found there. The temple was rectangular and faced E and traces of its tesselated floor and votive offerings can be seen in the Museum. Another larger temple is believed to have stood on the site earlier, as evidenced by a section of older wall which runs parallel to the temple about 1m away. A 12C castle also once stood here. A 14C Gothic chapel dedicated to St. Andrew now houses the **Museum**. This is well worth a visit for it contains some rare pottery, both Iberian and Greek; also coins, figurines, mounted skulls, jewellery and some of the best examples anywhere of Iberian writing on fragments of lead.

Ullastret village has a medieval sector (*casc antic*) with fine 13C fortified walls which are almost completely intact. Outside the walls is an impressive covered market square (*Llotja*); inside is the church of St. Peter (*Sant Pere*), a particularly good specimen of Romanesque with three arcaded apses and low relief carvings of sirens and animals on one arch near the main façade.

From Ullastret village drive a short distance S to *Canapost* which has an 11-12C church in two parts, the section with the trapezoidal apse being the earlier of the two. Inside are scant remains of mural paintings. From here take the road E to **Peratallada**, a lovely walled village in particularly good state of preservation with moated medieval castle literally hewn out of the hill (hence the name of this village; *pedra tallada* = carved stone). The castle began as a rectangular keep in the 11C. Next to this was built the palace of the feudal lords of *Cruilles*. Other houses followed and building continued over another four centuries. Today one can date the various structures from the shape of their windows. The whole complex has been well restored and much of it is privately owned.

The village which grew up around the castle has fine old houses, many with *Ajimez* windows, and a porticoed *Plaça Mayor,* somewhat transformed in the 19C. It is probably safe to say there is not one ugly building in this village which is a delight to wander in though perhaps a touch self-conscious. The parish church of *St. Stephen* (*Sant Esteban*) is an interesting one for it has two naves divided by massive piers; the N nave is Romanesque, the S one is transitional Gothic, and there is a particularly good S chapel with star vault and fine central boss. The two naves share one external façade. The church contains the 14C tomb of *Gilabert de Cruilles* with polychrome heraldic shields.

Continue along the same road a further couple of kilometres to *St. Julia de Boada,* worth a visit to see what must be the tiniest and most primitive of all churches. It is a pre-Romanesque (10C) gcm, and its massive walls bulge with age. Nothing is quite straight, which is part of its charm. It really is imperative to get inside this church and the lady living next door keeps the key. The triumphal arch is slightly horseshoe- shaped (betraying *Mozarabic* influence) and is echoed by a second similar arch leading to the single apse. There are vestiges of simple painting on one of the arches. The exterior of the church bears no decoration whatsoever and the single door is also slightly horseshoe-shaped.

Continue to a T-junction and turn right 3km for **Pals** which is another well-preserved fortified village. It once had a 9C castle but the story goes that stones from the ruins were taken to rebuild the parish church alongside in 1478. Now all that remains of the hill-top castle is a distinctive cylindrical tower known as *Tower of the Hours* (*Torre de les Hores*). The church itself is not special though it does preserve the Romanesque façade of its predecessor. All around is a network of extremely picturesque streets with immaculate façades of medieval houses including the *Ca de la Pruna* which contains a small museum. A walk along the '*Archaeological Way*' (*Passeig Arqueologic*), which follows the outside of the ramparts, is recommended especially when the sun is low and the colours intense. Notice the defensive arrow slits in the walls and the way in which the stone was hewn out of the surrounding bedrock.

This wealthy village, like *Peratallada,* keeps itself in an excellent state of preservation, conscious no doubt of the proximity of the *Costa Brava* resorts and tourist potential. It is unlikely that any bars or tatty shops will ever be allowed to spoil the architectural harmony. Everything is perfect. Almost too perfect. Even the Siamese cats are the same colour as the stone.

Continue a km S and turn right for **La Bisbal d'Emporda**, capital of the comarca of *Lower Emporda* and once the residence of the bishops of Girona. The splendid 12C Bishop's Palace still stands in the heart of the old town, with castellated walls and central court. It has suffered somewhat through the centuries from successive restorations and alterations, the windows perhaps most of all. It is nevertheless regarded as an outstanding example of medieval civil architecture. The old town has one or two nice Gothic-Renaissance buildings and the Baroque church has a distinctive door. A market is held every Friday in the town centre. Today *La Bisbal* is known as the ceramics capital of the region and several streets are duly lined with displays of hand- made pottery in styles to suit all tastes.

2km up the *Daro* valley from La Bisbal is the once walled village of *Cruilles*, distinguished by its fine cylindrical watch tower, the only surviving vestige of the 11C castle. It is 25m high and now stands solitary in the middle of a plaça. Next to it is the 18C parish church with its own bell tower rivalling the castle one in height but not in beauty. 1km outside the village is the *Monastery of St. Michael* (*Sant Miquel*) founded by the lords of Cruilles in 1040 and with its Romanesque church surviving. This is a large basilica-style building with nave and two aisles, three apses and a cupola over the crossing. The church is most famous for what is no longer there: its superb painted beam showing a procession of monks and a wooden image of Christ in Majesty have both been taken to the Museum of Art in Girona.

From Cruilles you have a choice of continuing along the Daro valley for 16km to *Cassa de la Salva* and then turning N 13km for Girona (a pretty route), or returning to *La Bisbal* and taking the speedier main road (255) to Girona via *Pubol.*

GIRONA TO BARCELONA:

A.   Coastal route via Costa Brava resorts

Take the NII southwards out of Girona for approximately 14km where you turn off left for *Caldes de Malavella*. This is a spa town which the Romans called *Aquae Voconis*. There are substantial Roman remains on the surrounding hilltops of *Sant Grau* and *el Puig de les Animes* and the town itself has three sets of modern thermal baths (*balnearios*), the biggest of which is *Vichy Catalan* in an imposing Modernist building. There is also a much restored Romanesque church (*Sant Esteban*) with nice Renaissance door, and remains of a medieval castle.

Continue 7km to the small town of *Llagostera* which prospered in the 19C with a sizeable cork industry thanks to the abundant cork oak forests in the vicinity. Some notable neo-classical and Modernist buildings date from this period, as does the *Casino de Llagostera*. It must have prospered before that time too for it possesses a noble 15C church in typical Catalan-Gothic style with chapels between the internal buttresses. In front of the church are a few remains of its medieval castle.

4km further on, take a left hand turn to *Romanya de la Selva* (7km) to see one of the best surviving megalithic dolmens in Spain – **la Cova d'en Daina**. Probably dating from around 2,000BC, this amazing structure stands in a cork forest, just off the road, about 1km N of Romanya. (Frustrated dolmen-seekers can relax; this one is well signposted). It consists of a

179

GIRONA TO BARCELONA

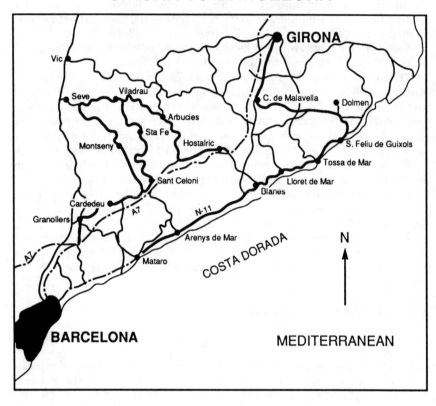

complete circle of standing stones, in the middle of which is a long narrow burial chamber. There are three vast stones placed horizontally over the chamber.

Back on the main road there are 6km to go for *Sant Feliu de Guixols*. For the purposes of this Guide the Route turns southwards after that towards Barcelona. (The coast road also goes N through the popular resort town of *Platja d'Aro* as far as *Palamos* where it turns inland.) The thousands of sheltered inlets along this dramatically beautiful coastline have always attracted invaders, first the Greeks, then the Romans, later the pirates and now the tourists. The tourists are of course welcome and their invasion is made easier by the presence of an international airport S of Girona city and a smaller one at *Empuria-brava* on *Roses Bay*. The one-time natural harbours, places such as *Sant Feliu* and *Blanes*, are now all but blotted out by huge conglomerations of hotels, apartments and camp sites. Sometimes the intensity of colour, the contrast between rugged rock formation and tranquil blue sea can be heart- rendingly beautiful. But all too frequently aesthetic pleasure is turned to irritation (occasionally outrage) by the insensitivity of the developers whose ugly holiday blocks, casinos and fast- food restaurants bestrew the coastline. That said, the Costa Brava beaches are wonderful and the facilities for water sports are probably second to none.

Sant Feliu de Guixols is one of the largest resorts, once a modest port relying on the cork industry for its well-being and before that, the site of a 10C monastery. Still standing is the monastery church, rebuilt in the 14C but retaining much of its original W end. In front of this façade is an interesting porch, known as *Porta Ferrada*, with slightly keyhole (ie Mozarabic) arches below and pure Romanesque triple arches above. No-one knows what purpose this elegant structure served or indeed why it has been allowed to remain standing. S of the church in a large neo-classical building is the Municipal Museum with prehistoric remains and a collection of local paintings. And in the middle of the Plaça is the lovely Baroque arch of *St. Benedict* (*Sant Benet*). Sant Feliu also has some Modernist buildings, the most notable of which is a casino called '*La Constancia*', a bullring and an excellent beach some 3km N of the town centre known as '*Sant Pol*'.

The corniche road between Sant Feliu and *Tossa de Mar* is spectacular, sometimes scaling the high cliffs, sometimes plunging down almost to the water's edge. But it can be hideously hot and slow in high summer. **Tossa de Mar** is an attractive resort managing to preserve its old town (*Vila Vella*) more or less intact amidst modern development. The 12C walls are distinguished by three very fine cylindrical watch towers and a stroll amongst the medieval houses, redolent of times past and now mainly occupied by fishermen, can be a delightful experience after a day spent on Tossa's marvellous horseshoe-shaped sandy beach which lines the bay. Inevitably the tourist shops are there too, but they do not detract from the intrinsic charm of the walled section. Here too is a fine museum, housed in a 16C governor's palace with archeological pieces, but best known for its quite considerable collection of modern painting and sculpture. Tossa, like *Cadaques* further N, was a favourite haunt of European artists in the early part of this century and the museum is proud to own one or two fine examples of their work, including some paintings by *Marc Chagall*, alongside works of foremost Catalan painters. Whilst exploring the old town, notice too the many fortified houses, mainly Gothic, built to withstand the onslaughts of Barbary pirates, as indeed were the walls and the towers, and a castle, now replaced by a lighthouse. The origins of Tossa are Roman and a villa has been excavated at *Els Amettlers* with some good mosaic floors, one of which is inscribed with the name of the owner and of the town. The villa is thought to date from the 4C.

After Tossa the road weaves somewhat tortuously to Canyelles beach (*Platja de Canyelles*) and then drops down to follow quietly along the coast. The next resort, **Lloret de Mar**, announces its ancient pedigree with a Roman sepulchre marked by a small rectangular tower, at the Tossa end of town. But it is a brave spirit who plunges into this vast collection of anonymous white hotels and apartments, discos and restaurants, to search for more relics of the past, at least during the high season. For those who do, there awaits a 16C parish church of *Sant Roma*, much modified and with Modernist chapel added; also one or two neo- classical and Modernist buildings in the region known as *Paseo de Mar*, and even a small nucleus of narrow streets and 17C houses behind there. Lloret's outstanding success as a seaside resort probably has something to do with the fact that a road connects it directly with Girona (and therefore with the airport). It has a bullring, a casino and a fabulous sandy beach.

Having left Lloret there are two features to look out for from the road: one is the neo-classical sanctuary of *Santa Cristina* built on the beach in the 18C and still the focus of an important procession in honour of the saint on 24 June; secondly there are the scant remains – a foundation or two and a cylindrical tower – of Lloret's medieval castle of *Sant Joan*.

Blanes, the largest and most southerly of the Costa Brava resorts, has everything: a kilometre of beach held in the arms of the bay, a picturesque fishing port (and active fishing industry), a marina to take advantage of the splendid sailing conditions, and even a fine botanical garden – *Mari Murtra* – with some 3,000 species of exotic and Mediterranean plants and fine views of the bay glimpsed from its hillside paths. Blanes has also managed to preserve vestiges of the original town, including its castle of *Sant Joan*, a Gothic church of *Santa Maria* and a viscount's palace alongside. The old section of town, once walled, is proud of its Gothic fountain (in the *Carrer Ample*) and its medieval market place, still used by fishermen today.

At *Malgrat de Mar* the coast road joins the N11 from Girona. Malgrat has lost its identity (if it ever had any) in a clutter of tourist blocks. It is distinguished only by its 16C parish church of *Sant Nicolau* with Baroque façade added two centuries later. *Pineda de Mar* and *Calella* originated as stopping places along the royal road from Barcelona northwards. Both retain significant old quarters, mainly 18-19C but with some Gothic buildings left; they also have 18C parish churches and lively fishing industries. Pineda can even boast four arches of a Roman aqueduct and *Calella* has a nice seafront and a municipal park. The two towns are virtually joined now by a continuous string of apartments. Just visible on high ground between them are the ruins of the 13C castle of *Montpalau*, said to cover an Iberian settlement.

A more complete castle can be seen in the next town – **Canet de Mar**. This is in fact an early 20C re-creation of a medieval building which once stood there, masterminded by the celebrated Catalan architect, *Lluis Domenech i Montaner*. Its multitudinous towers and turrets, its minute castellations and satisfying shapes look very well against the dark back-drop of pine forest and it contains a collection of Catalan paintings which can be visited. Canet is an interesting town which once had a flourishing cloth industry as well as an active fishing trade. During the prosperous 19C and early 20C several interesting eclectic and Modernist houses were built. These are now in danger of disappearing from view under the wave of recent development which symbolises the new form of prosperity – tourism.

Also of interest is the one-time fishing port of **L'Arenys de Mar**, conserving in its *Church of Santa Maria* one of the best Baroque retablos anywhere in Spain – the work of *Pau Costa* (1706-1711). To afford such a rare treasure Arenys must at one time have known considerable wealth. And it did, particularly in the 18C and 19C when it built boats which were used all over the Mediterranean and even as far afield as South America. The town also preserves two fine watch towers from the 16C, undoubtedly built with pirates in mind, and one or two vestiges of earlier walls. Much of the story of Arenys, from its medieval origins through its period of industrial success to the present day, can be seen in the *Museum of Federico Mares* housed in an ancient hospital.

Mataro is proud of the fact that it had the first ever railway in Spain (in 1848) which connected it with Barcelona. It is a large unlovely town of some 100,000 people with an important textile industry. Its origins are Iberian and the Romans turned whatever they found there into an *oppidum*, or fortress. The best evidence from the Roman period is a ruined villa known as *Torre Llauder* which has a good mosaic. Apart from that there is little to tempt the visitor to hang around, except perhaps the monumental 15C basilica *Church of Santa Maria* containing one or two paintings, and some Modernist houses by such masters as *Puig i Cadafalch*.

Anyone wishing to come off the main road for a change of scene (and pace) may wish to turn inland up the scenic 1415 road from Mataro to *Granollers*. At 4km is the small town of *Argentona* containing a whole lot more of Puig i Cadafalch's work, including the house he built for his own use in the summer, and an imposing mansion called *Can Curi*. He also restored the 16C church, next door to which is the *Museu del Cantaro*, containing some 1,500 wine pitchers from all over Europe. At this point you may decide to extend your excursion 9km over the mountains to *La Roca del Valles* dominated by its recently restored castle and continue to Granollers; or you can simply return to Mataro by the same mountain road; or you can take the minor road from Argentona back to the N11 by way of *Cabrera de Mar*, with impressive *Plaça del Poble* and a Museum containing Iberian finds from nearby *Burriac*. On the way notice the ruined castle of Burriac on the right.

Thereafter there is everything to be said for leaving the N11 and joining the Motorway so as to pass quickly through the unattractive suburbs of Barcelona and end up at the important junction of *Plaça de les Glories Catalanes*.

B. Inland route via Montseny Region

Take the A17 motorway southwards from Girona as far as *Hostalric* (33 km), a historic town with some of the most imposing ramparts to be seen anywhere. It was originally built as a royal stopping place along the road from Barcelona to Perpignan and its location between the two massifs of *Montseny* and *Montnegre* have given it strategic importance since it was founded in 1145. For this reason it has suffered in most of Catalonia's devastating wars and many of its ancient buildings have been destroyed. The medieval castle was completely rebuilt in the 18C in the manner of the French architect, *Vauban*, with characteristic star-shaped walls to facilitate maximum visibility over the surrounding area. The castle was used as a military garrison until the beginning of this century but is now a municipal building.

Stay on the 253 road out of Hostalric. To the right is the very beautiful region of **Montseny** – the highest massif in the Catalan pre-littoral range. It is a region of thickly forested hills (mainly oak and beech and with some conifers on high ground), deep gorges and abundant natural springs. Significant differences in height, and therefore temperature, provide the Montseny with an astonishing variety of flora and fauna varying from the typical Mediterranean species to those of Central Europe. Its natural inaccessibility, its fertility and abundance of water have meant that man has lived here undisturbed, cultivating the land and working the forests, since time immemorial. Remains of Iberian settlements, early Christian churches, castles and an abundance of traditional *masias* bear witness to the different periods of occupation.

In modern times the delicate balance of man and environment has become endangered, and in 1978 UNESCO declared the area (some 30,000 ha) a 'Biosphere Reserve'. It is the only such Reserve in Catalonia and is administered jointly by the Barcelona and Girona provincial authorities. It is run as a Nature Park, with plenty of information centres, museums, marked paths for walkers and several good camp sites.

After Hostalric take the next right turn to *Breda* which has an 11C *Monastery of Sant Salvador* with 32m high Romanesque bell tower, Lombard style blind arcading and twin windows. The church itself is Gothic with internal buttresses and polygonal apses. It has a charming cloister contemporary with the tower with paired columns. Behind the cloister is the old parish church of *Sta. Maria* which is now a museum containing ceramics and paintings by a local *noucentist* artist, *Josep Aragay i Blanchart* (1889-1973). The town is an important ceramics centre.

Continue N to *Arbucies* (on the edge of the Park). Overlooking it from the S side is the fine hilltop castle of *Montsoriu* built by the viscounts of *Cabrera*. A substantial amount of curtain wall remains making a wildly romantic silhouette from afar. The village of Arbucies has a nice porticoed square and one or two Modernist houses, an ethnological museum and an Information Centre. There is also the pre-Romanesque *Church of Sant Pere Despla* which has recently been restored, during which time fragments of original wall paintings were discovered, said to be some of the oldest in Catalonia.

After Arbucies the road winds its picturesque way over the *Col de Ravell* (820m) to *Vilardrau* (16km). Just before getting there, take a right hand turn to the hilltop village of *Espinelves* (1km) which has a 12C church with particularly fine 3-storey bell tower with arcatures resting on brackets with small heads. This tiny village has solved its security problem not by locking the church but by placing a glass screen across the entrance, through which the visitor can gaze at the simple interior, and even put on a light for 100 ptas. (The minor road continues past three more small 11C churches, to Vic (see Route 8)). To complete this Route, return to the main road and continue 6km to Vilardrau, a peaceful little town, well equipped with hotels and restaurants and proud of its *Church of Sant Marti*, rebuilt in 1769 but preserving both Romanesque and Gothic arches on the S side.

There is a choice of two routes now to take you through the heart of Montseny and back to the Girona-Barcelona road. Both offer spectacular views and interesting distractions on the side, and only the reader can choose which one to take.

For the first, ending up at *San Celoni*, return 3km and take the right hand turning to *Santa Fe*. The road runs between the massifs of *Tura de l'Home* (1712m) and *Moron* (1300m) and takes you to the centre of the Nature Park. You will pass the ancient Benedictine *Monastery of Sant Mercal de Montseny* with 12C church now turned into a restaurant. Santa Fe has a nature school, an Information Centre, an abundance of marked routes, a camping area and a rather expensive hotel in a pseudo-Gothic building. This is an excellent walking area and the hotel itself carries large scale maps and guides. The contrast between the verdant and voluptuous wooded landscapes of Montseny and the grey industrialised coastal sprawl, a mere 30km away, never ceases to amaze.

The corniche road between Santa Fe and San Celoni (22km) is an excellent one and passes close to the medieval village of *Fogars de Montclus* with round tower of ruined hilltop castle nearby. The town of San Celoni is worth a quick look if only for its parish church with striking Baroque façade. Dating from 1762 this is covered with carved plaster decoration in the form of a retablo: the familiar figure of Charity (*Caritat*) and Good Works (*Bona Obra*) are well in evidence at the bottom and above them is a quite delicious stucco gallery full of musicians. This whole wall could so easily have been over-decorated; in reality the balance between stylised figures and blank space seems about right.

For the second route go westwards from Vilardrau to *Espinzella*, a remarkable fortified village with walls dating back to the 12C. There is a Romanesque chapel and a large Gothic mansion with fine windows approached by a flight of steps. Continue westwards to *Seva* which has an information centre and a fair number of hotels, chalets and restaurants spotted amongst its 18C buildings. Turn southwards for *El Brull* and the centre of the Montseny park. El Brull has an 11C church in good order outside but with interior much modified and its main treasure – a mural with scenes from *Genesis* and the life of Christ – taken to the Episcopal Museum in Vic. Above the church are one or two walls remaining from El Brull's 12C castle. There are many fine traditional *masias* in the neighbourhood. This is also an area of archaeological interest: at *Turo de Montgros* (on the outskirts of El Brull) a long section of wall has been excavated believed to be part of an Iberian castle.

Continue to *Montseny* (10km), a medieval village turned tourist resort with information centre, hotels etc. Less mountainous than Santa Fe, standing as it does approximately equidistant from the three main massifs, Montseny village is a good starting point for walks and has tracks going off in all directions, one of which leads to the large camp site of *Fontmartina*, at the foot of *Turo de l'Home*. Follow the *Tordera* river southwards to *Sant Esteve de Palautordera*. Before arriving, notice on the left the hilltop ruins and round tower of the 12C castle of *Montclus* and, on the right, the *Castle of Fluvia* rebuilt in the 17C and preserving within its walls a lovely Romanesque church with three cloverleaf apses. Sant Esteve itself has an 11C church with Gothic façade and chapel.

A few kilometres further on is the somewhat larger village of *Santa Maria de Palautordera* documented as early as 862. Its old centre is now mainly Gothic, including the *Carrer Mayor* (with some fine pointed windows) and the church with polygonal apse. Its bell tower is said to be an expansion of what was once a medieval watch tower. The 15C builders seem to have removed all traces of the town which was there before.

Your foray into the Montseny Region ends as you rejoin the main road – or the motorway – from Girona and continue 28 km to Barcelona. The only sizeable town on the way is *Granollers* which has little to recommend it save its distinguished 16C grain market (*lonja*) with tiled roof held up by elegant Tuscan columns.

INTERIOR ROUTES

ROUTE 8

BARCELONA TO VIC: ENVIRONS OF VIC: VIC TO RIPOLL

There is a direct route to Vic from Barcelona – 67km straight up the N152 – speedy but with little of outstanding interest on the way. Or you can take a longer, more leisurely drive along the 1415 road via *Caldes de Montbui* and *l'Estany*, which will include medieval villages, Romanesque churches, a monastery or two and some good *masias* along the way. Both routes entail leaving Barcelona from the *Plaça de les Glories Catalanes* from which the N152 is signposted, and travelling northwards as far as *Bellula*. At *Canovells* close by, there is an 11C church worth stopping for with Lombard arcading on the apses and an exceptional doorway with archivolts and carved animals.

For the **fast route**, continue on the N152 to *La Garriga*, notable for its abundance of Modernist houses standing in their own gardens, built by the rich and famous at the turn of the century for summer use. The busiest architect seems to have been *Manuel Raspall i Mayol*, four of whose houses stand together in a group known as *La Manzana Raspall*. There is also, on the S side of town, a 12C church near to which are the excavated ruins of a Roman villa. (It is worth remembering that the N152 follows the tracks of the main Roman road from Barcelona to Vic and northwards). Pass through *Aiguafreda* and on to *Centelles* noticing the remains of *Cruilles* castle high up on the right between the two. *Centelles* (slightly off the road), is an old town with some good stone doorways, a 16C monumental gate and a Baroque church.

Tona was first documented in 889 and a few vestiges of the original town and castle can be seen near the much altered Romanesque church of *Sant Andreu*. But Tona reached its *apogée* in the late 19C when people came from far and wide to enjoy the abundant sulphurous springs. The numerous Modernist chalets and houses in and around town bear witness to the once popular pastime of taking the waters which seems now to have given way to the more pressing needs of industry. Tona is no longer the pleasurable spa that it was. It stands, incidentally, at the W end of one of the best routes into the *Montseny Region* (see Route 7). From Tona there are 10km to go before reaching Vic.

For the second, less direct and far more **rural route**, turn left at Bellula on to the 1415 to **Caldes de Montbui**. Caldes, as the name suggests, is another thermal spa. It was known to the Romans as *Aquae Calidae* and they built there a substantial bathing establishment which has recently been restored and displays some of the huge quantity of coins and pots which have been discovered in the area. The hot springs are still appreciated today and there are two modern *balnearios*. Much of the medieval town has also been preserved. It focussed around the main hot spring – *Font de Lleo* – and some sections of the encircling rampart also remain.

Caldes was once capital of the *Comarca* and had a sizeable hospital (*Santa Susanna*) which today houses an archaeological museum containing a lot more of the Roman finds. Its Baroque church is worth visiting for its remarkable doorway and its 14C *Christ in Majesty* repaired after it was all but destroyed during the Civil War, and noted for its fine carving of the hair and beard (which is original).

From Caldes a drive up the mountain road as far as *Sant Sebastia de Montmayor* is recommended to see the 12C Romanesque church of that name. In the form of a Greek cross (with four equal arms) it has three apses and a square bell tower over the crossing. After that short diversion continue to *Sant Feliu de Codines* with charming 16C and 17C houses in the centre and some good Modernist ones as well. On leaving the town, take the very scenic mountain road sign-posted to the right to *Sant Miguel del Fai* where a church of that name (part of a former Benedictine monastery) has actually been built into the rock of a cave. Its façade is Romanesque and its setting of rocks and waterfalls is memorable and well worth the drive up.

Return once more to the main road and continue across the high plateau to Moia which is dominated by its huge Baroque *Church of Santa Maria* and has several interesting old *masias* on the outskirts including, in particular, a splendid Gothic one known as *Castellnou de la Plana* with its original water mill still functioning deep inside a subterranean chamber. At Moia there is a mountain road (N141) going off to the right to join the main Barcelona – Vic N152. But we recommend you continue northwards to *L'Estany* (the main jewel of this route) before turning off right to Vic on a minor road.

L'Estany lies in a wonderful setting, in a high valley surrounded by impressive peaks. It was here, in 1080, that the Bishop of Vic caused an Augustinian Canonry to be founded, of which the 12C church still stands. It was restored in the late sixties to its original late Romanesque style, having suffered both Gothic and Baroque additions and considerable damage from an earthquake. It now has a nave, transept and three simple apses each with a single window and minimal ornamentation.

The church is distinguished by its very lovely **Cloister** with perfect arches, ten on each side, resting on pairs of columns. The capitals, some seventy-two of which are excellently preserved, represent some of the liveliest and most beautiful medieval carving anywhere in Catalonia. Those on the side nearest the church are the oldest and very properly present the story of the life of Christ. Elsewhere there is a rich diversity of themes, both sacred and profane, with jugglars and musicians, men and beasts, flowers, and all kinds of ceremonial scenes. It is an exhilerating account of life as it was lived in the 12C and 13C.

Next to the church is a small museum which gives an interesting insight into the various periods of architectural 'improvement' and the task of the recent restorers. In the immediate vicinity of the church are one or two picturesque medieval houses which would have been residences of the Augustinian monks until they moved away from the community in 1592.

After L'Estany continue 5km N to the crossroads where you will turn right for Vic. Just before this, on a hilltop, stands the very early church of *Sant Feliu de Terrassola*. Archives in the cathedral of Vic mention its consecration in 1093 but its origins are thought to go back to 927. Over the centuries it has suffered a confusion of additions and destructions and this is ably explained by the farmer who lives in the adjoining house and who welcomes visitors every day in the summer season (Sundays only during the rest of the year). The second apse was added in the 12C and there was every intention to put in a third but this was never done. The fortified tower was added in 13C because of feudal struggles with neighbouring parishes; in the 18C the apses were removed and the church was given a heavy Baroque altar (of which there is a photograph) at the W end. During the civil war, when clerics hid in tunnels under the church and were fed daily by villagers, the church was badly damaged. In 1975 work started on restoring it to the original pre-Romanesque shape, the apses were rebuilt at the E end and the unsuitable Baroque addition was blocked off. The original font, which had been discovered in thirty-seven pieces, has recently been meticulously repaired by the farmer and his wife and stands in its rightful place once more as solid evidence of their devotion. At the time of writing this church has a regular congregation of eight people.

Take the next right turn for **VIC** (19km). Vic is one of Catalonia's most prestigious and interesting towns with a history which goes back to the fierce Iberian tribe of *Ausitani*, whose capital it was. They resisted the Roman onslaught for over 30 years before finally succumbing to superior strength in 183BC. The Romans called the town *Ausona* and filled it with fine buildings including a temple. In 516 under the Visigoths it became the seat of a Christian diocese until overwhelmed by the Moors 200 years later. The Moors were finally dislodged by Wilfred the Hairy in 879 who then started to build a new city roughly where the cathedral now stands, which was called *Vicus Ausonae* and which was to dominate the surrounding countryside both clerically and politically throughout the Middle Ages and beyond. In the 14C *King Pere III* surrounded it with defensive walls, vestiges of which can still be seen. In recent times a modern city, with important small industries such as food processing (especially sausages) and tanning has grown up around the nucleus which is now encircled by a continuous series of *Ramblas*.

A walk around the old quarter is a rewarding experience and should start with the **Cathedral**. There are some cathedrals which are architecturally superb and deserve a serious visit on these grounds alone irrespective of what is inside, and there are those whose structure is less distinguished but which contain one or more outstanding features which should on no account be missed. Vic cathedral belongs to the second category.

The 11C building was entirely reconstructed between 1780 and 1803 in neo-classical form and only the crypt, Gothic cloister and Romanesque bell tower remain from the original. Outside, the 6-storeyed tower is a delight with Lombard-style arches and perfect proportions. The main, W, façade is however very disappointing and it is important not to stand and dwell on its shortcomings but to go inside: here, covering all the walls, are the incomparable masterworks of the Catalan artist *Jose Maria Sert* (1874-1945).

The church is like a museum dedicated to this great painter and the heavy fluted columns in sombre colour provide the perfect setting for his ochre tints and powerful images. It is interesting to learn that these paintings are actually Sert's third attempt. He first conceived the idea when he was twenty-six and was looking for a church or palace to decorate. The Bishop of Vic invited him to embellish his relatively recently completed cathedral. Sert went to Paris for inspiration and ended up selling his first works there because he was not satisfied with them. He came home and started again only to have the paintings totally destroyed by fire when the cathedral was ransacked during the Civil War. Once more he set to work to cover the walls and died in 1945 leaving only a small area (the lunettes above the cornice) to be completed by his pupil, *Miguel Massot.*

Sert's paintings have been compared to those of Michelangleo for their sublime power. He evokes the well-known scenes from Old and New Testaments but with so much detailed attention paid to the people who are watching and participating that you, the onlooker, feel part of the drama too.

The W wall depicts in the centre the moment when *Pontius Pilate* washes his hands and the crowd hails the thief *Barabbas.* On the left is the road to *Calvary* and on the right the chasing of the money-lenders from the temple. The ruined cathedral itself appears as background to all this, as if to say that man's inhumanity has not changed. The biggest painting of all is at the E end and represents – on five planes – the crucifixion scene, the burial of Christ, and the ascension. Here again it is the onlookers which command the attention, including a moving picture of Mary watching Jesus ascend. Everyone's personal involvement is depicted as never before: a facial expression here, a pointing finger there, speak more poignantly than ever the written word could do.

Local people who knew the artist say that his second cycle of pictures, painted in his prime and enriched by the Paris experience, were even better. Suffice to say that the present scenes, admirably lit and well set off by the plain white vault and the ochre tones of the columns, are a rewarding and unforgettable sight.

Another joy awaits the visitor and that is the marvellous 15C alabaster retablo by *Pere Oller* of Barcelona, which stands at the end of the ambulatory. Quietly hidden away, and presumably even more hidden away during the Civil War, it has escaped both restoration and devastation. Its twelve panels, divided by statues of the saints, represent familiar biblical scenes in the finest detail. Below are fourteen apostles and prophets, not just standing, but all engaged in doing something or, at the very least, holding something by which they can be recognised: there is Mark surrounded by books, James with his pilgrim's hat and staff; and notice the long, thin, ascetic face of 'doubting' Thomas, said to have been the most intelligent of all the apostles. Opposite the retablo is the tomb of the cleric who commissioned and then paid for this work.

The Romanesque crypt has also survived intact (because it was hidden for over 500 years) and can be entered down the steps in front of the high altar. The simple pillars have very primitively carved capitals, some said to be Visigothic. The cloister is another survivor: it has three storeys, austere Romanesque below, elaborate Gothic in the middle and a neo-classical top added later. The three periods weld together very harmoniously and the only unfortunate note is struck by the huge monument to a 19C philosopher which has been placed in the middle and is right out of scale. The cloister contains the tomb of the artist, Sert, and above it has been placed his very last work – a small and immensely moving picture of Christ and the thief talking together, both crucified.

Alongside the cathedral, close to the belltower, is the **Episcopal Museum**, only open for three hours each day (between 10 and 13 hours) but well worth a visit. It contains a good collection of frescoes, retablos, polychrome wood figures and altar frontals, starting with the earliest (11C-13C) in Room I and working through another seven rooms to the early 16C. There are many treasures, particularly amongst the earlier periods, and the whole collection is well lit, well displayed and avoids becoming overbearing. Early works include a fine *Last Supper* from Seu d'Urgell, some charming renderings of Adam and Eve and a recurrent theme of St. Michael and the Devil weighing their souls (which are depicted as miniature versions of themselves). There is also an alabastar retablo by the 14C artist, *Bernardo Saulet* (in Room II) consisting of 20 panels and much revered, though the detail seems less fine than that of the *Soler* retablo in the cathedral. Gradually, as centuries pass, the works become more vivid, more exuberant, more obsessed with tempting devils and martyrdom and gushing blood as the fertile Gothic imaginations take over. Despite the increasingly gruesome tendency there are some joys and the Last Judgement by *Ramon de Mur* in Room IV is one such.

Two minutes' walk from the cathedral and museum is a **Roman Temple** which was discovered in 1882 during the demolition of the 11C castle of the *Montcada* family which had been built all around it, using what was left of the temple as an interior patio. One or two walls of the castle remain hard up against the temple, as does one wall of the 11C *Sant Sadurni chapel* (now integrated into a later church) which once served the Montcada family.

All around are recognisably medieval streets, managing somehow to remain sheltered from the modern sector of town which you know is near at hand but fortunately cannot hear. One street, *Carrer del Albergueria*, (close to the cathedral) claims to date back to the 10C. Just below this street is the 11C *Queralt bridge* which marks the spot where the road to Barcelona once left the city of Vic, following the tracks of the original Roman road. The bridge has been many times repaired and crosses what remains of the river *Meder*, a mere trickle now since its waters have been dammed higher up. Here modern life *does* impinge and it is outrageous that factories on the opposite bank are (at time of writing) allowing their effluent to pour out quite freely, thus turning what was once a beauty spot into a smelly and polluted sludge.

Incidentally this point affords a good opportunity to look up at the Cathedral's Gothic cloister from outside: one is particularly struck by the extreme delicacy of the columns looking as if they could quite easily be snapped in two. Also visible from here are remnants of the 14C walls which once encircled the old city.

Walk back into the centre, past the cathedral and down *Carrer Sant Sadurni* or any parallel street and you reach the lovely arcaded *Plaça Mayor* (also known as *El Mercadal*), probably one of the finest squares in Catalonia. Since time immemorial it has been the animated centre of Vic's commercial life and it still has a fascinating Saturday market. Buildings range from 16C to the present day, though the town hall with clock tower has 14C origins and fine pointed arches on the ground floor to prove it. There are several well placed cafés from which to admire the square whilst enjoying a drink and a dish of *tapas.* (*Cafe Nou* boasts over 100 varieties).

Environs of Vic

Vic has roads radiating from it in all directions and any one of these will take you into glorious mountain scenery, through tiny villages past gems of Romanesque churches and the occasional monastery or castle ruin. Here are 3 suggestions. But the visitor can take virtually any road in this richly endowed and beautiful countryside and not be disappointed.

1. Take the 153 road NE-wards through *Roda de Ter* and *Santa Maria de Corco* to *Rupit.* The last part of the drive is wild and particularly beautiful. The village of Rupit hangs on the rock face, curving round the line of the valley, with the river far below. It would be hard to find anywhere a village which is so much at one with its mother rock. A wander through its gently stepped streets is a delight. Moreover, for all its remoteness, Rupit has three modest hotels (two *hostales* and one *fonda*) and seems to have achieved, at least for the moment, just the right balance between retaining its natural charm and catering for visitors.

    If you return to Vic by the same road you will have covered about 70kms. Or you can branch off right to *Manlieu* (just before Roda de Ter) which will be slightly shorter and bring you on to the Vic-Ripoll road a little further north. Manlieu is however a modern industrial town with little charm. (Or you could continue from Rupit on the same road as far as Olot – see Route 6).

2. Take the 153 again and after 6km branch off right to *Tavernoles* where there is a somewhat modified 11C church. Continue from Tavernoles to the *Parador de Sau* which overlooks the reservoir of that name. From here there is a 4km track to the 11C Benedictine *Monastery of Sant Pere de Casserres*, standing on the very tip of a peninsula jutting out into the reservoir. The large church has been remarkably well preserved with a nave and two aisles and three well-decorated apses; it is considered

to be one of the best examples of Lombard Romanesque anywhere in Catalonia. There is also a cloister (in rather poor condition). The only way back to Vic is by the road you have come (32km in all).

3.   Take the 141 road E-wards from Vic and after 4km branch off right to *Sant Julia de Vilatorta* and immediately right again to *Vilalleons*. Here there is an 11C church with Lombard arching, a belltower and good doorway. Go back to Sant Julia and continue E-wards to see two more Romanesque churches – at *Sant Sadurni d'Osomort* and *Espinelves* (a lovely hilltop village and church described on page 184 as part of the Montseny excursion in Route 7). If you return to Vic, you will have done about 40km.

Vic To Ripoll (37km)

The road follows the Ter valley which is liberally scattered with ancient farmhouses (*masias*) and castle ruins. You may be tempted, about half-way up, to take the right-hand turning to *Torello*, a market town with an evocative old quarter which has a nice plaça and doorways. You should then continue 3km to the village of *Sant Vicenc de Torella* where the much restored 11C parish church has a very lovely 3-storey bell tower with Lombard decoration, which has thankfully remained unchanged. Remains of the medieval castle of Torello are just visible on a hill to the NW.

For Ripoll see Route 6.

ROUTE 9

BARCELONA TO PIUGCERDA VIA TERRASSA, MONASTERY OF MONTSERRAT AND MANRESA. EXCURSION TO CARDONA

From the *Plaça de les Glories Catalanes* in Barcelona take the A18 motorway to (22 km) **Terrassa**, a dauntingly large industrial town which nevertheless contains some significant treasures in the shape of three of the oldest churches in Catalonia. They stand side by side in the district known as *Sant Pere de Terrassa* on the N side of town. It is best to go into the centre and then follow signposts to *Esglesia Sant Pere*.

Sant Pere de Terrasa, originally settled by Iberians, became the Roman *Municipium Flavium Egara*. Under the Visigoths, in 450AD, Egara was the seat of a Christian bishopric – with eight bishops – and prospered greatly until

BARCELONA TO PUIGCERDA

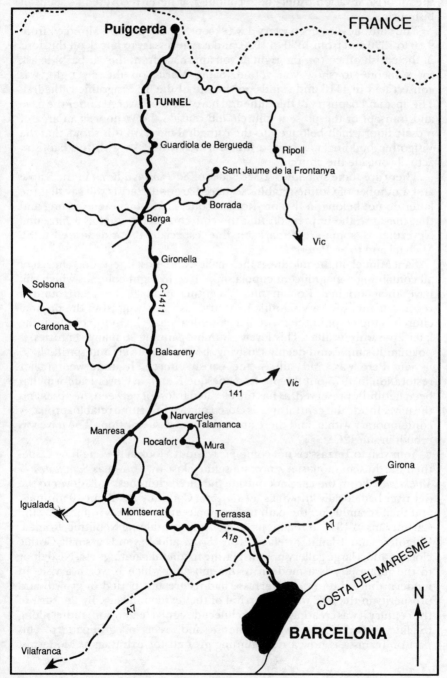

the Moorish invasion. After the reconquest, it never recovered its status of bishopric.

The churches are open every day (except Sunday pm and Monday) from 9.30 to 1330 and from 1530 to 1930, and it is necessary to knock on the door of the parish office (on the right as you approach from the car park) to ask for someone to show you round. **Santa Maria**, on the far right, was consecrated in 1113 and stands on the site of the 5C Visigothic cathedral. The apse and baptistry of the cathedral have been discovered under the nave and transept of the present church and outside the W door is an area of mosaic floor which belonged to the cathedral nave. All this shows that the Visigothic building was built a little further to the W, with the baptistry actually outside the church.

There are some splendid 12C frescoes of *St. Thomas à Becket* in the S apse and a number of Gothic retablos scattered around. Purists will say that the latter do not belong in this pre-Romanesque and Romanesque setting and that they give the impression that the church is being used as a museum. Nevertheless, some are remarkably fine, especially those dedicated to St. Michael and to St. Peter.

Sant Miquel, in the middle, is the smallest and most interesting church of all containing a magnificent cupola supported by eight columns which still have their original Roman and Visigothic capitals. They surround a reconstruction of the Visigothic baptistry. Also surviving from the original church is the crypt in the form of a clover-leaf chapel. On top of this is the later apse with its altar. This lovely church, spanning so many centuries, is poignantly simple and deeply satisfying, both aesthetically and spiritually.

Sant Pere was, and still is, the parish church. It underwent major restoration in 1975 but the pre-Romanesque E end, in clover-leaf form, has been faithfully preserved, as has the elevated transept between the apses and the nave. Inside the central apse is closed off by a fine stone retablo, probably contemporary with it, and there are remains of a mosaic floor. The nave was rebuilt in the 12C.

Your visit to Terrassa is not complete without a look at the one-time castle, then Carthusian monastery, now museum, close-by, known as *Sant Jaume de Vallparadis*. From the car-park outside the three churches, walk down to the dry river bed, locally known as '*El Torrente*'. Continue for about 10 minutes, and then scramble up the path to the monastery which was founded by the Carthusians in 1344. It retains its chapel, now containing Neolithic, Roman, Visigothic and Islamic artefacts from *Egara* and beyond, a small Gothic cloister, and a large gallery now displaying medieval paintings etc. Next door to the monastery is a modern textile museum which is worth a visit. In modern times the town of Terrassa had its greatest period of growth and prosperity in the 19C with the arrival of the textile industry. By the turn of the century it was creating a new, architect-designed 'extension' rather along the lines of Barcelona's own, with houses and streets in a grid pattern. This part of Terrassa is now a rich hunting ground for extravagant Modernist buildings, including the lovely wavey *Masia Freixe* in the *Sant Jordi Municipal Park*.

For the more traditional eye there is a late 16C parish church containing a good Renaissance sculpture of *El Sant Enterrament* (the holy burial) as well as some striking modern pieces. And you might just be fortunate enough to spot, amongst all the later development, the single remaining cylindrical tower of the first (10C) castle of Terrassa.

From Terrassa take the 1213 road (which passes under the motorway) to *Monistrol de Montserrat* to visit the famous **Monastery of Montserrat**, perched high in a cleft in mountains of the same name. One can either take the rack railway up from Monistrol (which is the terminus of the train from Barcelona), or drive up the steep zig-zag road for 7km.

Although the Monastery building is somewhat disappointing aesthetically, and much of the quintessential spirituality has been lost in the inevitable layer of tourist commercialisation, the setting is of unique and spectacular beauty. *Mons Serratus*, or the Serrated Mountain, is aptly named. An isolated and barren ridge of limestone conglomerate formed into extraordinary folded shapes by centuries of wind and water erosion, the range extends for over 10km and its saw-toothed outline is visible from a great distance.

First sight of the Monastery poised precipitately on its high ledge and bounded on three sides by surrealistic pinnacles and boulders provokes the question WHY THERE? Ancient legend relates that an image of the Virgin was brought to Barcelona by St. Peter and this was hidden in the mountains by shepherds in the early 8C to protect it from the invading Moors. The image was later rediscovered by more shepherds who tried to take it to Manresa. However, when it reached the ledge where the Monastery now stands, the image refused to go any further. Realising they had witnessed a miracle, the shepherds fell on their knees and then built a simple chapel to enshrine their holy statue.

The Benedictines arrived in the 9C and the first documentation about the shrine of Montserrat dates from the year 888. In 1025 they converted the shrine into a monastery and Oliva, Bishop of Vic and Abbot of Ripoll, became its first abbot. The monastery grew rapidly in importance and in 1409 was given the status of an independent abbey, separate from the episcopal authority of Ripoll. By 1490 it had its own printing press (probably the earliest in Spain) and became a centre of learning throughout the Catholic world. Kings and princes made pilgrimages and endowed it with rich treasures, invoking the blessing of the Virgin before going to war. Christopher Columbus took with him a hermit from Montserrat and so-named one of the first islands he discovered in the New World. King Philip II was a great benefactor and totally rebuilt the church in the late 16C. In 1811 disaster struck in the form of Napoleon's army which, in all the horror of the Peninsula War, sacked and almost completely destroyed the building. The monks abandoned it and the holy image was removed to Esparraguera nearby. In 1844 they returned and began reconstruction. This was necessarily a very slow process and towards the end of the century involved the young Catalan architect, Antoni Gaudi, who is said to have derived the inspiration for his masterpiece, *La Sagrada Familia* in Barcelona, from the very Montserrat mountains he worked alongside. Apart from the interruption of the Civil War, reconstruction work continued until 1968 which was when the new monastery façade was finally completed.

- Today there are some eighty Benedictine monks living there, tending the holy shrine of the Virgin and practising various traditional crafts such as bookbinding, pottery and distilling a herbal liqueur called *Aromas de Montserrat* (on sale in the shops). They also write and publish theological, scientific and artistic works and attend to the needs of a quantity of visitors who come on retreat each year. Fortunately for the monks, their rich and edifying existence is played out behind closed doors and away from prying tourist eyes.

Another very important part of Montserrat is the inspiring *Escolania Boys' Choir* (first documented in 1223) which sings in the church every day around noon and again in the evening, usually at 19 hours. The choir school is located in a building behind the church and holds fifty boys. It is closed to the public.

A visit to Montserrat starts with the *Square of the Cross* (*Plaça de la Creu*) so-named because it contains the unexpectedly simple stone cross carved by the modern Catalan sculptor *Josep Subirachs*. Passing buildings containing rooms for pilgrims, and a disconcerting array of souvenir shops and cafés, you come to the largest square of all – that of *Santa Maria*. Straight ahead is the rather forbidding façade of the *Monastery*. The three upper balconies display designs by the sculptor *Joan Rebull* representing (left to right) St. Benedictine, Pope Pius XII and St. George (patron saint of Catalonia).

To the left of the monastery is a rare and lovely sight which should not be missed (though frequently is, by those who are unaware of it): that is the two remaining arms of the Gothic cloister, dating from mid 15C. There are two storeys with pointed arches below and flatter ones above. The capitals are ornamented with primitive designs and in each of the spandrels is a face. The columns are slender and the whole displays a purity of line and medieval simplicity which is sadly lacking in other parts of the complex.

Another remnant of past times is the 11C entrance to the original Romanesque church to be found through the main entrance porches on the right. On your left is a modern statue of St. Benedict. You are now standing in the atrium with graffito decorations dating from 1952, those on the right showing principal Christian shrines and those on the left representing the main events in Montserrat's history. It is worth entering the small baptistry which has a pleasing mosaic interior completed only in 1971. Ahead is the church façade, designed by the Catalan architect *Fransesc Villar* in 1900. The

Montserrat. Monastery and mountains. Bages.

sculptures of Jesus and the twelve apostles add a touch of interest to the otherwise heavy and uninspiring design.

Inside the church itself (consecrated in 1592) the atmosphere is dark and rather oppressive. The wide nave has round arches and six chapels. The most highly ornamented section is the Sanctuary with choir stalls reserved for the monks, and the main altar (weighing 8 tons) is made from local Montserrat rock. Over the altar is a 16C ivory image of Christ which has been attached to a modern cross. High above that, presiding over the whole church, is the heart and soul of Montserrat – the 12C statue itself. To come close to this beautiful and simple representation of the Virgin and Child (known as *La Moroneta* because the wood has become blackened with the smoke of candles throughout the centuries), it is necessary to go back out of the church and enter a side door on the S side of the main one. Skirting three 19C side chapels, you come to a fine staircase with alabaster gate and candlesticks and mosaics representing saints who were virgins (on the right) and saints who were mothers (on the left). This leads up to the throne room with Venetian mosaics and nine silver lamps representing the eight Catalan dioceses and Montserrat itself. The ornate silver throne was donated by the people of Catalonia in 1947.

But it is the serenity and simplicity of the image itself which holds the eye, with its blackened face and robes of rich gold. The figure of the Virgin is said to be original; that of the Child was restored in the 19C. The faithful are invited to kiss the image's hand through a hole in the glass casing so the queue inevitably moves rather slowly at this point. Just below the throne room is the chapel for which the architect Gaudi was partly responsible. The fine dome, painted by *Joan Llimona*, depicts pilgrims paying homage to *La Moroneta.*

Returning to *Plaça Santa Maria* you will find two Museums: one contains a collection of archaeological pieces from Egypt (including a splendid mummy dated 650-300 BC), Mesopotamia and Palestine, together with many prehistoric artefacts from Catalonia itself. Also on show are some of the many fine jewels and other gifts which have been offered to the Virgin over the centuries. The second museum contains a wide range of paintings, with two fine *El Grecos* – Santa Magdalena and St. John Evangelist, a *Zurbaran* and three *Picassos* (two from his early, Malaga, period, and one displaying a dedication by the artist to Montserrat written in 1961). Thre are also two paintings by *Sert* including a version of the Descent from the Cross (which appears in Vic cathedral), and a very stiff drawing by the young *Salvador Dali.*

Approximately 3km along the Igualada road is the tiny 10C *Monastery and Church of Santa Cecilia.* It nestles at the foot of the bluff and is a simple and refreshing joy after the somewhat overwhelming charms of the Montserrat complex. The church has been well restored and its three apses with Lombard arching are in excellent condition. The typical Romanesque belfry is curiously placed to one side. This was a separate Benedictine monastery until 1539 when it was taken under the control of the much more powerful

Montserrat. Now the building is occasionally used as a young people's hostel. The road between the two monasteries offers a close-up view of some of the most spectacular and surrealistic rock shapes and the term "folded mountains" takes on a whole new meaning, especially at sundown when silhouettes are especially sharp.

After Santa Cecilia continue along the same mountain road to **Manresa**, a modern industrial city with an ancient quarter down by the river which is worth a short visit. It was probably the Roman *Menorisa* and throughout the centuries has played a prominent role in Catalonia's many battles because of its strategic location at the crossroads of the main N-S and E-W routes. It was used by the Christian armies in the 9C during their victorious campaign against the Moors and was later built up into a fortified city. It stood up bravely against the French invaders in 1811 and suffered greatly as a result. By the middle of this century it was rebuilt and greatly enlarged. Rapid industrialisation and growth have brought about an untidy sprawl of a city today but the small medieval quarter (*Ciutat Vella*) holds one or two features, not least its huge dominating fortress *Church of Santa Maria* (known as *La Seu*).

Typically Catalan-Gothic in style and built on the foundations of a 10C Romanesque church, *la Seu* is the work of the 14C architect *Berenguer de Montagut* (who also designed *Santa Maria del Mar* in Barcelona). On entering the church one is struck by the immense width of the nave (one of the widest in Europe), by the slightly ethereal pink light overall caused by the abundant (and sometimes lovely) stained glass windows, and by the heavy octagonal columns. Closer inspection will reveal three outstandingly beautiful retablos; on the S wall is the masterpiece – *El Espiritu Santo* – created for the tanners' guild in 1394 by *Pere Serra*. (The three scenes in the bottom panel are not part of the original work though are thought to belong to the same period); in the apse are two more: one on the S side is by *Cabrera* (1406) and is dedicated to Saints Michael and Nicholas; the other, by *Arnau Bassa* (1346) stands right behind the altar and represents Saint Mark.

A walk around the outside of the church is also rewarding, and the many marks on the walls where buildings have been added and taken away again are almost a history lesson in themselves. The S wall has some particularly good gargoyles and an early Gothic door with medieval beasts climbing over it (looking like snails). The 19C W front is exceptionally ugly and has been discreetly cordonned off with an iron railing. The cloister, accessible through a metal door, is pleasant enough; substantial sections of the original Romanesque cloister are in process of being uncovered behind one of the walls and this is the exciting part. The delicate twin columns and primitive carving of the older work make a refreshing contrast with the staid and heavy carving all around.

One or two mansions have been restored in the medieval quarter standing below the church and there remain some vestiges of the original city walls.

There is also the distinguished 17C *Palace of Justice* with its classical façade and the slightly less impressive *Town Hall* (18C) which stands on the main square (*Plaça Mayor*). Oldest of all is the town bridge (*Pont Vell*) which crosses the river *Cardener* at the SE corner of the *Cuitat Vella*. It was built in the early 14C on the foundations of an older one (just visible under the water) which is thought, in turn, to have replaced a Roman bridge. Recently some modern buildings alongside were pulled down and it is now possible to appreciate the picturesque hump-backed silhouette in all its simple glory, unspoilt by later intrusions.

After Manresa we propose a short EXCURSION into the countryside to see the picturesque monastery of *Sant Benet de Bages* plus one or two village churches, about 46km in all. Take the 141 NE-wards and after 10km turn right to *Navarcles*. The monastery is quite difficult to find. Once in Navarcles, take a right turn opposite *Currer Monestır*, cross a bridge over the *Llobregat* river and then turn right. Sant Benet de Bages (12C) is a former Benedictine monastery whose cloister, with paired columns and intricate carved capitals showing biblical and mythological scenes, is a romantic delight. Several monastery buildings remain but the church itself is very dilapidated except for its splendid doorway with carved capitals and three archivolts – a typical late Romanesque feature.

Talamanca is the next village along the road and has a 12C church of *Santa Maria*, of no particular interest except for the rather fine carved capitals on either side of the main door. The village itself seems to have been built inside what is left of its original castle whose round castellated tower still stands in the centre.

The village of *Mura* lies up a right-hand turn some 4kms beyond Talamanca. Its 12C church, *Sant Marti de Mura*, is much more rewarding than Talamanca with a particularly lovely *Epiphany* in the tympanum of the main door, some very imaginative carved capitals and good examples of arcatures on the apse. This church has been restored many times but retains a poignant and unspoilt simplicity. From Mura you can either continue to the village of *Rocafort* and then back to *Talamanca*, or return from Mura the way you have come. If you are really keen you can continue from Rocafort in the direction of *Sant Vicenc de Castellet* for on the way, at the village of *El Marquet* is the pre-Romanesque, Mozarabic church of *Santa Maria de Matardars*. It has a rectangular apse and horseshoe arches between it and the two side chapels – an interesting example of the early touching of two cultures.

Back at Navarcles turn left and then right on to the N-bound C1411 which follows the Llobregat valley. After about 12km you reach the small town of **Balsareny** with its 11C church of *Sant Esteban* standing below an even earlier castle. The church is very simple indeed – single nave, one apse completely devoid of decoration, and a side chapel added in the 16C which is now full of relics. The principal reason for stopping here is the **Castle**, visible for miles around on its hilltop and said to have been built originally by Wilfred the Hairy, founder of the House of Barcelona, in 883, possibly on the ruins of a Roman military camp. It was destroyed by the Moors and then rebuilt, and rebuilt again many times over. It is now in an excellent state of repair and has been turned in to a private museum, only open at weekends and overseen with much pride by a caretaker who also acts as guide. The rooms are stuffed with paintings and furniture of various periods and there are piles of documents in Catalan dating back to the early 11C and still waiting to be catalogued. All the ceilings are of painted wood and look distinctly Moorish; there is also a gem of a period tiled kichen, a dining room with English grandfather clock and a delightful courtyard which is rented out for weddings. The tour is a pleasurable experience, as much for the memorable patter of the guide who insists on addressing even two people as if they were a group of thirty, as for the intrinsic value of the various exhibits.

At Balsareny there is a road going W across the mountains which eventually joins up with Route 4. It is a very beautiful road and passes through two important sites: *Cardona* and *Solsona*. The latter has been included as part of an excursion from Route 4. Cardona, only 31km W of Balsareny and the main route N-wards, is included here. *Suria*, halfway along the road, has a pleasant medieval sector and remains of a castle.

Cardona, on the right bank of the river Cardoner, is recognisable from afar by the distinctive hilltop outline of its Castle and Church; the Castle, now containing what must be one of the most atmospheric paradors in Spain, was first documented in the 8C when it was built as a defence against the Moors. Captured by them in 826, it was not reconquered and rebuilt until 880. Many times destroyed and rebuilt thereafter, it fell eventually into long-term decay until reconstructed and opened as a parador in 1975.

Standing a little apart from the main complex is the small and utterly simple *Minyona Tower* which one can both enter and climb to the top of. The smallness of the space inside is evidence enough of the immense thickness of the walls and consequent total impregnability of this 12C tower, which at some time had also been used as a dungeon. It was decapitated in the 18C. Also visible in this are sections of the original castle on which later versions were imposed.

The 11C collegiate **Church of San Vicenc** alongside is a superbly restored specimen of the Lombard Romanesque style. It was constructed by order of the *Bishop of Urgell* over an earlier church, and occupied by a community of Augustinian canons. It has a huge nave, some 46ms long and nearly 20ms high, three apses, two side aisles, a transept and the oldest complete dome in Spain with four shell formations in the squinches below. There is also a remarkable crypt (from the earlier church) with alabaster windows and very small columns with primitive cushion capitals.

The interior of the nave is well lit by natural light coming through the plain glass windows and there is absolutely no superimposed embellishment to distract the eye from the pure and majestic architecture line. From the W end it looks as if the two side aisles curve slightly outwards, which may well be an optical illusion. In the S aisle, a patch of original floor has been uncovered.

Outside, the three apses are the main joy with typical Lombard arches, cut very high, as the main decoration. There is also a small Gothic cloister under restoration. It is hard to believe that in the 18C (probably at the same time as Minyona Tower was reduced) this church was converted into an army barracks – under the punitive regime of Philip V – and remained under military occupation until 1802. (The cathedral at Lleida and many similar hilltop buildings suffered the same fate). Its place as parish church was taken by *Sant Miquel* in the town below, another large, bare edifice, lacking the refinement of *San Vicenc* and now showing evidence of years of neglect.

Parts of the medieval town of Cardona are worth exploring, especially the arcaded *Plaça Mercat*, narrow streets leading off *Carrer Mayor*, and the old town gate of *Portal de Graells*. The town is however primarily famous for its rock salt 'mountain' alongside the river which appears from above like some huge grey-white excrescence on the landscape – almost a disfigurement. It is said to be a unique geological feature and salt has been mined here since Roman times. It is even possible to visit some of the old mine shafts and galleries on application to the director. The Salt Museum in town is of doubtful value but worth a visit if only to complete the picture. The town has one or two ancient and colourful festivals, most exciting of which is *Corre Bou* on the second Sunday in September, when local young bloods test their courage against the bulls which are released to run through the streets.

Back on the main Route, *Puig Reig*, 12km N of Balsareny, is a modern industrial town retaining the ruins of its 12C castle on high. Close to the ruin is the Romanesque *Church of Sant Marti* containing some 13C frescoes. *Gironella* (8km) sits astride the Llobregat river and has a good medieval bridge, and several modern ones, tying it together. Apart from an interesting contemporary church, there is not much to see here.

Just S of Berga (turning left off the 1411) is the very early Romanesque church of *San Vicenc de Obiols*, with Mozarabic horseshoe arches supported by simple columns and 8C primitive capitals. Outside the church are some anthropomorphic tombs excavated in the stone, in one of which a 7C Visigothic coin was found.

Berga, capital of the *comarca*, is a historic town, home of the Iberian tribe of *Bergistanos*, and proud to have been the birthplace of the 12C poet and troubadour, *Guillem de Bergueda*. The old quarter, at the foot of the castle ruins, retains its 14C gate of *Santa Magdalena* and some nice 16C houses along the *Carrer Mayor*. The ancient fiesta of *La Patum* which lasts several days around *Corpus Christi*, is great fun: people dress up as outsize chickens, and other monsters, and dance to the beat of a kettle drum.

There are three recommended EXCURSIONS from Berga. One is to drive up the hill (NW of town) to the *Santuario de Queralt*, as much for the lush beauty of the road, and the views, as for the sanctuary itself which has suffered numerous additions and restorations.

The second excursion is to cross the Llobregat, by way of a fine Gothic bridge, and drive E-wards on the C149 alongside the *Baells* reservoir, to *Sant Quirze de Pedret*. This is one of the finest pre-Romanesque churches in Catalonia, dating from the early 10C and preserving still a primitive and tranquil beauty despite 12C modifications. Its rectangular nave connects with the square central apse through a severe horseshoe arch. Similar arches lead to the side aisles (added later), each of which has its own small round apse. 10C and 12C frescoes have been removed from the apses and can be seen in the Museum at Solsona, as well as the *Museu de Arte de Catalunya* in Barcelona.

The third is to continue along the C149 as far as Borrada and then turn N-wards to *San Jaume de la Frontanya* which stands in a wild mountain setting just 24km from Berga. In complete contrast with the primitive intimacy of the last church, this one is large by comparison and is as fine a specimen of the Middle Romanesque period as can be seen in the area. The key is available from the *hostal* up the road, though it has to be said that the interior lacks interest. It is the outside which is superb with classic examples of Lombard banding placed high up around the three apses and the fine 12-sided lantern. There is no other decoration and the building exudes a quiet majesty which is in no way diminished by the rocky bluff behind it. It was once part of an Augustinian canonry.

Back on the 1411, continue N-wards to *Guardiola de Bergueda* and on to *Puigcerda* by way of the *Cadi Tunnel* (see Route 5).

ROUTE 10

BARCELONA TO LLEIDA VIA CERVERA AND TARREGA; EXCURSION TO THE ABBEY OF VALLBONA DE LES MONGES

This route takes you across the central agricultural plateau of Catalonia which is a region of almonds, olives and cereal crops, dotted with hill-top villages and countless Reconquest castles. There is everything to be said for leaving the ugly Barcelona suburbs behind as quickly as possible. From *Plaça*

BARCELONA TO LLEIDA

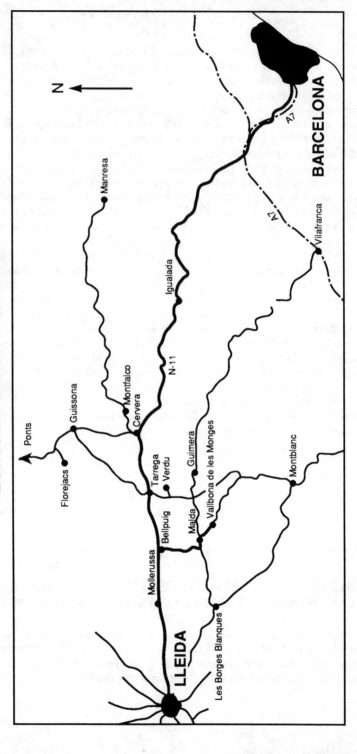

d'Espanya follow signs for the N11 or, better still, the motorway, A7, leaving the latter at the Martorell exit (27km).

Martorell is a large industrial town at the confluence of the rivers *Anoia* and *Llobregat*, and you may be tempted to by-pass it altogether. It had Roman beginnings, and then grew in medieval times alongside the royal route from Catalonia to Aragon. Its one significant monument is the fine bridge over the two rivers, known as *Pont del Diable* (Devil's bridge), still standing on Roman foundations and with a Roman triumphal arch at one end. The gateway in the middle is medieval and the bridge has been many times destroyed (most recently during the Civil War) and rebuilt.

Continue along the N11 (the Motorway turns S-wards to Tarragona at this point). Notice on the right, as you drive towards *Igualada*, the extraordinary outline of the Montserrat massif (see Route 9). Igualada is another large industrial town, preserving from its past two ancient gates, a medieval quarter with arcaded *Plaça Vella*, and a 17C church of *Santa Maria*, in Renaissance style with Gothic chapel. There is also a museum which traces the industrial development of the town from prehistoric times to the present day.

The small town of **Cervera** was chosen by Philip V in 1714 as a suitable location for Catalonia's only university, the previous long-established universities in Barcelona and other cities having been abolished by him as part of Catalonia's punishment for supporting the losing side in the War of Succession. For just over 100 years Cervera had the doubtful honour of being the only university town in the Province. Today the university building is part occupied by a secondary school. It has a very grandiose Baroque façade behind which are two courtyards, one in good order, the other more massive and more neglected. From here there is a good view of the elegant neo-classical interior facade with fine pediment between the two identical towers.

But it is the medieval aspect of this town which is exceptionally attractive. Cervera is small and compact and easily explored on foot; one can leave the car somewhere in the vicinity of the University and then walk straight on down to the *Carrer Mayor*, a charming and well-kept street with houses dating from the mid-16C or earlier, many with pretty windows and monumental doorways or with plaques recording some historical event which took place there. At no.15 there is a small museum. The real find, however, is the dark and forbidding **Carrer de les Bruixes** (**Street of the Witches**). Turn left and then right off *Carrer Mayor*: at a much lower level has been preserved a 13C street, covered and with tiny doors and windows either side behind which people lived. The play of light and shade where the sun does manage to penetrate through spaces in the low roof adds magic. And black magic seems to be the mood throughout, with here and there an effigy of a witch or a black cat to remind you where you are. This street is remarkably clean and damp-free, despite its low level, and so far the temptation to turn it into a tourist attraction has been resisted.

Both *Carrer Mayor* and *Carrer de les Bruixes* emerge into the *Plaça Mayor*, a tiny arcaded square overlooked by the imposing bulk of the 18C *Town Hall*, known as *La Paeria* with Baroque façade. Notice particularly the delicious carved figures holding up the three first-floor balconies (five under each), said to represent popular local dignitaries of the time. Right behind the *Paeria* (touching it in fact) is the Gothic *Church of Santa Maria* with octagonal tower and a Romanesque porch from the earlier church of *Sant Marti*, with primitive tympanum design showing the saint giving his cape to a poor man. Opposite the Romanesque porch is a mirador offering a good view of the surrounding plain and an even better one of the church's 14C roof structure and tower.

A curiosity worth exploring is the tiny 11C round church of *Sant Pere Gros*, on the outskirts of Cervera (SW). This strange building looks more like a fortification than a church. It has two slit windows, a small external apse and one door. Only the belfry on the roof proclaims its true purpose. It was in fact once part of a Benedictine priory and is considered one of the best examples of a Romanesque circular church in Catalonia.

It is worth continuing down the road which follows the *Ondara* river a few kms more to see the ancient castle-village of *Granyanella*. This is a typical example of a common phenomenon in these parts, where a village grows up around its castle and then, as the castle falls into disuse, it actually cannibalizes it, using the very stone to build more houses. Two circles of curtain wall are still discernible in Granyanella as well as some of the original castle gates, but the houses are now inside, as well as outside, built into the walls in some cases and following the overall circular design. In place of the central keep there now stands a water tower.

Return to Cervera. 5km to the NE (along the 141 road to Manresa) and worth the short detour is *Montfalco*, a noble and picturesque specimen of castle-village on a hill – visible for miles around. The village, making use of the thick, thick castle walls, is quite dark and creepy in places. There seem to have been several periods of house building: the first presumably immediately after the retreat of the Moors and there was no longer need for defence (the church was built at this time); more was built in the 16C and 17C, each time chopping off a bit more castle wall or arch so as to create space inside and to make use of the stone. And building is going on even now, as several houses outside the walls are being restored.

A very charming village which has grown up at the foot of its ruined castle and church is *La Curullada* (W of Cervera on the Tarrega road). It has made use not only of chunks of stone but of great formal balconies right out of proportion to its cottages. There is a truly wonderful panorama from the hilltop over this remote and wild countryside spotted with reminders of its heroic past.

To anyone wanting more of the same we recommend the following EXCURSION of some 50km which ends up at Tarrega. Take the 311 road

N-wards out of Cervera to *Tarroja de Segarra*, with a particularly nice main plaça with stone seats; continue to the town of *Guissona*, with large arcaded plaça and neo-classical church; keep going N until *Palou de Sanauja* where turn left for *Florejacs* and *Sitges*, both splendid castles which were turned into noble mansions in the 17C; return to Guissona and take the Tarrega road SW-wards through *Concabella* where the castle walls have square windows with medieval human and animal faces carved into the moulding. From here turn right to *Pelagalls* – a tiny village distinguished by its 12C church with exceptional door with three columns on either side bearing capitals decorated with birds and ears of corn; the tympanum is special and shows Christ in Majesty with two smiling angels; return to the Concabella crossroads and turn right for Tarrega.

Tarrega is a busy market town with one outstanding monument which stands just off the *Plaça Mayor*. It was once the Palace of the *Dukes of Floresta* and is a splendid specimen of civil Romanesque architecture (not often seen because not often preserved). It has been well restored recently by an insurance company who now occupy it. The façade is dominated by a bold doorway and three double-columned windows with typical Romanesque moulding. Above these there are beautifully carved figures and there is a top storey with six columns. Facing this building is a 16C house with good contrasting pointed windows.

There is a reproduction Gothic cross in the middle of the Plaça Mayor and a 17C town hall giving on to it. Nearby is the neo- classical *Church of Santa Maria* and there are several picturesque arcaded streets and little squares in the vicinity, particularly the porticoed *Plaça de Sant Antoni*. There is also a Jewish sector, a sprinkling of Modernist houses and a Museum (*Museu Comarcal*) housed in an 18C mansion and containing an archaeological exhibition. After Tarrega you have a choice of simply continuing along the N11 to the next town, *Bellpuig* or of taking an EXCURSION to the important Cistercian Abbey of *Vallbona de les Monges* and surrounding villages (approx 45km).

Take the 240 road S from Tarrega and after 4km turn left to *Verdu* which has a delightful *Plaça Mayor* with arcades and stone pillars gently leaning this way and that. Verdu has grown up around its 12C castle of which the circular tower and part of the outer wall remain, the latter converted into dwellings. The 13C *Church of Santa Maria* has a single nave without transept, with low barrel vault, massive pillars and no decoration whatsoever. The fussy rose window at the end and the two Gothic side aisles added two centuries later serves to emphasise the heavy tranquillity of the central section. Notice the good W door with typical Romanesque carved capitals of the Lleida School. Verdu is well known for its distinctive black pottery, especially wine pitchers (*cantaros*) which were once used all over Catalonia. Today it is all more of a curiosity and there are several workshops and stalls along the road where the visitor is welcome to browse.

Return to the crossroads and turn left, and left again, to *Guimera*, a medieval castle-village characterised by its network of streets burrowing their way through original walls and often beneath original archways. The walls lean inwards, the streets are often stepped, the whole is a symphony of muted colour and gentle shapes, with everywhere a vista for the eye to follow. It would be hard to find anywhere a more picturesque village to walk through.

Come back from Guimera to the crossroads once more, noting the romantic ruin of *Ciutadella* castle with Square Tower on the left. Continue W-wards through *Sant Marti de Ruicorb*, with Baroque church full of twisted columns and cherubs eating grapes (not recommended), to *Malda*. Malda's castle was turned into a noble residence in 1682. Behind its palatial façade is a much older defensive structure with arrow slits and a keep. Even the parish church has had a clumsy 18C façade stuck on. Old bits of stone and wrought iron balconies have quite obviously been fixed to modern buildings. There is a strange feeling in this village that nothing is quite what it seems. Only the *Carrer Mayor* is truly unchanged.

The **Abbey of Vallbona de les Monges** lies 7km to the SE. It is one of a trio of Cistercian communities in Catalonia, the other two being *Poblet* and *Santes Creus*. Documents record that a mixed community of hermits came here as early as 1135 and lived according to the Rule of St. Benedict. In 1175, by which time the community had become exclusively female, it was incorporated into the Cistercian Order and given its first Abbess, *Oria Ramirez* from Navarre. From that moment on, the Abbey received maximum attention and privileges from Catalan royalty and also from Rome. *Kings Alfonso I* and *James I* (the Conqueror) lodged there frequently, gave it their personal protection and poured money in to the creation of sumptuous buildings. In 1200 *Pope Innocent III* decreed that the community should come directly under control of the Cistercian Order in France, thus bypassing day-to-day control by Catalan ecclesiastical authorities.

By the late 14C the Abbey had purchased vast areas of surrounding land and the then Abbess stood at the head of the '*Barony of Vallbona*'. The prosperous community attracted the daughters of the noblest families in the land: there were at least 150 nuns, plus countless lay sisters and associated helpers. Intellectual and charitable interests, as well as spiritual life, were dynamically pursued and there was a prestigious library, a school, a hospice for pilgrims and a hospital and pharmacy for the poor.

The year 1573 saw an end to the Abbey's privileged isolation in a hitherto uncultivated valley. Villagers were transferred there from neighbouring Montesquiu precisely to cultivate the land and two-thirds of the Abbey's buildings were given up to create the new village of *Vallbona de les Monges*. This gave rise to present-day phenomena such as the adjacent street surmounted by two huge arches, which once formed part of the Abbey store-house. The reduced monastic Community survived the various social pressures put on it throughout the succeeding centuries and there are still today some thirty nuns sustaining the spiritual and cultural traditions which were established eight centuries ago.

The Church and Cloister are open to visitors every day and are approached by way of a charming *plaça*. This was once the cemetary and several tombs of the Abbey's earliest benefactors can be seen standing up against the wall on columns. There are two magnificent Romanesque doorways giving on to the Plaça: *Portal de los Muertos* (Door of the Dead), which is now blocked off by a tomb; and *Portal de la Esglesia* with archivolts and a fine tympanum showing Virgin and Child between two angels.

The *Church* is typical of the Romanesque-Gothic Transitional style and has recognisable elements of both periods. One is struck on entering by the grey simplicity of the narrow nave in typical austere Cistercian style. Over the crossing is a magnificent 8- sided Cimborium with eight windows and a domical vault constructed in the last 13C and said to be the best preserved structure of its kind in the whole of Catalonia (the guide goes further and says it is unique in the world). The second tower, also octagonal and distinctly Gothic in style, was added over the nave a century later. The church is full of tombstones, mainly of abbesses; on either side of the main altar, set into the wall, are the royal sepulchres of *Queen Violante of Hungary* (second wife of James I) and of their daughter, *Princess Sancha*.

The *Cloister* (which you pay 50 ptas to enter) is trapezoidal with all four of its wings slightly different. The E and S wings are early and late Romanesque, the older of the two with plain capitals, the later with carvings of plants and fruit; both have rounded arches but a Gothic vault with fine bosses which were added when the church was renovated in the 14C. The N wing is pure Gothic and the remaining W wing is 15C Renaissance.

The Gothic *Chapter House* has a tranquil beauty all its own with some very fine carved tombstones set in to the floor, many belonging to past Abbesses. It is interesting to note that the less ornate, but dated, tombstones in the floor of the cloister belong to the humble nuns, who were buried anonymously.

There is the usual array of dependencies – refectory, kitchen, library, writing room (*scriptorium*) etc, all of which have been transformed so many times through the centuries and are currently being changed yet again to make room for new living quarters for the nuns. There is also a small museum containing church treasure and embroidered articles; and also a medieval pharmacy.

From Vallbona, go back to Malda; then turn left to *Balianes* and right to Bellpuig (where you rejoin the main Route). *Bellpuig* was part of a Barony in the Middle Ages, that of *Cardona- Anglesola*. So it is not surprising that one of its proudest monuments is the *Mausoleum of Ramon Folc de Cardona-Anglesola*, Viceroy of Siciliy and Naples, who died in 1522. Made of marble in the form of a Triumphal Arch with scenes of battle all around and the recumbent figure of the Viceroy over a central sarcophagus, it stands in the *Church of Sant Nicolau* (St. Nicholas) and is one of the best pieces of Renaissance sculpture in Catalonia. A second monument worth a short visit is the 16C *Convent of Sant Bartolomeu* on the outskirts of town. It has two good cloisters, the first quite simple, the second with pointed arches separated by buttresses, and a gallery of twisted columns with finely worked capitals above. This is one of the very few examples of late Gothic work in the Region. The top storey, in Renaissance style, was added in 17C.

Mollerussa, 10km to the W, was once a stopping place along the royal road to Aragon from Barcelona, but has lost all trace of its medieval past beneath modern development. 23km W again is Lleida (see Route 4).

INDEX

INDEX